VISUALISATION IN POPULAR
FICTION 1860–1960

Visualisation in Popular Fiction explores the important but neglected tradition of illustrated fiction in English. It suggests new analytical approaches for its study by offering detailed discussions of a range of representative texts including Mary Webb's *Gone to Earth* and Daphne du Maurier's *Rebecca*.

Among the issues Sillars explores in this study are:

- the implications of Roland Barthes' ideas of narratology as they apply to this compound form
- Victorian 'narrative' paintings and how they were understood or misunderstood by their contemporary 'readers'
- the use of illustration in children's stories
- the role of illustration to reinforce reader ideology in Edwardian fiction magazines
- the use of visual narrative in comic strips
- the translation of novels to film.

An insightful and provocative work, *Visualisation in Popular Fiction* will be of value to students of literature, cultural studies, visual art and film.

Stuart Sillars is a writer and freelance lecturer. Previous publications include *Art and Survival in First World War Britain* (1987) and *British Romantic Art and the Second World War* (1992).

NARRATIVE FORMS AND SOCIAL FORMATIONS

(formerly published as *READING POPULAR FICTION*)

General Editor: Derek Longhurst

The enjoyment of thrillers, romances or Westerns is no longer the secret vice it used to be. *Narrative Forms and Social Formations* offers a polemical, challenging and provocative contribution to our understanding of popular fiction and the pleasure it gives its readers. Each volume draws on contemporary critical theory, historical contexts and the nature of readership and production to address key questions concerning the relationship between popular narrative and issues of class, gender, race, nation and regionalism.

In the same series:

EMPIRE BOYS: Adventures in a Man's World
Joseph Bristow

GENDER, GENRE & NARRATIVE PLEASURE
Edited by Derek Longhurst

MURDER BY THE BOOK: Feminism and the Crime Novel
Sally R. Munt

VISUALISATION IN POPULAR FICTION 1860–1960

Graphic narratives, fictional images

Stuart Sillars

London and New York

First published 1995
by Routledge
11 New Fetter Lane, London EC4P 4EE

Simultaneously published in the USA and Canada
by Routledge
29 West 35th Street, New York, NY 10001

Typeset in Garamond by
J&L Composition Ltd, Filey, North Yorkshire
Printed and bound in Great Britain by
Biddles Ltd, Guildford and King's Lynn

British Library Cataloguing in Publication Data
A catalogue record for this book is available from the British Library

Library of Congress Cataloguing in Publication Data
Sillars, Stuart
Visualisation in Popular Fiction 1860–1960: Graphic
narratives, fictional images / Stuart Sillars.
p.   cm. – (Narrative forms and social formations)
Includes bibliographical references and index.
1. English fiction–19th century–History and
criticism.   2. Popular literature–Great Britain–History and
criticism.   3. English fiction–20th century–History and
criticism.   4. Popular literature–Great Britain–
Illustrations.   5. Art and literature–Great
Britain–History.   6. Illustrated books–Great Britain–
History.   7. Illustration of books–Great
Britain.   8. English fiction–Illustrations.   9. Visual
communication.   10. Graphic arts. I. Title. II. Series.
PR878. I4S57   1995
823'. 80923–dc20   94–22787

ISBN 0–415–11914–6

For Laurence
my son

CONTENTS

PLATES

ACKNOWLEDGEMENTS

Many people have contributed to the growth of this book and it is a pleasure to be able to record my thanks to them. The staffs of Cambridge University Library and the English Faculty Library in Cambridge were their usual models of erudition and humanity; the former's photographic department produced some of the illustrations, the remainder being made by the University Audio-Visual Aids Unit.

Passages from *Rebecca* by Daphne du Maurier are reproduced with permission of Curtis Brown Ltd, London on behalf of the Estate of Daphne du Maurier. Copyright © 1938 by Daphne du Maurier Browning. Plates 5, 6, 7, 8, 12, 25, 27, 28 and 29 are reproduced by kind permission of the Syndics of Cambridge University Library; Plate 31 reproduces material from *PC 49*, © 1994, Fleetway Publications, reprinted by kind permission of Hawk Books. The remaining illustrations are taken from the author's collection.

The production of the book was much assisted by the help of Sarah Dann, Derek Longhurst, Talia Rodgers, Tricia Dever, Sarah-Jane Woolley and Sheila Kane. I also owe much to many students and colleagues who listened and argued during the book's gestation.

What credit there is, I am delighted to share; the responsibility for errors, omissions and stubborn perversities must remain my own.

Stuart Sillars

1

THE NATURE AND FUNCTION OF VISUALISATION

Alice was beginning to get very tired of sitting by her sister on the bank and of having nothing to do: once or twice she had peeped into the book her sister was reading, but it had no pictures or conversations in it, 'and what is the use of a book,' thought Alice, 'without pictures or conversations?'

(Carroll 1982: 1)

Alice's question, at the beginning of a book which itself contributed much to the tradition of Victorian book illustration, conceals an important assumption – that, by 1865, when the text was written, the illustrated book had become a primary form of literary entertainment. Defining the use of a book *with* pictures would by implication have been no trouble at all to Alice – it provided something that was more entertaining and less taxing than a book with neither pictures nor conversation. But when we move out of this world of Victorian certainties, to ask what the visual text contributes to the verbal, and what is the nature of the dual discourse that is produced by an illustrated text that truly unifies the two, the answer is far from straightforward.

What exactly does a picture do in a book? How does it modify the response of the reader to the written word? Does it enable him or her to enter more fully into the created fictive world, or does it present that world as more of an artifice? Does it amplify the concepts and structures of the words, or does it offer separate ones of its own, as a sort of visual commentary? If the two work together to provide a new discourse, how is it assimilated and how best analysed?

All of these are insistent questions. This book sets out to attempt to answer them by looking at works of popular illustrated fiction as it is most broadly interpreted – an interpretation which includes fiction for adults and children, magazine fiction, strip comics and film, as well as popular novels which are illustrated after their first appearance, and those which, although they do not contain any visual images, nevertheless make complex use of the psychology of visualisation.

Given the prominence of illustrated fiction as a major force in publishing since the early nineteenth century, it is surprising that it has not attracted critical attention greater in depth and in quantity. Despite the fact that many of the novelists who remain solidly within the established canon of literary studies produced work that was illustrated on its first appearance, mainstream literary study has resolutely refused to accept the visual dimensions of such texts. David Cecil's *Early Victorian Novelists* (1932) and Kathleen Tillotson's *Novels of the Eighteen-Forties* (1954) make no mention of the visual components of the novels they discuss – novels which include *The Old Curiosity Shop* and *Bleak House* in which the illustrations are of fundamental significance in the reading experience, and *Vanity Fair*, a novel which perhaps has more claim than any other of its age to be considered as a single discourse of word and image since both are the product of the same 'author'. The reason for this neglect is perhaps implicit within the reference in my last sentence to 'the reading experience'; this is not something that English critics have taken seriously until recently, with the coming of Wolfgang Iser (1978) and Stanley Fish (1980). Perhaps the Leavisite doctrine of the primacy of the text as instrument of cultural transmission is responsible, in two ways, for the neglect of illustration. First, it stresses the unique significance of the written word; secondly, its moral earnestness inevitably nudges it away from the apparent frivolity of the curlicues and caricatures of engravings which were, after all, something which appealed to the Victorian public, an organism hideously non-Leavisite in nature and taste.[1] There is perhaps another cause which is more relevant to the immediate context of the present discussion. Illustration is something which explicitly links the canonic novels of the 1830s, 1840s and 1850s to those which are, in traditional circles, regarded as of merely sociological interest since they belong to that dangerously profligate sub-culture, popular literature. Here indeed is a common pursuit rejected by those in search of transmitting the uncommon.

2

Whatever the reason, the gap is there. Even the Open University, with its stress on interdisciplinary studies, has produced a course in which a Victorian novel is presented for study with no mention at all of the visual texts which constituted a part of it at its first appearance.[2] There are, of course, some honourable exceptions, chief amongst which is J.R. Harvey's *Victorian Novelists and their Illustrators*; and works on individual authors and novels have furthered our awareness in specific directions,[3] even if this is often in the effort to construct bibliographic or publishing history. Yet if we move out of the subject of illustrated fiction within the canon to consider its counterparts in popular fiction, there is little which goes beyond the bibliographic to the extent even of considering the work at all. Given the sheer bulk of the material involved, this is a serious omission.

The importance of illustration in popular fiction is self-evident. Many of the runaway publishing successes of the first half of the nineteenth century were books conjoining text and illustration. Magazines and periodicals of all sorts published illustrated fiction either, in the earlier years, in serial instalments or, from the last two decades of the last century, as self-contained stories. Books and magazines for children continued and developed the tradition of illustration. The habit of visualisation has continued into the twentieth century with the practice of producing fine editions of an established author's work with specially commissioned illustrations; and, in the middle years of the century, before the tyranny of the electronic narrative, the comic-strip become one of the most pervasive influences on child readers, dependent as it is upon compelling visual images to convey action. Even in a society dominated by electronic narrative, the prevalence of films based upon books has been a potent form of visualisation in popular culture. These circumstances make the nature and function of illustration in popular fiction of all these kinds something which the serious critic may no longer ignore.

II

The full nature of the complex relationship between word and image within the context of what can reasonably be called the illustration of texts is apparent if we return to the figure who is generally cited as the originator of the illustrative print in its modern sense in England: William Hogarth. Hogarth's prints are clearly of fundamental importance in the tradition of illustrated fiction for a number of reasons concerning their nature and the circumstances in which they were produced and distributed. First of all there is their conception as series of prints: from *The Harlot's Progress* (1731–2) onwards, Hogarth's engravings were produced in sequences of from four to twelve plates conveying a continuous narrative usually in the discussion of events concerning the same cast of characters. Often a text in the form of short verses was engraved with the image. Seen alongside one another – as they often were when framed and hung by their purchasers – they present a sequence of stages in a narrative, using the kind of structure which surfaces much later and in simplified, more intimate form, in the comic strip.

To this must be added the way in which we approach Hogarth's prints. As has been remarked frequently (see e.g., Paulson: 1975; Cowley 1983), Hogarth's prints have a 'reading structure' which necessitates that the onlooker begin at the left hand side and pass across the image to the right, taking in the denotative, narrative and connotative significances of its elements along the way. This explains why the engravings are lateral reversals or mirror images of paintings – which in many cases they antedate: in the painting the composition and other painterly values are significant, but in the print it is narrative and symbol, perceived in the sequential reading, which dominate.

The reading that is demanded is by no means simple: we need to decode emblematic references, specific allusions to contemporary figures, links made by parallel visual structures, and subtleties of irony and satire caused by features such as glance, posture, juxtaposition or separation of figures. That Hogarth could confidently make such demands upon his readers shows that subtle habits of absorbing a range of kinds of visual data were well established in the print-buying public, if not at the outset of Hogarth's career, then certainly by its end. Yet we should not assume from this that all of Hogarth's readers were skilled in the kind of iconographical elucidation that is necessary if we are fully to grasp the targets and effects of much of his satire. As a contemporary source makes clear, the images worked at several levels, with a 'plain literal sense' that is apparent to even the least perceptive reader alongside more complex levels of signification: 'The Story should be such as an ordinary Reader may acquiesce in, whatever Natural, Moral or Political Truth may be discovered in it by Men of Greater Penetration' (*The Spectator* No. 315, 1 March 1712). The truth of this is not difficult to grasp. A wholly untrained eye may discern the scenes of moral corruption in the various progresses; one with a grasp of the contemporary underworld will discern references to specific criminals and locations; one with a grasp of Catholic iconography will be aware of the ironic use of, say, a chalice or monstrance; one with a connoisseur's familiarity with European painting will understand and relish the comic presentation of, say, three whores in the classical *topos* of the three graces. This gives to Hogarth's work something fundamental to eighteenth and nineteenth-century popular prints and the Victorian illustrated novel which in large measure derives from them: the appeal to people of a wide range of backgrounds and experiences in reading and decoding visual narratives. Hogarth's desire to appeal to even 'men of the lowest rank'[4] is made clear in his production of *Industry and Idleness*, a sequence of twelve prints opposing the careers of the good and the idle apprentice. This was popular in its destination if not in its origin: that it had a clear moral intention should not be counted against it, since this was apparent too in all of Hogarth's productions and is another link between his work and a good deal of later illustrated fiction, Charles Knight's *Penny Magazine* being perhaps the most outstanding example, as will shortly become apparent.

Discussion of notions of popularity brings us on to the second important aspect of Hogarth's prints: the circumstances under which they were produced and sold. The sequences were sold by subscription, with half the cost being paid by the purchaser on subscribing and the remainder on receipt of the prints. This was a method which Hogarth followed for his subsequent sequences, and which was a common approach at the time. Johnson's *Dictionary* and Pope's *Iliad* were among the better-known works which were produced in a similar manner. This had the simple but crucial advantage for the artist and publisher – in Hogarth's case the two were the same but this was not always the case – of providing finance to begin the project and bear some of the costs of production. What Hogarth was doing, in effect, was anticipating the commercial feature which ensured the popular success of the Victorian best-selling novel – producing it in serial form so that some of the costs could be covered at an early stage of printing and circulation. But this does not mean that the prints were only available to those who could afford to subscribe to them. Their display in the leading print shops, of which there were many in London and other major cities, and their production in cheaper editions after their first appearance, gave them much wider currency.

In Hogarth's prints, we have the development of a complex reading structure, often with the aid of a verbal text, and frequently within a sequential presentation of frames. An awareness of a multiplicity of reading levels and experiences shows not only Hogarth's moral zeal but also his sound grasp of the practicalities of publishing. All of these are features of importance in the nature and circumstances of Victorian and later illustrated fiction. This does not, however, place Hogarth outside the current of his own time. His references to contemporary figures from the criminal classes, and his satiric attacks upon those in authority or who show signs of the pomposity attached to it, link him to Fielding: the novelist himself makes explicit and detailed references to the working of the artist's satiric intent in comparison with his own in both *Joseph Andrews* and *Tom Jones*. Thackeray, himself a caricaturist and illustrator whose abilities are today too often neglected, was fully aware of the link in devoting a chapter in his *English Humorists* (1853) to 'Hogarth, Smollett and Fielding'.[5]

The reference to Thackeray should not, of course, suggest that Hogarth's influence and popularity continued to be felt only in 'serious' literary circles. In 1796 *The Comick Magazine*, a monthly aimed at a popular readership, advertised as its major attraction the presentation of one of 'William Hogarth's Celebrated Humorous, Comical and Moral Prints' with each issue. The prints were reproductions of *Industry and Idleness*: that the magazine was aimed at the new literate apprentice classes would suggest that Hogarth's moralities were still capable of arousing humour among those without an education enabling them to grasp the classical allusions and iconographic complexities nearly fifty years after their publication.

Links between verbal and visual texts continue to be strong in the generation of satiric print-makers to follow Hogarth, most especially James Gillray, Thomas Rowlandson and the brothers George and Robert Cruikshank. Gillray's work, like Hogarth's, sometimes appears with lines of verse: more often, it incorporates words into the image by using speech bubbles or larger explanatory captions. Yet this in no way contradicts a more serious literary origin. *Sin, Death and the Devil* is a good example of the complex

6

levels on which Gillray's prints often work. Dated 9 June 1792, it is a representation of the figures of the Queen, Pitt and Thurlow presented as a parody of the figures and composition of Hogarth's *Satan, Sin and the Devil* (1735–40; oil on canvas, 29 x 24, Tate Gallery, London), a painting illustrating *Paradise Lost*, Book II, lines 648–59. These lines are presented in handwritten form above the image, which shows Pitt as death and Thurlow attacking him with a mace while the Queen, with the keys to the Back Stairs hanging instead of serpents from her waist, endeavours to keep them apart – a reference to the Regency crisis and Pitt's attempts to assume the power of the crown. A line at the foot draws attention to the provenance of the imagery, mentioning the Milton Gallery proposed by Henry Fuseli.

What we have here is quite a subtle relationship between word and image – indeed, it is almost a satiric attack on the nature of illustration itself. Not only does it present the text which it illustrates – illustrates in a parabolic and satiric manner, albeit – but it also depends for its effect on the distance between the words and the image, the former serious and complex, the latter comic and satiric. This difference can be grasped even if the onlooker has no knowledge of Milton, or is not familiar with the bathetic borrowing of Hogarth's design.

Gillray's subtle elision of word and image is of major importance in the growth of English illustration, albeit that his work did not achieve a circulation as wide as that of Hogarth or of Rowlandson and Cruikshank: the link that is established is one of much intellectual depth as well as satiric intensity, and his influence is felt in the work of Blake as well as that of later artists. His prints attacking Boydell's *Shakespeare Gallery*[6] and M.G. Lewis's gothic horror novel *The Monk* (1796) show a fine sense of contemporary taste; though they are not explicitly relevant to the present study as they do not illustrate literature, they are important in illustrating popular attitudes to literature, and so reveal another aspect of the supple relation between verbal and visual text upon which later illustrators were to build.

Gillray's productions are only one strand of a large and diverse stream of work in which word and image are brought together to cumulative effect. Thomas Rowlandson was a significant contributor to this range. With Augustus Pugin he produced the plates for *The Microcosm of London* (1808) issued by the coachbuilder turned publisher Rudolph Ackermann from his print-shop in the Strand. Its significance lies in the fact that it is one of the earliest productions in which an illustration – here a hand-coloured engraving of a London landmark – is accompanied by a short passage of text, the whole being issued in twenty-four serial parts. It thus created a mechanism for publication – image with contextualising prose – which came to be one of the dominant modes for fiction in the middle decades of the century.

Almost at the same time as working on this serial publication, Rowlandson was contributing illustrations to a venture which did much to establish the other mode of fiction publishing of the age. This was *Dr. Syntax in Search of the Picturesque* which appeared in the *Poetical Magazine* in 1809. Each episode paired a hand-coloured plate by Rowlandson, satirising in a mild, good-humoured manner the concern for picturesque scenery made fashionable by William Gilpin[7] with text by William Combe. Although written in verse, this was fictional in nature as it presented the narrative of a journey and attendant anecdotes: along with Ackermann's London prints, this was largely instrumental in establishing the pairing so crucial to later illustrated fictions. Like the *Microcosm*, however, it also established the primacy of the image over the text, something which was to have important reverberations in the serial fictions of the 1830s.

The third member of the triumvirate, George Cruikshank, had established a reputation as a caricaturist by presenting Napoleon's retreat from Russia and the absurdities, political and social, of the Regency, in images which again employed speech bubbles and brief texts in the form of captions. These were issued in a collection of serial parts by John Miller and William Blackwood in 1818; but it was three years later that Cruikshank began to produce the most influential work in terms of impact upon illustrated fiction. This was *Life in London*,[8] in the plates of which Cruikshank was joined by his brother Robert, and for which a prose text was written – after the plates had been produced – by Pierce Egan (1820–1), who had conceived the idea and who published the twelve monthly serial parts between October 1820 and July 1821. That Egan the publisher produced the text is an index of how little significance it had in comparison with the plate, which presented the major action of each episode, and to which the prose served merely as a contextualising introduction. The publication was an immense success. It spawned over sixty stage versions before 1840, and Egan listed sixty-eight pirated treatments, including prints and songs, in 1828:[9] the plates were reproduced as trays, snuff-boxes, fans, screens and handkerchiefs, and an outbreak of overturning night-watchmen's sentry-boxes was recorded in the month when the print showed 'Tom Getting the Best of a Charley'.

Important though these publications were, however, there were several others which showed the linked discourse of word and image developing in other ways. One which continued the moral impulse of Hogarth was the *Penny Magazine*, founded by Charles Knight as the organ of his Society for the Promotion of Useful Knowledge, in 1832. It included factual articles, but made full use of illustrations,[10] and appealed to the new urban classes who were hungry for learning. In this it succeeded: by the end of the first year it was selling 200,000 copies and, although this dropped to 40,000 in the mid-1840s, it had shown that there was a large market for a serious well-produced, illustrated magazine for a class of people hitherto not catered for. In later years it was to spawn many descendants, most particularly magazines aimed at children, and family readerships of a range of ages; its moral zeal would not always be followed by its later imitators, but it did establish that it was both practically possible and financially viable to produce an illustrated magazine of this sort. It was a moral counterweight to periodicals such as the *Newgate Calendar*, a serial account of London low-life which had been issued since 1774, with luridly explicit illustrations. A sequel, *The New Newgate Calendar*, was issued in 1826, and a selection appeared in 1840. It used the inevitable pretext of prurient journalism, that it was merely exposing vice and folly: but its scurrilous nature did much to ensure the skilful reading of dual discourse of word and image amongst those who had no interest in more elevated literary topics, and so had a role to play in the growth of the illustrated text as a popular cultural product.

Another significant development was a group of publications which, with hindsight, can be seen as the early stages of what we would now regard as the comic strip in their use of word and image. Harrison's *Comick Magazine* has already been mentioned in connection with Hogarth but, apart from this link, there was little in it to suggest a visual narrative, let alone one in which word and image combined. The earliest production in this area was William Heath's *Glasgow Looking Glass*, a four-page tabloid first issued on 11 June 1825. It contained a series of separate images – 1s for uncoloured prints, 6s for a hand coloured version – on political and social topics, very much as a more popular version of the political prints of Cruikshank and others. This was by no means cheap, yet that the magazine prospered is shown by its change of name to *Northern Looking Glass* in August of its first year, and its distribution by no less a figure than Ackermann in London. A year later, Heath moved to Thomas McLean, Ackermann's publishing rival, to produce *McLean's Monthly Sheet of Caricatures*. Similar publications followed: *Figaro in London* in 1831, and *Every Body's Album and Caricature Magazine* in 1834. Both included caricature prints, but the latter made the significant advance of having some comic strips, sequences of frames which shared characters and action and thus moved towards the modern comic.

By the early 1820s the production of visual images with accompanying prose – in self-contained monthly parts, as articles contained in weekly or monthly magazines, or as caricatures with speech balloons or captions – was not only firmly established but had in some celebrated cases become a publishing phenomenon. In every form, the visual image remained the dominant partner; but the link with the text was very precise, since the words provided a narrative context, developed a plot to the climactic moment shown in the print, or provided speech to extend or explain the visual meaning. The ground was thus prepared not only for the serial fiction with illustrations which was to dominate the fiction market in the 1830s, but also for the comic strips which were to become important at the end of the nineteenth century and for most of the twentieth. Another point is important here, since it is one which recurs throughout the rest of this study: the illustration of works of fact and fiction, the involvement of artists as illustrators in works of both 'high' and 'popular' art and the interweaving of elements of what we would now call comic-strip art with prints making serious satiric points all reveal that the new dual discourse sprawled right across a number of genres and contexts, so that the separation into categories fundamental to much traditional literary and art historical study is quite impossible when dealing with illustrated texts.

These separate streams converge and develop into the flood tide of the Victorian illustrated novel during the 1830s. At the beginning of the decade, novels were usually produced in two or three small volumes, often in a plain or 'trade' binding, so that the purchaser could have them rebound in his or her personal library style.[11] Most novels, including those of Scott, had no illustrations when first published, but the practice developed of inserting prints of appropriate subjects into the bound volumes, a process known as 'Grangerising' after the most celebrated practitioner. Some print-makers sought to exploit these two movements by producing engravings depicting scenes and locales from Scott's novels, which were sold to be tipped in to the volumes.

Constable's edition of *Novels and Romances of the Author of Waverley*, published in seven volumes for 4 gns in 1824, for example, has title-page vignettes by Alexander Nasmyth, but no illustrations in the text. My own copy of this has engravings tipped in to the text, 'The Tower 1670', for example, which not only bears the names of the artist D. Roberts and the engraver E. Findon, but also the title of the novel to which it should be applied, *Peveril of the Peak*. The print also has the line 'London, Published Feb;y [*sic*] 1831 by Charles Tilt, 86 Fleet Street' – a clear indication of the way in which the growth of illustrations had a retrospective effect on novels produced earlier.

These prints, however, were merely presentations of the topography in which the events of the novel took place, and can hardly be called illustrations in the larger sense of a visual presentation of the action: they are perhaps as much the result of the growth of interest in places following from the cult of Picturesque tourism as the product of a concern for illustrations in novels, so the fact remains that illustration was not a feature of the novels of Scott and others in the 1820s and before. Why these and other texts did not contain illustrations is a separate topic of considerable interest, to which I shall return in a later section of this chapter: for the moment, my point is that, before the great explosion of publishing in serial form, illustration was not a feature of the novel, even those novels which, most especially in the case of Scott, could justifiably be called popular.

The dominance of illustrations in the novel from the 1830s onwards is largely the result of the writings of two men, Charles Dickens and Harrison Ainsworth, working in conjunction with the illustrators George Cruikshank, Robert Seymour and Hablot Knight Browne ('Phiz'), and a variety of publishers among whom Richard Bentley and John Macrone were prominent.

Dickens' *Sketches by Boz* grew out of some nine short pieces he had published in the *Monthly Magazine*, beginning with 'A Dinner at Poplar' in December 1833. These were not illustrated, and it was John Macrone's idea to commission the writer to produce the text to accompany illustrations by Cruikshank on the theme of London life. This was a shrewd attempt to cash in on the success of *Life in London* by exploiting the skills of both writer and illustrator in depicting urban scenes for the new urban middle classes. That the two were to be equal partners is suggested by early ideas for the title, which included *Sketches by Boz and Cuts by Cruikshank*. The first series appeared in February 1836, and sold so well that a third edition was issued a year later and a second series was commissioned, taking the form of two volumes, which would bring the complete work into the three-volume format of a novel, giving it the semblance of a self-contained work of fiction rather than the series of collected sketches which, as Dickens himself realised, it still was.

Dickens' success with *Sketches by Boz* led to several other commissions. The most significant of these was *The Pickwick Papers*, which appeared in twenty monthly parts from April 1836 to November 1837. From its eighth issue, *McLean's Monthly* had numbered among its artists Robert Seymour, a caricaturist in the mould of Gillray and Cruikshank. The close links between caricature print, comic magazine and serial novel are made quite clear when we recall that, when *The Posthumous Papers of the Pickwick Club* were begun in 1836, it was the plates of Robert Seymour that were seen as the main attraction, and not the prose of Dickens.

The publication had its origin in Seymour's suggestion to the publisher Edward Chapman for a book of humorous plates concerning a sporting cockney character, with accompanying text. Dickens was apparently chosen as the writer only after several others had refused,[12] and was offered a set fee for the production of a sheet and a half of text for each monthly part. This rate of payment is of interest in showing the degree to which the format of the issues was dependent upon considerations of production, in which the plates clearly took precedence: the sheet was the single large sheet of paper which, when folded, would produce sixteen pages of text. A sheet and a half would give twenty-four pages; the four plates, which of course would be printed on one side only, would provide the other eight pages for a thirty-two page gathering which, stitched into a simple paper cover, would make up each number.

At first the venture was not a success. Of 1,000 copies of part 1, only 400 were bound; the print run for part 2 was cut to 500. Seymour was experimenting with steel engraving plates instead of copper, and they began to disintegrate while being worked on. Seymour's suicide after the second number brought matters to a crisis: Dickens suggested saving the publication by changing the format to thirty-two pages of text and two plates in each monthly part. It was a solution both practical and artistic: costs were cut because of the reduced expenditure on plates, and the text was given space to develop lines of character and action independent of the illustrations, which could then depict scenes chosen from the story, instead of the words providing merely a commentary on four visual elements which were the major interest of the episode. This was to become the standard form for illustrated serial parts from then on. A major part of the success was the employment of 'Phiz' or Hablot Knight Browne as illustrator. Lacking the reputation of Cruikshank or Seymour, he was content to follow Dickens' instructions: the shift in dominance from image to text was significant. Sales rocketed to 26,000 in October 1837 and, for the final number in November, a total of 40,000 was sold.[13]

Although the influence of *Pickwick*'s success was considerable, we should beware of seeing it as the progenitor of the Victorian illustrated novel: another work produced at roughly the same time has a claim to at least an equal share in this title. A short while after the appearance of the first series, Macrone published the fourth edition of Harrison Ainsworth's first novel, *Rockwood*, a combination of fashionable low-life and respectable historical fiction in the manner of Scott, recording as it did Dick Turpin's ride from London to York. The appearance of this fourth edition only two years after the novel's publication indicates its popularity, but it is largely significant because it included twelve etchings by George Cruikshank. It thus has some claim to being the first nineteenth-century novel for which narrative illustrations were commissioned after the text's completion, instead of being a work of fiction written alongside or even after the creation of the accompanying visual images.

In the succeeding years both Dickens and Ainsworth produced work in which illustration is of central significance. In 1837 Dickens took on the editorship of *Bentley's Miscellany*, including from the second number an episode of his new novel *Oliver Twist* with illustrations by Cruikshank. The same year, Ainsworth's *Crichton* appeared with illustrations by Browne. When Dickens resigned from *Bentley's* in 1839 he was replaced by Ainsworth, who began his serial *Jack Sheppard* which was also illustrated by

Cruikshank. The popularity of all these was great, as was the rivalry between writers and illustrators. When *Bentley's* fell from its opening circulation of 8,500 to 5,000 in 1842, Ainsworth – whose *Guy Fawkes* was thought to be to blame – was dismissed as editor and Richard Bentley, the proprietor, took over himself. But when Cruikshank stopped illustrating for the paper, the circulation was about a third of its earlier figure.[14]

In these texts of the late 1830s it is hard to establish whether illustration or verbal text came first in producing characterisation and event. Certainly, the origination of the narrative was the subject of considerable acrimony between the writers and artists. Ainsworth and Cruikshank discussed the matter publicly in the correspondence columns of *The Times* in 1872 (9, 11, 13 August). Elsewhere, Cruikshank claimed that 'Mr Ainsworth and I were *partners*, holding equal shares' in *The Tower of London* (1841), asserting that all the illustrations were printed before the text was set, 'and sometimes before the Author *had written his manuscript*'.[15] From the surviving correspondence between the two men[16] it is clear that Ainsworth gave Cruikshank an outline of the plot, which Cruikshank would then develop in detail for his illustrations, whereupon Ainsworth would write the text including the illustrated material.

Dickens' relations with his illustrators seem at this stage to be similarly close. In the preface to later editions of *Pickwick* he asserts that 'Mr Seymour never originated or suggested an incident, a phrase, or a word, to be found in this book' (Dickens 1986: 886 n.2), going on to say that he saw Seymour once only, never received a letter from him, and can call Chapman as a witness of the truth of his assertions. What is significant here is not the truth or otherwise of this claim, but the mere fact that Dickens thought it necessary to make it. It shows that he wished to remove himself from the earlier convention in which text followed image, and move towards a position where the writer is the instigator because, as he says elsewhere in the Preface, 'it would be infinitely better for the plates to arise naturally out of the text' (Dickens 1986: 885).

What is also striking is the fact that Dickens clearly sees himself in the tradition of the visual moralist. This is shown most precisely in the following paragraph, discussing the actuality of life in London slums, from the Preface to *Oliver Twist*:

I had never met (except in HOGARTH) with the miserable reality.
It appeared to me that to draw a knot of such associates in
crime as really did exist; to paint them in all their deformity, in
all their wretchedness, in all the squalid misery of their lives; to
show them as they really were, for ever skulking uneasily
through the dirtiest paths of life, with the great black ghastly
gallows closing up their prospect, turn them where they might;
it appeared to me that to do this, would be to attempt a
something which was needed, and which would be a service
to society. And I did it as I best could.

(Dickens 1949: xv)

Two points are striking here: first, Dickens assumes without
question that the 'reality' of urban vice and squalor is that which
is presented by Hogarth – a statement of the 'truth' of the image
which reveals much about the impact of the earlier artist's work
upon the writer, and also of the larger power of the transmitted
vision of truth rather than the external truth itself at a time when
engravings were the major source of reproduced visual data.[17]
Secondly, the language of the passage reveals that Dickens himself
is presenting reality in terms of a series of visual images translated
into literary structures, something which is one of the most
outstanding features of his use of language. J.R. Harvey (1970:
34–5) argues that this was a detrimental result of the influence of
the caricature school, which moved Dickens to produce an exaggerated style out of a need to prove superiority over the engraved
image. Certainly it is evidence of the way in which the visual sense
is absorbed into the writer's style because of the prolonged
popularity of the popular moral print; but that the visual sense
has become wholly literary in its style and structure is suggested in
the balancing periods and careful rhetorical growth to climax in the
passage quoted above, and its personal dismissal which approxi-
mates to a mediaeval *diminutio* at the end of the passage quoted. All
of this makes clear the major point that underlies the squabbles
between Ainsworth and Dickens on the one hand and their
illustrators on the other: that the writers saw the visual sense as
a key element of their work and, in analysing the texts as we have
them, we need to be aware of word and image, text and engraving,
as a single composite text.[18] That the Preface was written after the
completion of the novel, and is thus a retrospective analysis of
the writer's approach, does not, I think, invalidate it: rather, it

15

strengthens the importance and widens the currency of the views it expresses, since Dickens is writing with a particular readership in mind and saying what he assumes they wish to hear. This serves to emphasise the degree to which verbal and visual have become linked in the popular imagination, with all the concomitant skills of reading that this union implies.

These key works of the 1830s established the genre of the illustrated novel as a primary form which covered most of the areas hitherto separated by boundaries of income. Those who had not bought the monthly parts of *Pickwick* could purchase it, after the serial run was completed, bound in cloth for a guinea, half morocco for 24s 6d, or full morocco with gilt-edged leaves for 26s 6d. Ainsworth's novels were available in similar range. *The Tower of London* appeared in thirteen parts over twelve months in 1840, the last being a double issue – an approach that was to become a frequent way of concluding the run of a serial novel. In the same year it was published in a single volume by Richard Bentley; and in 1842 an edition with the forty steel engravings and fifty-eight woodcuts by George Cruikshank was produced. Dickens' periodical *Master Humphrey's Clock* was founded in 1840, and was the first place of publication for *The Old Curiosity Shop* and *Barnaby Rudge*. Thackeray's *Vanity Fair* appeared in monthly parts between 1847 and 1848, with illustrations by the author, before subsequent issue as a single volume. Whether in serial form or as a single publication in one, two or three volumes, the illustrated novel was established as the major mode of popular fiction from the 1830s to the 1850s.

As well as popular taste, technical developments were largely responsible for this. The technique of putting a steel facing on the copper plates used for engravings and so prolonging their life was known from 1823 but was by no means perfect until many years later, when the steel engraving became a major form. Wood engraving, using the hard end-grain of the wood instead of the face used for woodcuts, had been developed by Thomas Bewick at the turn of the century. By the 1830s it was being used to produce runs of up to 100,000 copies and, in the late 1850s and 1860s, became the dominant mode of production for illustrations. The production of collections of wood engravings became fashionable in the 1860s, either as separate plates or as illustrations to works of fiction.

Printing techniques also advanced, with the development of a succession of steam presses and the use of stereotypes to produce copies of a typeset page and so make possible multiple production. This resulted in an explosion of magazines from the later 1850s onwards, ranging from the moral tone of *The Leisure Hour* (1852) and *The Sunday at Home* (1854) through the commercial concerns of *Cassell's Illustrated Family Paper* (1867) to the overtly recreational *Ally Sloper's Half Holiday* (1884) and *Comic Cuts* (1890), the forerunner of the twentieth-century comic which, in 1896, produced its first colour issue. They have in common more than the fact that they all use illustrations: they all create to some degree a unified discourse of word and image.

All of this makes quite credible Carroll's assumption of his readers' familiarity with the delights offered by a book with pictures: the insistent question of how we may critically approach such unified discourse is one to which we must now turn.

III

The growing exploration of semiotics in the second half of the twentieth century has brought the disciplines of literature and art history closer together, and, alongside the change of direction in art history[19] from studies of attribution and tradition to a concern for visual images within a larger socio-political context, this would seem to be a suitable starting point for a critical method in approaching illustrated fiction. A key part of such a methodology is a quest for a theory of literary visualisation which allows it to be placed within the patterns of literary theory which have formed in the second half of the century. A consideration of the degree to which a theory of the unified discourse of word and image has developed – or, at least, what elements of such a theory may be constructed from theoretical discussions of the nature of narrative in its verbal form – is thus a useful starting point for any analysis of the structures and ideologies of illustrated fiction. Once again, however, there has been little interest in this field, with the important but perhaps unsurprising exception of Roland Barthes.

Barthes' work shows a considerable range in itself, moving from the more precisely semiotic analysis of imagery in which Saussurean linguistic analysis is still of prime importance to much more general semiological discussion which accepts a much wider range of approaches, culminating in his final work, especially *Camera Lucida – Reflections on Photography* (1982), in a stress on a deeply personal phenomenological stance. The wider range of semiology and its implications in terms of approaches to the dual text of image and text is something to which I shall return later in this chapter: but before moving in this direction it is of value to explore the stricter methodology expounded by Barthes in his earlier writing. This is important for the reason that, since word and image combine to form part of a larger narrative discourse, it is valid to investigate the ways in which a common ground in linguistic structure may be established as an approach to the new discourse which together they provide.

We may ground this investigation in two areas of Barthes' writing. First there is his essay 'Introduction to the Structural Analysis of Narratives' (Barthes 1977: 79–124), which we might see as a paradigm for the discussion of the structure of images as they contribute to prose narratives; and, secondly, there is his exploration of the semiotic significance of imagery in the essay 'Rhetoric of the Image' (ibid.: 32–51).

In the first of these two essays, Barthes postulates a functional distinction between units of a prose narrative. He suggests that constituents fall into two main groups, functions and indices. Functions are those parts of the verbal structure which concern elements of event or action: they are further divided by Barthes into nuclei, or cardinal functions, which we may paraphrase as major changes of event; and catalysers which, as the word suggests, have more a facilitatory than an initiatory role in the continuance of action. The second group, indices, are to do with character or setting. They, too, are of two orders. Indices proper contain data of fundamental significance, whereas informants give intelligence of less import, or qualify or amplify that which has already been conveyed by a index proper.[20] Is it possible that this division may give us a way in to the analysis of the operation of illustrations as some kind of parallel units within the narrative syntagma?

To answer this it is helpful to consider Barthes' discussion of the nature of images in the other essay. Here, Barthes postulates two relationships between word and image. 'Anchorage' occurs when the words accompanying the image have the function of denotating or locating it, the most frequent example being a caption to a press photograph. 'Relay' is more complex, occurring when word and image each contribute separate but related units to single syntagma, which is often in its turn part of a larger diegesis (Barthes 1977: 38–41).

This poses the question of whether, in the illustrated novel, the relationship between word and image may ever be as simple and one-dimensional as Barthes' 'Anchorage'. Certainly it would seem unlikely, since such a relation would inevitably throw the main significance on to the image, into which the verbal unit is subsumed as a kind of enabling device to complete the denotative significance, as Barthes' example of the caption to a newspaper photograph makes clear. I would suggest that this kind of relation is not one that need concern us long: it is something which is perhaps present in the collections of images with accompanying text which were popular in the early years of the nineteenth century – the tradition from which Dickens strove to escape in *The Pickwick Papers* – although, even here, the link is likely to be more complex. Even when captions occur in illustrated fiction, they do not constitute the whole of the verbal half of the equation: the reader's knowledge of character, action, locale and a number of other signifieds is necessary for the illustration to fulfil its true semiotic purpose and thus contribute to the reading experience.[21]

This assumption made, we are left with the relation of relay as the main structural link between word and image, which we may explore within the range presented by Barthes' concerns with functions and indices as units of narrative. These are made clearer by Barthes' subsequent discussion of the levels of significance of a visual image, which may be separated for the purposes of analysis into denotative and connotative.

Straightaway, though, we encounter a difficulty. Barthes' essay is primarily concerned with an image from commercial photography used with an advertising slogan. Its signification is multivalent, but does not approach the complexity present within a drawing, as he makes clear. In a drawn illustration, every apparently denotative element is also connotative, since it is the product of the style of an individual and the culture which produces it – to varying degrees depending on how far we accept the validity of Barthes' claim of 'The Death of The Author' (Barthes 1977: 142–8). An illustration is an idiolect because of its style and structure as much as in the network of signification it sets up: ultimately there is no such thing as a purely denotative element within it. Analysis thus becomes a matter of factitiously teasing out the separate layers of connotative signification, to sort out the signifieds which are implicit within style and structure – which are, of course, in essence inseparable.

This should not, I think, present too much difficulty in terms of the practical analysis of images and their operations within the novel. We may construct the layers as follows. First there is the layer of denotation – which depends upon the reader's knowledge of a set of conventions of signification much the same as that postulated by Gombrich's idea of the 'beholder's share' (1960: *passim*). An acceptance of this level of denotation at such a level that it becomes unnoticed – an acceptance that image is object, not a series of lines or tones – is part of the idiolect, the outlook of the individual formed by the dominant cultural mode of his or her day. This would account for the ease with which early nineteenth-century onlookers accept as quite 'natural' images in, say, Rowlandson's aquatints to *Dr Syntax*, elements which we now consider remote in their stylisation: and why, slightly later, readers of *Sketches by Boz* assimilated the comic caricatures as similarly 'natural' when to a late-twentieth-century – that is, post-photographic, post-filmic and post-computer-graphic – idiolect they appear self-conscious and exaggerated to a degree.

From this, there is the level of narrative significance – the level of 'meaning' which is usually described in popular accounts of narrative as 'action'. To understand this we need to be able to grasp denotation as signifying event – to see what is going on in an illustration. When we look, for example, at a man running from another lying on the ground, we need to be able to construct a causal relationship between the two. For this, we need a knowledge of the other key feature – inseparable from other elements of fictive progress but conveniently done so by tradition in criticism of the novel – that we know as 'character'. In this instance, the denotation of a person will carry signifieds of personality – good, evil and various degrees between – which will enable us to place him or her within the 'action' that is being shown, and perhaps draw conclusions about his or her contributions to its present, past and possible future course.

A further level is provided by what we might term the emblematic or iconologic level of signification – the presence of visual elements which we first read as denotative of specific objects, and then endow with a larger moral or referential significance because of the tradition of encrypting within which the idiolect of the image exists. In Renaissance painting, for example, this allows us to read quite naturally a dove as the holy spirit, or light passing through a window as the virgin birth.

At a more complex level are the signifieds which do not work in the convention of a named emblem. These are suggestions of mood or atmosphere, or possible future event, which occur through juxtaposition of objects, placement of characters, or elements of composition, rhythm, chiaroscuro, and all the other components of a visual construct. To these, of course, we need to add the cumulative effect of such elements, the way in which, to a reader who has a grasp of the idiolect, such elements work together to produce an effect or response. This collective structure, the series of relationships to which Barthes refers as the 'rhetoric of the image', is something of key importance when we come to address the issue of how we decrypt and respond to an illustration and place it within a complex narrative structure.

All of these layers of signification are, of course, present in an image which does not have any literary conjunction, an image which is 'pure', lacking a text to provide relay or anchorage. When we add the knowledge of the text to these signifiers, they become more complex not only in the dimensions we have discussed in the preceding paragraphs but also in the relationship between the style of the verbal text and that of the image. When we consider the complexity of all these relations, Barthes' ideas of 'function' and 'index' as applicable to illustrations as units of narrative do seem somewhat simplistic. Yet, if we accept that the levels of stratification constructed above are a useful fallacy when it comes to analysing connotative functions in images, might we not also accept their value – a kind of facilitating validity – when looking at illustrations as units of narrative? Might we then hope to arrive not only at some kind of rudimentary rhetoric of the image, but also at some sort of narratology, or structural analysis of narrative, for use in the analysis of narratives which are constructed of verbal and visual units which are equal partners in the discourse?

How does this work in practice? An illustration chosen almost, but not quite, at random will allow us to explore the validity and value of the approach. This is the plate showing the body of Little Nell after she has died in Chapter 71 of *The Old Curiosity Shop* (1951: 538; see Plate 1). This occurs near the end of the chapter, where her father calls into the room those who have gathered to see her in her illness. Accepting for the moment the fiction of a purely denotative level, and taking for granted an acceptance of the stylistic as natural and representational, we see a young woman lying on a bed; a book is in her right hand, some flowers rest on the bedclothes and some leaves are on the pillow. At the left there is some kind of carved headboard; to the right there is a gothic arch with an open window, a washstand and a rudimentary account of the wall of the room, on which is hanging some sort of cupboard or cage. These are the most basic denotatory elements, couched in the style of a mid-Victorian line engraving.

A contemporary reader, sharing the idiolect of the artist, would instantly recognise this as a pious representation of a young girl dignified in death. One who has read the novel would know more: this is Nell on her deathbed, lying at peace. Event and character are inseparable, since her death is another version of the innocence and goodness that has run throughout her life. This is, perhaps, the simple function of 'anchorage' suggested by Barthes, a kind of caption; yet, since it is not supplied by a short passage of text, but by our knowledge of the world of the novel which encompasses Nell, it can hardly be seen as separate from the more complex elements which tie the image to the text which immediately surrounds it.

Before we explore these, however, we should note some of the emblematic elements which a contemporary reader would have had no difficulty in decoding. The book on the bed is without question the Bible; the hourglass in the window an emblem of Nell's death since the sand has all run from the upper into the lower chamber, showing that time has run out for her. The open window is an emblem of the free passage of the spirit; and the carved headboard a representation of the Madonna and Child to imply the purity and saintliness of Nell, and so adding the suggestion that she lives on in a Christian heaven.

Most of these are elements which can be read without recourse to the novel: they are part of the shared idiolect of illustrator and contemporary observer. The exception is the identification of Nell and her nature: but, since this would be gained from a reading of the part of the novel which precedes the scene depicted, it is not part of the immediate moment of the illustration. It is, if you like, a narrative placement at a deep level which in a way is analogous to the assumptions made about the onlooker's idiolect. The verbal text which accompanies the illustration is of a different order, since it locates the image specifically within the narrative, revealing other

levels of signification and 'meaning' within it. The paragraph above
the illustration reads thus:

> Her couch was dressed with here and there some winter
> berries and green leaves, gathered in a spot she had been
> used to favour. 'When I die, put near me something that has
> loved the light, and had the sky above it always.' Those were
> her words.

(1951: 539)

The flowers and berries in the illustration are revealed as an
embodiment of Nell's wishes. To this we must add their larger
signification as an emblem of spirituality: when we know that they
are '*winter* berries and leaves' we know that they are evergreens, and
this turns them into signifieds of eternal life which, within the
image's 'rhetoric', amplify and redefine the idea of spiritual release
shown in the open window. Word and image here work together,
the one giving specific reference, the other supplying visual detail
and emblem. ᵃˢ ᵒᵇʲᵉᶜᵗˢ associated with and serving to indentify something
else.

The illustration does, however, go beyond the confines of the
text in one important measure. A few words after the passage
quoted above, the chapter continues: 'Her little bird – a poor
slight thing the pressure of a finger would have crushed – was
stirring nimbly in its cage; and the strong heart of its child mistress
was mute and motionless for ever' (1951: 539). This allows us to
understand the significance of the rectangular object to the right of
the illustration: it is a bird-cage. In a sense, the text is essential to
clarify the denotative meaning of the illustration in this regard; yet
designative
the link is much more important and more dynamic than this
purpose of mere identification. On close examination we can see
that the door of the cage is open and that on the window sill there
is a bird. When read together with the text, the image is revealed as
an extension of the verbal image of the bird continuing in life,
which gives it added force by showing the bird set free. This in
turn amplifies the image of the soul's release from the body in
death that is presented by the open window.

The relation between this sentence and the image thus couples
our ability to 'read' the illustration at a simple denotative level and
our symbolic decoding of the signification of open cage door and
freed bird, with the result of extending the verbal image into
another statement of release. We cannot easily separate denotative
from connotative here; and neither can we easily set apart this

section of the illustration from other passages, because of the image's arrangement of lines and tones – which, in its turn, is another level of existence of the image. The door of the bird-cage opens towards us and to the right; the window opens away from us and to the left. The two forms thus balance each other in the composition of the illustration, the one leading us to the other, and so enhancing the link between the two visual statements of release.

This is one example of how something that appears simply an element of design is also fundamentally denotative and at the same time has a major function in the connotative role of the illustration. Similar complexity is found if we try to separate Barthes' function from index here. The idea of release is an element of narrative advancement, albeit not of major significance, so it is a catalyser, facilitating our larger grasp of Nell's freedom in death; but it is also a comment on the release achieved by Nell as a result of her goodness and purity, so it is an informant. This single element of the visual statement is thus reinforced both by other emblems in the illustration and by the knowledge of the plot and of Nell, which we have not only from this passage of this chapter but from the novel as a whole. Denotative, connotative, plot, character, catalyser, informant – all of these come together in a complex structure of elements within the illustration and in its interchange with the verbal text.

If we now try to place the illustration as a whole within Barthes' notions of functions and indices, the inadequacy of the use of such distinctions becomes immediately apparent. It is a major event in the narrative, so it could be called a cardinal function. But it is also to do with character, so it is an index, with, as discussed above, the use of some of the emblematic details as catalysers. We might perhaps take this further and say that the various elements of the illustration perform various roles as functions, catalysers and the rest: yet this would seemingly only give us a kind of taxonomy of visual statement, which would not do much to advance our grasp of the relationship between text and image. It would seem that, suggestive as they are, Barthes' categories for a system of narratology work well with the small units of verbal discourse, but cannot properly be assimilated into the analysis of illustrations. It is perhaps inevitable that, just as every denotator is a connotator in illustration, so every function is also an index, since we can rarely separate action from character in the visual presentation of narrative.

This does not mean that Barthes' earlier approach is not of value: certainly, a grasp of the different orders of elements which constitute an illustration is essential if we are fully to explore their significance. They are a valuable basis: but, for reasons of the multivalence of significance which have become clear in the preceding paragraphs, I do not find them a useful approach in the analysis of the compound discourse of word and image which is the subject of this present study since they seem to draw attention away from the image and text and to the process of categorisation. Certainly, the progression of Barthes' own work would seem to confirm this: his later writings on imagery show a strong movement towards a concern for semiology in its broadest sense, reflecting a great diversity of visual significations and 'languages', in place of a semiotic approach which rests on defining precise equivalences with grammatical structures. These other significations involve social and political elements of the image, and a whole range of other 'meanings' resting on areas such as gender, ethnicity and the relationship of power and idea which the image creates between itself and its beholder. In the image of Little Nell, for example, some critics might find the depiction of the woman typical of the infantilisation of women seen throughout Victorian painting and a good deal of fiction; others might relate it to a Freudian reading of Dickens' own sexuality.

Issues of this sort are complex enough in an image not linked to text: add a verbal discourse, and the complexity becomes even greater. Yet this does not mean that a concern for the rhetoric of illustration does not have its place: Meyer Schapiro's absorbing study of mediaeval biblical illustration, and the relationship postulated between reader and illustrated figure by the use of figures in profile and figures presented full-face, (Schapiro 1973: *passim*, esp. 37–49) makes clear that an awareness of these elements is fundamental to any analytic discipline. In the studies that follow, I have used a range of approaches to image, text and ideology which try to reflect this diversity while remaining aware of what we might term the larger syntagmatic nature of the placement of illustrations within a dual discourse of image and text.

Exactly what this may mean in practice, when an illustration contributes to the continuum of the narrative and so modifies our reading experience, may be shown by further exploring George Cattermole's illustration of the dead body of Little Nell in *The Old Curiosity Shop*. Coming at the end of the chapter, it provides us with a moment of stasis, of contemplation, almost, in the face of the death of the character. That the engraving is placed sideways in the original edition, with the consent and to the satisfaction of Dickens, is also significant.[22] We have to turn the book around to take in the image, and in so doing we suspend the continuum of the verbal discourse. This presentation of a moment of stasis within the text is only one function of the image, which also extends and deepens the verbal text in the ways explored above; but we might say that it is the larger, overall role that it performs in the reading process, and might well have some sort of cathartic operation for the original readers who are not frightened of the charge of sentimentality that hovers around the episode for a twentieth-century reader.

This is only one of a significant number of larger roles an illustration might perform – either singly or, more often, in complex combination. The moment of contemplation seen in the image of Little Nell is also seen, for example, in the detailed study of the departure of the Micawbers in *David Copperfield* (1948: 832; see Plate 2) with a use of detail to present character at a nodal point of the action which is of considerable importance in the reading experience, and which occurs frequently in illustrated novels of this period. Yet there are many other roles for illustrations. Even if we restrict our concern to the high tide of Victorian illustrated fiction alone, the roles are various. Illustration can heighten suspense by delaying a key moment of the text, as for example in the illustration by Boz to *Oliver Twist* (1947: 390) which shows Fagin trapped on the roof, the rope already about his neck. This illustration advances the narrative by restraining it, forcing us to contemplate what will happen next; and at the same time it is perhaps also a moral statement, stressing the nemesis that is to fall on Fagin in response to his misdeeds – a reading that original beholders would almost certainly have given to the image. The caption, 'The Last Chance', enhances both narrative and moral delay, reinforcing the image's effect still further.

This image is an example of another fundamental point which any discussion of illustration must embrace at an early stage: the selection of moments of the fictive discourse for illustration. What is and is not illustrated, and the placement of illustrations in the verbal text, is of course influenced by commercial and technical considerations: but it is also something of very considerable importance in the creation of the dual discourse that results, and hence of the reading experience.

Illustrations may perform a role that is more general. Consider, for example, the frontispiece to *Bleak House* (1977: xxii) which shows the house itself gaunt and isolated in swirling fog. Close to it comes the famous opening of the novel in which, in the whole of the first paragraph, there is not a single finite verb, the whole being held together instead by present participles which explore the murk of the city. Here verbal and visual text combine to convey what is the symbolic and literal core of the novel – the real and moral fog that engulfs the characters of the novel. The lack of incident in the illustration is far more than mere scene setting of the sort found in the tipped-in plates to Scott's novels.[23] It is a visualisation of the stasis caused by the fog which is shown also in the verbal text, where the absence of finite verbs is also the absence of tense, so that the two are close parallels in the statement of physical and moral paralysis. Here the stylistic parallel discussed earlier is of major importance in constructing the dual discourse of word and image, and in affecting the reading experience so profoundly at the very start of the novel.

The subtlety of this should warn us against assuming a simple use of illustrations for 'atmosphere' – a kind of untramelled index, in early Barthesian terms – since this is rare, especially in Dickens. He does not, for example, choose to present us with an illustration of the desecration of Staggs's Gardens by the coming of the railway in the early chapters of *Dombey and Son* – his concern is not so much for the material detail, but for the spiritual result of this desolation.[24]

Sometimes, an illustration can embody the text's ideas in other ways; by extending them in the provision of new elements, by making explicit ideas only suggested indirectly in words, or by presenting an ironic counter-current to the written text. The image showing the return from the wedding in *Dombey and Son*, (1950: 447; see Plate 3) for example, subtly extends the images of negativity which pepper the chapter by including, in the background, a funeral hearse, a punch and judy show, and a ragged street band, all of which deconstruct the formal prosperity of the foreground bridal procession, but none of which is mentioned explicitly in the text. The illustrations to George du Maurier's *Trilby*, by the author himself, often add an ironic dimension in revealing the pomposity of the characters.

The most complete example of this rather savage relationship, in which the rules of the Victorian materialist novel seem to have been totally abandoned, occurs throughout Thackeray's *Vanity Fair*. The Preface makes quite clear the dominant conceit of the novel: the presentation of the characters as puppets by the author as puppet-master. The title page and frontispiece even depict the puppets in their chest and the puppeteer manipulating them. Throughout the novel, the illustrations present the characters as unreal, wooden figures, in a kind of Victorian anticipation of Brechtian A-effect where we are constantly kept away from sympathising with the novel's cast. Yet there is in some way a strange parallel between the final illustration of *Vanity Fair* and the depiction of the death of Little Nell discussed earlier, as both significantly extend the verbal text, albeit in different ways (see Plate 4). Thackeray's final image shows Becky and Amelia putting the dolls back into a toy box, except one, a portly male figure in frock coat, who lies on his back with his legs against the box. This seems to be an overt reference to the death of Jos Sedley, referred to on the preceding page. In the verbal text, there is only a suggestion that Becky has been responsible for his death: in the visual, the link seems to be more explicit. The completion or extension of the verbal text by the visual thus presented performs an almost exactly opposite moral function in the *Old Curiosity Shop* image: there, the presence of the figure of the Madonna on the headboard suggests that Nell's death is a beginning rather than the ending so heavily stressed in the accompanying paragraphs.

All of these are individual examples of ways in which illustrations may contribute to the workings of a unified discourse of word and image, with the resultant ideological and moral effect upon the reader. The role of illustration within a complete fictive structure is, of course, incalculably greater and broader, and demands extensive and detailed study.

Nor should it be assumed that the absence of illustration in a novel also means the absence of visualisation. Running parallel to the convention of the illustrated novel which I have considered here is another stream which does not use illustration – a particularly rich stream, in that it includes Mary Shelley, the Brontës, Elizabeth Gaskell and, after the failure of *Romola*, George Eliot. In novels of this tradition, the visual sense becomes part of a continuum of experience presented within the verbal discourse with an intensity of which external visual treatment would be incapable: Chapter 6 explores the ways in which this may be seen to operate in a twentieth-century bestseller.

The sub-title of Joanne Shattuck and Michael Wolff's pioneering and influential study of the Victorian periodical press, *Samplings and Soundings*, sets the right tone for the remainder of this present study. Instead of trying to provide an encyclopaedic and inevitably fictive 'history' of the roles of illustration in popular fiction, I have instead tried to select for detailed exploration individual works which typify some of the problems and issues which need to be addressed in the study of the dual discourse of word and text, and of the ideological constructs it is seen to present. The first study explores the way in which the reading habits of the public affected not only social journalism of the late 1860s but spilled over into academic painting, continuing the elision of genres mentioned in the preceding section of this chapter and so revealing the extent to which reading illustrated text had permeated the culture of the time.

Chapter 2 explores illustration in children's fiction not in the customary manner, but as a reflection of changing ideas of children and of larger ideologies. Illustrated magazines of the 1900s are next discussed by way of a close examination of a typical number. The way in which the addition of illustrations some little while after the production of a novel can significantly relocate its ideological stance is next discussed with reference to a bestseller of the 1920s; there follows an exploration of the role of visualisation within the psychological continuum created by the narrative in a novel without illustrations. The final chapters take as their subjects the nature and function of visual elements in representative comic-strip fiction of the 1950s and a key film from the so-called British realist cinema of the 1960s, to look at the way in which visual structures respectively extend and redirect the narrative impulse of their verbal texts. These are offered both as ends in themselves, and as examples of the kind of approaches that are possible.

The field of illustrated fiction is extensive. As a foundation of popular reading for over a century, it deserves greater critical attention than it has in the past received. The aim of this book is to suggest some directions which this exploration can follow.

2

GRAPHIC NARRATIVES

By the mid-1860s, the illustration was firmly established as a part of the narrative structure of the novel. Generally produced by the artist in close collaboration with the writer, it offered a means of comment as well as a redefining of viewpoint which ensured that the reader, while remaining a privileged observer outside the sequence of events, was nevertheless offered guidance as to how the events offered in the discourse should be perceived. If we add to this complex reading experience the circumstance that novel reading was socially quite pervasive, ranging from those who bought the complete three-volume edition of the novel for 31s 6d on its appearance right the way across to those who contributed a halfpenny a week to buy a shared copy of a fortnightly part of the latest bestseller, we must conclude that the combination of printed text and single visual image was one of the dominant cultural modes of the time. A specific index of this can be provided by comparing A. & C. Black's twenty-volume edition of the *Waverley Novels*, published in 1860, with Constable's six-volume edition of 1824. Each volume contains over thirty illustrations, either wood or steel engravings, taken from the much more expensive Abbotsford Edition: their provision in a small format edition, cheaply bound and aimed at a much larger reading public, clearly indicates the much greater importance of illustrations.

It is clear, then, that the illustrated text was a way in which the emotional journeys and mythic patterns contained in the novel were experienced by a wide range of readers. From the 1860s onwards, however, the established combination of text and image took on a separate but clearly related function, becoming an instrument through which facets of contemporary reality could be brought into focus and made more immediately accessible. At about the same time, illustration began to take on another dimension of its pervasive importance as a cultural product; from the conventions of the magazines it spilled over into academic painting and became an artefact of the wealthiest society homes. A scrutiny of this expansion of influence reveals the degree to which the visual sense and the narrative had become inseparable not only in the act of telling a story, but also in the act of presenting aspects of external reality and voicing critical opinions about them. The key element in bringing about this role of the visual image is the illustrated periodical.

On 4 December 1869 the first number of a new magazine appeared: *The Graphic*, 'An Illustrated Weekly Newspaper: Price Sixpence or by post Sixpence Halfpenny'. Illustrated journalism was not new: The *Illustrated London News* had been in existence since 1841, as had *Punch, or the London Charivari*, and both had their imitators. By the sixties, the journal with wood engravings was a well-established source of information and what we would now term 'feature' or 'background' pieces, concerned not with breaking news items but with expanding on recent events or discussing issues of topical interest. But what was new about *The Graphic* was the way in which it used skilled, representational artists of the highest calibre to produce the drawings from which the engravings were made, and the way in which they approached their subjects. To understand what made *The Graphic* both part of this tradition and different from it, we need to look briefly at the complex set of circumstances and influences from which these magazines grew, and the nature and function of their illustrative engravings.

In their earliest numbers both *Punch* and the *Illustrated London News* had used illustrations which were crude in both content and execution, resting heavily on the tradition of the caricature sketch which the novel illustrations of the 1830s had developed from the popular prints of an earlier generation. By the 1860s, techniques of both wood engraving and illustrative drawing on which it might be based had developed greatly, partly due to the growth of a ready market for such work in illustrated journals and partly through chance. This flowering came to be known after the decade in which it occurred, the 'sixties style' stressing dark, close textures caused by infinite variation of the spacing of engraved lines, often alternating with free and imaginative use of white paper to give the characteristic lighting effect referred to in the name of 'black and white art' by which it was also known. Add to this the intense emotional narrative effects of the second generation pre-Raphaelites, and it is clear that the 'sixties style' is a complex medium well suited to the presentation of dramatic incident and feeling.

The new style was most strikingly apparent in illustrations of literary writing. Two of the most celebrated works, from which the new style is often thought to have derived, are William Allingham's *The Music Master* (1855) and the edition of Tennyson's *Poems* published by Edward Moxon in 1857. Although these are both volumes of poems, they should not be regarded as distinct from popular literature: Tennyson's poetry was at that time at the height of its popularity, and Allingham's fairy-verse was also well known, albeit as the result of one lyric beginning 'Up the airy mountain / Down the rushy glen'. Both volumes contained wood engravings after drawings by Rossetti, Holman Hunt and Arthur Hughes, the concentration and intensity of which established the rich textures of the sixties style and instigated a flood of followers. Because of the publishing market of the time, this did not simply mean pictures in volumes of poetry, novels bound as one or three volumes, or any other single form. It included plates or cuts – separate pages or illustrations incorporated in the text – in serial parts of a novel published as separate chapters or groups of chapters in a magazine. Important magazines in this regard were *The Cornhill* and *Good Words*; and, since these carried both fiction and factual or feature articles, the interchange between the illustrations of the two forms was perhaps inevitable. From this, the influence broadened to the illustrated news magazines so that, by the middle years of the decade if not before, the standard of engraving in periodicals such as *The Illustrated News* and *The Illustrated Times* was far superior to that of twenty years previously. The same is true to some degree of *Punch*, both in the full-page drawings on social or political themes known as 'cartoons', as opposed to the smaller humorous drawings or 'sketches' – what we would now call cartoons. And the interplay of artists and engravers producing the material was as considerable as in earlier decades: the list of figures who produced work for *Punch*, the illustrated fiction journals and those carrying news or descriptive features, and illustrations for books of poems or other anthologies is long and distinguished, including John Tenniell, Richard Doyle and a range of other figures.

All of this means that, by the time of the foundation of *The Graphic*, the new style of dense, dramatically lit engraving with high articulation of emotions was firmly established as a part of fiction and in social reportage. Thus the reader, in his or her experience of the discourse offered in such material, is not only presented with visual styles which may be very similar in both 'fact' and 'fiction' passages; he or she also encounters a relationship between word and image which is fundamentally the same in both, and thus a type of discourse is shared between notional 'fact' and 'fiction' which colours and in many cases directs the reader's approach to the outside world.

This merging of forms is something which is particularly significant in one of the most celebrated illustrations to appear in the first number of *The Graphic*. This issue contained a great range of illustration. Some of it was quite self-contained, such as the title-page engraving 'Egyptian Girl (from a painting by Richter)'. Other images had a clearer origin in recent events: the King of the Belgians receiving a civic address, Pope Pius IX in council, a series of views of the recently opened Suez canal, along with portraits of Ferdinand de Lesseps and the Khedive of Egypt, and a view of the 'Wreck of the Spindrift', a sailing ship recently gone aground. Engravings of 'The Pasha's Couriers' by W. Thomas and a portrait of Queen Victoria, 'from life by the late George H. Thomas', completed the visual material, with the exception of one image which stood apart for its visual quality and subject matter: 'Houseless and Hungry', a wood engraving after S. Luke Fildes (see Plate 5).

Some of these engravings accompanied a descriptive article in the magazine – on the Suez canal or the changing nature of the papacy, to take examples from the first number. Those which were not part of such an article were still given a prose commentary, generally printed not alongside but a few pages distant, grouped with other commentaries in a section headed 'Our Illustrations'. These passages ranged from a single paragraph to well over a full column of print, about 2,000 words in length. I stress this because it reveals that the verbal text had something approaching the importance of the passages accompanying the engraving in a much earlier print-publication: in *Dr Syntax*, for example, there is one plate for each canto of verse, a passage of between four and eight pages; in Dickens' *Sketches by Boz*, each plate is accompanied by a passage of about 3,500 words. That the prose in *The Graphic* is shorter is perhaps inevitable given the publication of the illustration in a magazine made of several discrete articles rather than as a self-contained periodical part; but that it is still extensive suggests that it is part of the same tradition of publishing. It also reveals the importance of *The Graphic*'s prose passages to the practice of reading the illustrations, implying that the two texts, verbal and visual, form a single discourse which invites a very particular kind of response from the reader.

What we need now to address is the relationship of the verbal and visual texts, to explore the particular kind of discourse they together offer, and what this tells us about the visual sense in the new magazine as it is related to the visual sense in the novel and within the larger context of the way external reality – particularly social and moral problems of the day – was presented and perceived.

In discussing the effect of this illustration and its text, an awareness of its sources is helpful, since it shows that there is a mixture of 'fact' and 'fiction', the genres of the exploratory, social issue journalism of the emergent magazines and of the illustrated novel, in their antecedents. Fildes himself gives what seems to be a clear account of the origin of the illustration in a scene he himself witnessed. In the summer of 1869 Fildes was still a student at the Art and Science Department in South Kensington, but was increasingly producing work for the illustrated papers, some of which depicted street life in London. William Luson Thomas, then developing his plan for *The Graphic*, asked him to produce a drawing on any topic. Fildes' account continues:

> Some few years before, when I first came to London, I was very fond of wandering about, and never shall I forget seeing somewhere near the Portland Road, one snowy winter's night, the applicants for admission to a casual ward. It lived in my mind, and as I sat there in my room I tried to reproduce it.
> (How 1893: 119–20)

Two years after this, however, Fildes recalled the origin of the illustration somewhat differently:

> I had been to a party, I think, and happened to return by a police station, when I saw an awful crowd of poor wretches applying for permits to lodge in the Casual Ward. I made a note of the scene, and after that often

went again, making friends with the policeman and talking with the people themselves. That was my chance, and I at once began to make studies for my Graphic picture.

(Thompson 1895: 5)

That the circumstances of the origins of the composition should not be recalled exactly by the artist after a lapse of well over twenty years is not perhaps surprising: but the uncertainty of Fildes' memories suggests that other explanations of the genesis of the image might be just as valid as the artist's own. Fildes' stress that Thomas did not stipulate the subject – 'Anything you like . . . as long as it's effective and a good drawing' are the instructions the artist quotes – also seems unlikely. Weight of circumstance would seem to support a quite different view: Thomas, after all, was an experienced editor about to launch a major illustrated journal, Fildes was a young illustrator who had already produced a few fiction illustrations and some scenes of London street life. It seems far more reasonable to suppose that the commission would have been specified, if only in fairly general terms, within the area of Fildes' known interests and the social concerns of the paper.

This general vagueness in Fildes' account makes it at the very least plausible that other factors and influences were involved in the choice of the subject. The artist's own interest in street life in London is one dimension of a larger awareness that had been current for some time. It is important to distinguish this from the 'street cries of old London' motifs familiar from eighteenth-century prints, or the comic excursions of *Life in London*: since industrialisation street life was something accompanied by dirt, squalor and for most middle-class onlookers a fear of attack that perhaps equates with late twentieth-century mistrust of late-night city travel. What, then, were the sources that Fildes might have been aware of, if not necessarily influenced by, when producing his first *Graphic* drawing?

One of the most important roots of the social inquiry illustration was Henry Mayhew's monumental study *London Labour and the London Poor*. The first three volumes of this appeared in 1851; the third, *The London Street Folk*, included an engraving, 'Asylum for the Houseless Poor, Cripplegate', subtitled 'from a sketch' (Mayhew 1851: 419; see Plate 6). The draughtsmanship is representative of Victorian engraving at its simplest and least expressive, yet it contains many elements of Fildes' composition. The groups of figures stand before a clearly identified building embellished with classical columns, which reappear vestigially in Fildes' backdrop. The pose of the male figure at the right, with arms folded against the cold, is echoed in the figure just to the left of centre in Fildes' engraving; and the general range of characters – male and female, of a diversity of ages and backgrounds, as far as we may judge from the crude sketch – is something explored further by the later artist. These may well be chance resemblances, of course, or likenesses based on the actual nature and postures of the figures outside the casual wards. Yet there is enough similarity to suggest a possible influence and, given the popularity of Mayhew's work even at its publication and Fildes' avowed interest in street scenes, it seems at the very least likely that the young student of illustration would have seen a copy.

Interesting though it may be in passing, my main purpose here is not to establish a source for Fildes' composition: instead I am concerned with the relation between illustration and text. Mayhew's writing follows the practice he had established in the earlier volumes of his survey, in presenting interviews or 'statements' from individual people. The accounts of the people waiting for admission to the asylum which accompany the illustration include this from a native of Somerset:

> I walked up one street and down another. I sometimes got under a doorway, but it was impossible to stand still long, it was so cruel cold. The sleet was coming down one night, and freezed on my clothes as it fell. The cold made me stiff more than sleepy. It was next day that I felt tired; and then, if I came to sit down at a fireside, I should drop asleep in a minute. I tried, when I was dead-beat, to get into St. Giles's union, but they wouldn't admit me. Then the police sent me up to another union: I forget the name, but they refused me. I tried at Lambeth, and there I was refused. I don't think I went a day without some small bit of bread. I begged for it. But when I walked from St. Alban's to London, I was two days without a bit to put into my mouth. I never stole, not a particle, from any person, in all my trials. I was brought up honest, and, thank God, I have kept so all my life.
>
> (Mayhew 1851: 420)

After the conclusion of this statement, Mayhew continues:

I then took the statement of a seaman, but one who, from destitution, had lost all the distinguishing characteristics of a sailor's dress of the better description . . . He stated: – 'I am now thirty-five, and have been a seaman all my life. I first went to sea, as a cabin-boy, at Portsmouth. I was left an orphan at fourteen months, and don't know that I have a single relation but myself. I don't know what my father was. I was brought up at the Portsea workhouse. I was taught to read and write. I went to sea in 1827 . . . '

(1851: 420)

The seaman's statement goes on to record in some detail the misfortunes which have led him to his present position at the asylum. It is not unusual in its length, Mayhew's recorded 'statements' often covering a complete two-column page, over 1,000 words, and providing a detailed account of the speaker's life and suffering. The degree of genuineness of the stories, and the accuracy with which they were transcribed, are not at issue here; what is significant is that, in presenting an account of such people alongside an illustration in which they figure, Mayhew is creating a dual text remarkably like that of a Victorian illustrated novel. The autobiographical nature of the statements makes the link even closer, by presenting even in limited form the verisimilitude of recorded speech seen most evidently in Dickens but also as a major feature of characterisation in the work of other contemporary novelists.

What we have here is the unity of verbal and visual text to present a single stage of the narrative process revealed in the writing. The illustration acts as a kind of ganglion, a coming together of the narratives of a series of individuals which are presented in the written text. The seaman and the man from Somerset meet outside the asylum, and we are given a moment of frozen time to reflect upon their experience, in exactly the manner of a Victorian novel illustration which offers us this stasis. The illustration of Micawber's emigration discussed in Chapter 1 performs just such a role: it brings together a series of separate narrative strands and allows us to stand back from the sequence of events to contemplate character and emotion at a turning point of narrative sequence in the kind of blending of Barthes' function and index discussed earlier. The verbal narrative tells us what has happened so far; the visual allows us to share what

37

is happening now. That this technique is used in a work of factual inquiry reveals the degree to which this kind of dual discourse had permeated Victorian cultural production and consumption. Instead of tables of numbers, lists of impersonal statistics about 'the homeless', or arguments to convey causes and consequences of homelessness in the abstract, Mayhew offers us individual figures and their experiences, and unites their narratives with a visual statement at a key point where their 'stories' coincide. It is a kind of making real which allows us to share experience by presenting actualities as part of a story: the apparently factual is thus made more acceptable, and, paradoxically, more 'real', by being located within the dual text of a Victorian novel, revealing a subtle control of narrative progression, interplay of characters and above all the dual discourse of word and image which, as this chapter will later make clear, is fundamental to a grasp not only of Victorian popular fiction but also of Victorian narrative and moral painting.

   In this particular instance, the relationship between factual and fictional writing is shown to be even greater since there is a treatment in avowedly fictional form of what appears to be the same research material. In 1858, Augustus Mayhew had published *Paved with Gold: or the Romance and Reality of the London Streets*, a novel based on his brother Henry's work of social investigation. The early pages of this contain an account of a crowd outside the casual ward, along with an illustration by 'Phiz', the illustrator of Dickens and Ainsworth (see Plate 7). The illustration has familiar elements – the lantern, the range of people, the mother and child – and the caption, 'The Asylum for the Houseless', seems to fore-shadow Fildes' illustration. The image's emotional intensity is increased by its nocturnal setting, the falling snow and the narrow street in which the shelter is located, all of which add a sense of exposure and a feeling of emotional containment to the idea of displacement which is already strong in the scene and circumstances depicted.

   To this is added the quality of emotional involvement conveyed by the accompanying text. This is worth quoting at some length to establish the dual discourse of word and image.

   There they stand shivering in the snow, with their thin cobwebby garments hanging in tatters about them. Many are without shirts; with their bare skin showing through the rents and gaps, like the hide of a dog with the mange. Some have their greasy garments tied round their wrists and ankles with string, to prevent the piercing wind from blowing up them. A few are without shoes, and these keep one foot only to the ground, while the bare flesh that has had to tramp through the snow is blue and livid-looking, as half-cooked meat.

You can pick out the different foreigners and countrymen in that wretched throng by the different colours of their costume. There you see the black sailor in his faded red woollen shirt; the Lascar in his dirty-white calico tunic; the Frenchman in his short blue smock; the countryman in his clay-stained frock, with the bosom worked all over like a dirty sampler; and the Irish market-woman with her faded straw bonnet, flattened by the heavy loads she has borne on her head . . .

It was to this refuge that the policeman referred when he said to the woman whom he found half-frozen on the door-step, 'The asylum for the houseless is the only place for you.' It was to this refuge that the officer and the faint and weary creature were on their way – so faint and weary, indeed, that Heaven only knows what wretched fate would befall her if the bare hospitality of the place should be denied to her.

(Mayhew 1858: 11)

Here the verbal text once again draws us into a narrative sequence and allows us to engage directly with one of the characters depicted, adding another dimension to the involvement with the illustration seen in Henry Mayhew's work. In the novel, we are taken along to the asylum with the central character, and approach it through her eyes as much as through those of the detached omniscient narrator. There is effectively a dual viewpoint, allowing us both to experience the asylum as does the central figure, and also to recoil from it in horror. Involvement with the story and moral response to it are thus generated in the written text; and both are reinforced and echoed by the visual one, both in its mere presence, forcing us to stop at this key moment in the discourse, and in the way that it places us close to the shelter, allowing us to experience the moment more fully both as participant and onlooker. It is this dual perspective, which exists in both word and image, that makes up the peculiar force of the Victorian image–text narrative in both 'fact' and 'fiction'.

These two texts show that treatment of this theme – the narrative and moral moment of waiting outside the asylum – was clearly established by the time Fildes was required to select a subject for the new *Graphic*. It would be invalid to suggest that the three works show a clear progression from sociological enquiry through the novel to the new illustrated journalism: and clearly there is no such simple linearity of influence. Yet it is, I think, valid to say that this sharing of approach, not only in the actual elements of the composition of the illustration, but in the manner in which verbal and visual work together to create a composite discourse, shows that the practice of reading was, at this time, something which embraced the two elements not only in the novel but also in what we would regard as documents of social enquiry. It is within this context, and with this aspect of the Victorian reader's mindset firmly within our consciousness, that we need to consider Fildes' engraving and the accompanying paragraphs for the first number of *The Graphic*. Since the text has not been reprinted since its first appearance, I reproduce it in its entirety below.

The miserable people whose portraits are given on another page, are well-known to Londoners; for the sort of group they form may be seen outside certain police stations at a regular hour every evening throughout the year. They are some of the homeless poor for whom refuges are supported by the charitable, and on whose behalf Mr Charles Villiers, when President of the Poor Law Board, brought forward the measure known as the Houseless Poor Act. It is by virtue of that Act that the group before us will obtain food and shelter tonight. Before it became law, they would have slept on the strip of pavement by the workhouse of St. Martin-in-the-Fields, or burrowed beneath the dark arches of the Adelphi, or looked out separately for some door step with a covered porch, where they would have remained until morning, or until they were moved on by the constable on his rounds. As it is, they present themselves at a police station and ask for a ticket for admission to the casual ward of a workhouse. This is always given them, unless it happens that the inspector on duty chances to know that they are not in the urgent necessity they pretend; for the fundamental principle of the Houseless Poor Act is, that the destitute shall not spend their nights in the streets, and its provisions are no longer evaded as they were when it first passed into law.

The figures in the picture before us are portraits of real people who received the necessary order for admission on a recent evening, and whose names and last sleeping-place are all entered in the police books. They have nothing in common except hunger, destitution, and rags, and are fair types of the classes who drift into our casual wards night after night. The poor woman with a baby in her arms, and a ragged boy and a woebegone girl running at her side, is the wife of a dock labourer who is now undergoing three weeks' imprisonment for assaulting her. Already owing a heavy score at the general shop, and far behind hand in the weekly payments for the wretched room, which she together with her children and husband shared with others, the conviction of the family bread-winner was the signal for her being turned into the streets. It was clear that he could not earn money in prison, the creditors considered they had been forbearing enough, and had no inclination to increase their losses; so there was a summary ejectment, and four souls were cast destitute into the world. Hating the thought of separation from her children and becoming an inmate of the workhouse, the poor mother is on her way to Essex, where she has friends who she expects will help her. Her case serves to explain the unwillingness to prosecute, so often observed among wives who have been brutally ill-used, and which is sometimes commented on as inexplicable. But signal punishment for the husband means starvation.

The old man with thin worn features and a tall hat, who has just received his ticket and is slowly leaving the police office, has only been in London three days, and purposes to leave it in the morning. An unsteady son, who from being vicious has become criminal, is the cause of his being here at all, and the father having given his deluded boy every penny of the slender sum he brought with him, carries nothing but a heavy heart back to his native village. The two men who come next in rotation, and whom the policeman on duty is on the point of signalling to come in, are vagabonds. One calls himself 'an odd man on the look-out for a job,' the other avers that his health does not allow him to work, and that he subsists mainly upon what 'ladies and gentlemen who are good to him' choose to give. The policeman will tell you that this man is a well-known beggar, who must have been unusually unlucky in his vocation today, or he would not condescend to the meagre fare of the casual ward. Those folded arms, that shrinking mien, those legs clinging together as if to strengthen each other's weakness, that face and chin buried as they are in the shrugged shoulders, combine to form a tableau, the artistic merit of which seldom fails to make the public pay tribute. Very different is the bearing of the old man, who assumes a sturdy, rough-and-ready air, as if burning with anxiety to undertake some heavy labour, such as a railway-cutting, or the manufacture and transport of a load of bricks. This is another form of pretence. He is always out of work, always professing a readiness to be employed, and is one of the most accomplished shirkers in the labour-yard, where all these people are called upon to perform a prescribed quantity of work before leaving in the morning, in return for their shelter and food.

The wretched lad crouched on the pavement has, literally, no history. He never knew his father, and his mother got married and went to America as soon as he can remember. He was bred in the gutter, and he lives in the streets, sometimes hawking fusees, oftener hanging about cabstands, always without friends, and without a definite calling. There are thousands of such boys in London. The Chichester training ship is full of recruits who have been preserved from just such a life as the poor creature before us is leading; and not a night passes in which the casual wards would not supply scores of lads who are willing and eager to be reclaimed, and who, as experience shows, would develop into useful citizens if they could once be taught the rudiments of a decent life.

The middle-aged man with the bulbous nose and the quasi-respectable air, who rears himself against the wall and keeps his hands firmly in his trousers-pockets, with a half-humorous air of philosophic resignation; this man is a character. It is unnecessary to say he has seen better days, or that he has sacrificed comfort and position to drink. There is a rich huskiness in his voice, and a twinkle in his bleary eyes, which speak forcibly of tap-room eloquence and pit-house celebrity. Outcast as he is, this casual pauper is a keen politician, and will denounce the perfidy of ministers, and proclaim the decadence of England to any one who will listen. Supply him with gratuitous drink, and he will fawn upon you, bless you, borrow of you, and curse and abuse you, in rapid succession; telling all the while of the shameful conspiracies of which he has been the victim, and how impossible it is in this effete old country for a man of genuine talent to rise, or hold his own.

The mechanic who nurses his sleeping child so tenderly – a child whose comely features are full of girlish beauty – and the bowed and gaunt woman, his wife, are out looking for work. He has been ill, and was never very expert, so he found his place filled by one younger and more skilful than himself on receiving his discharge from the hospital; and he is now plodding his way to the neighbourhood of a distant town, where, as he has been told, such services as he can render are in demand. Of the two youths in the corner, one has been respectable, and the other belongs to the same type as the crouching boy: several additional years of vagabondage have passed over the head of the other, however, and he is past reclaiming. He has already graduated in petty larceny, and is now boasting of a successful raid upon 'a jolly green old lady as ever I see', to the youth by his side, who is far too much occupied in pitying himself to heed his companion's stories. There is a lurking grin on the face of the hardened young speaker in the scotch cap which is very characteristic; while the air of depressing woe with which the more gently nurtured youth peers into vacancy, makes one feel that he bitterly repents the folly which has brought him to his present pass.

All these people, with many others, received tickets, and were admitted into the casual ward of one of our greatest workhouses a few minutes after this sketch was taken. After submitting to a warm bath, they were each supplied with clean sleeping gowns; the clothes of the vagabonds and of the mechanic and his family being taken away from them for the night, and placed in a hot oven to destroy the vermin with which they were infested. A hunch of dry bread and a basin of water-gruel were given them for supper, and another hunch of bread and a supply of drinking water constituted their breakfast in the morning. When they had performed their allotted task of work, they were discharged; some to carry out their professed intention of seeking work, or of returning to the country, others to spend another idle, shiftless day in the streets or parks, and to present themselves next night at another metropolitan police office, to be examined and certificated, and subsequently bathed, sheltered, and fed.

(The Graphic, 4 December 1869, p. 10)

There are clearly some similarities between this and the passages accompanying the earlier illustrations; but there are also some significant differences. Instead of the autobiographical voices of Henry Mayhew, or the omniscient narrator of Augustus, there is an impersonal, almost official, voice. Inseparable from this is the difference in attitude to those described: the text steers a middle course between presenting the stories without comment and heavily directing our sympathies towards them which the two other accounts respectively represent. Instead, there is a tone of official detachment, attempting to present the truth of the circumstances of each of the figures described, whether professional beggar or abused wife. Yet, despite the apparently factual tone of the writing, both its own nature when considered independently and the relationship that it has with the illustration make use of elements which are the fundamental concern of Victorian fiction: the making real of a situation – both external and psychological – by placing it within a larger continuum of character and narrative.

Important here is the actual information contained in the passage. It is pertinent to ask about its origins and truth: yet there is no record of it being anything other than an invention of the periodical after the production of the illustration. In the 1930s, photographers working on *Picture Post* were sent out to record real-life situations which often approximated to that shown by Fildes. They were accompanied by journalists whose task was to provide information and a larger context – but the image was what counted. There is nothing to suggest that the same happened for *The Graphic.* Fildes' own accounts of how he came up with the subject say nothing of the presence of a journalist, or of his own inquiries about the figures and their stories. Thomas himself, in his account of the founding of the journal, is similarly silent. The only reference is Fildes' own assertion that the illustrations were 'written up to', suggesting that the account was added after the production of the illustration. Certainly, it is the kind of writing that might easily have been produced by a practising journalist who knew a little about the workings of the poor law and had a passing acquaintance with London street life. Whatever its origin, the individuation of the characters is striking. We are offered cross-sections through their lives, with a sketch of what has brought them here and a hint of where they will proceed, learning in this way of the old man with the 'unsteady son'; the 'mechanic' on his way to 'a distant town'; the vagabond who has 'graduated in petty larceny'.

This performs the general function of making the characters of the illustration come alive: we are offered something very similar to the narrative setting of one of the *Sketches by Boz*, or of an incident in a longer narrative in a serial novel. The passage gives the previous histories of the characters shown in the illustration before offering specific clarification of the moment presented in the image. In the third paragraph, for example, we are told that the policeman is 'on the point of signalling to come in' the two vagabonds, the verbal narrative extending our understanding of the structure. A similar expansion occurs later, when we are told what one of the two 'youths in the corner' is saying to the other. And the 'moment' of the illustration is given a kind of narrative closure by the last paragraph of the text, which suggests what will happen to the characters when they are sent off into the world after a night's safe lodging. A more complex linking function is performed in the third paragraph, in the sentence beginning 'the policeman will tell you that this man is a well-known beggar'. This is not merely a way of extending the information given us about the character: it also serves to draw us into the experience of the illustration by suggesting a direct dialogic link between its world and that of the reader, central to which is our familiarity with the figures as shown in the illustration.

All of this makes quite clear the fact that Fildes' wood-engraving is far more than a purely visual statement. It is one half of a dual narrative structure which makes use of the creation of character, the complex manipulation of relationship with character, and the diachronic progression and manipulation of closure in exactly the manner of a Victorian illustrated novel. The dual text offers us a cross-section through the lives of created characters in the frozen instant so common among Victorian illustrators as noted in Chapter 1. Yet, seen with the verbal text, it does not halt the narrative: the visual actuality of the moment, enhanced by details of speech and gesture clarified by the text, contributes to a continuum in which the verbal accounts of the characters' past lives and suggestions of their future treatment is inseparable from the verbal and visual statement of the moment outside the casual ward.

At this point it is worth repeating that this is apparently a work of social realism, a record of events in the streets of London as a statement of current social policy towards the homeless poor. Yet it makes this statement in the techniques familiar from the novel. Paradoxically, the fact that the characters are invented and given fictional life stories makes the scene depicted more real to the reader: instead of generalisations we are given particulars with which we can, if not quite identify, then in many cases sympathise. It may seem strange that, at a time when it was perfectly possible to produce documentary photographs of the realities shown here, an artist's presentation along with a text was preferred. Yet this should not surprise us in an age when many find the dramatisations of recent events in fictionalised television accounts – of the holocaust, say, or of the hostage crisis in the Middle East – more acceptably 'real' than factual and scholarly accounts. What is happening here is the use of a single discourse of illustration and text to make real through fictional presentation an aspect of contemporary reality otherwise difficult to grasp in human terms. The discourse of the illustrated novel is fulfilling a social and psychological function of considerable importance.

II

Novel reading, as we have seen, was a habit shared by all but the very lowest echelons of Victorian society. From the relatively restricted accessibility of *The Graphic* – its sixpenny cover price would have put it out of the reach of even the fairly well-off clerk classes as a regular weekly purchase – it is clear that the process of decoding text and illustration together is something ingrained into the reading habits of those from the higher social orders. The spilling over of this process into academic painting itself can be seen from the way in which Fildes developed 'Houseless and Hungry' into the large canvas *Applicants for Admission to a Casual Ward* which he exhibited at the Royal Academy in 1874. The success of this painting is well documented. At the Academy Summer Exhibition it was hung 'on the line' – at eye level – behind a rope barrier, with a police guard to marshal the crowds. It was then sold for £1,250 to Thomas Taylor, a north-country cotton magnate.

46

Instead of the detailed narrative of the earlier version in *The Graphic*, the painting was accompanied only by a short passage from a letter by Charles Dickens. Since 1798, the Royal Academy had allowed its painters to append short passages from prose or poetry to their work: Turner, for example, habitually exhibited paintings with passages from his own unfinished epic poem *Fallacies of Hope*, Thomson's *The Seasons* and occasionally from other writers such as Byron. Dickens' letter was not written with the painting in mind – it dates from 1855 – but in response to witnessing a similar scene of desolation: 'Dumb, wet, silent horrors! Sphinxes set up against the dead wall, and none likely to be at the pains of solving them until the general overthrow' (Forster, 1874 III, 53–4). The changes between the engraving and the painting are well chronicled elsewhere and are apparent from a comparison of the two images. That which is most significant in the context of narrative function is the addition of a series of posters offering rewards: £100 is offered for a runaway, £50 for a murderer and £20 for a dog; yet only £2 is offered for a missing child. This is a simple and direct statement of ironic condemnation of social values, which shows a grasp of the context in which the painting was to be seen. Instead of the leisurely narrative of *The Graphic*, there is a greater number of visual clues in the painting to suggest a moral standpoint. Yet the element of narrative is still strong: it seems unlikely that the many who filed past the image would have been unaware of the tradition of novel illustration, and they would surely have read it in a 'human' manner, considering the figures as people and not as part of a system of social welfare. The addition of the lines from Dickens seems to strengthen this: instead of a lengthy narrative we have a single general point to direct the onlooker's response – a sound bite instead of a full speech, if you like, to match the amount of time that each onlooker would have to take in the painting when filing past. Instead of a character description and cross-section through a narrative continuum, a different function is performed by the two 'literary' elements: the posters introduce an element of social criticism through the ironic value system they present, while the letter reinforces this in the resigned acceptance that no one will be 'at the pains of solving them', and adds a direct emotional comment on the horror of the system in its first sentence. Thus a new literary system is added to match the new circumstances in which the painting will be seen, to balance those provided for the earlier engraving.

It is, of course, a matter of conjecture as to how many who saw the painting were also aware of the earlier engraving. Yet in a sense this is not of material importance: what matters is that an image first produced with a powerful literary element as part of its impact is then translated to another medium, with a literary 'text' of reduced length but largely similar import. This suggests strongly that the reading habit of the novel has been carried over into what is ostensibly a purely visual medium, and that academic painting has become a further area in which the complex verbal-visual medium of the novel has come to be a dominant cultural product of the age. The success of Fildes' painting, I would argue, lies not only in the fact that people were aware of its basic form from the engraving: it lies in the way that the verbal-visual discourse has been radically simplified, pared down to the inclusion only of the lines from Dickens and the verbal clues implanted in the picture itself. It is much more immediate, making its points in a direct and unsubtle manner. This reveals Fildes' awareness of the different conditions under which it would be read, and thus constitutes a subtle modification of the rhetoric of the joint verbal-visual discourse. That Fildes made such modifications shows not only the pervasiveness of the dual discourse, but the artist's awareness of the need to modify the code when moving away from the more leisurely context of the novel. In this, he not only reveals the pervasiveness of the reading habit but also, in his act of modification, suggests that such subtlety may not always have been present in other painters who wished to produce narratives which are less reliant upon verbal clues.

Some idea of this may be gained by looking at some paintings roughly contemporary with Fildes' work and how they were read by their first audiences. Robert Braithwaite Martineau's *The Last Day in the Old Home* (1861: oil on canvas, $42\frac{1}{2}$ x 57, Tate Gallery, London) shows a family about to leave an ancestral home, the husband drinking a toast which is shared by his young son while the mother looks on in despair and the grandmother pays off an old family servant. The text is full of visual encryptings of the situation. In the foreground there is a handbill advertising an auction; the family portraits – in different historical styles to show the age of the family – each have a lot number pasted in the corner. The reason why the family must leave is revealed with similar directness: not only does the husband drink, but a painting of a jockey on a horse at the left foreground suggests that he also gambles. Here, literary clues are used in much the same manner as in Fildes' painting: instead of a parallel text, there are simple verbal elements to place the image within a narrative context.

This simplification of the verbal-visual discourse is not always present. Holman Hunt's *The Awakening Conscience* (1853: oil on canvas, $29\frac{1}{4}$ x $21\frac{5}{8}$, Tate Gallery, London), for example, was a victim of the public's inability to read the image. It was left to John Ruskin to explain the significance in a letter to *The Times*, in which he pointed to details such as 'the torn and dying bird on the floor' and the 'fowls of the air feeding upon the ripened corn' on the wall-hangings, all of which emblematise the ensnaring of the woman by the man on whose lap she sits. The discarded glove on the floor, the print of the woman taken in adultery, the music left unwrapped and abandoned on the floor are all emblems of the woman's seduction and imminent betrayal: yet, without a verbal narrative to explain this, contemporary onlookers were at a loss to read their significance.

Ruskin's explanations of paintings of this sort became an essential part of the exhibition season. Between 1855 and 1859, and again in 1875, he produced a small pamphlet called *Academy Notes* which he sold to the queues outside the Royal Academy: so highly did he regard this that he referred to it as 'one of the chief works which I have henceforward to do' (*Works* 14: 46). Here, for example, is his comment on a painting exhibited without title, but now known as *Past and Present*, by Augustus Egg (1858: oil on canvas, three panels, each 25 x 30, Tate Gallery, London):

> As I see that several mistakes have been made in the inter-pretation of this impressive picture in the public prints, I give the true reading of it, though I should have thought it was clearly enough legible. In the central piece the husband discovers his wife's infidelity; he dies five years afterwards. The two lateral pictures represent the same moment of night a fortnight after his death. The same little cloud is under the moon. The two children see it from the chamber in which they are praying for their lost mother, and their mother, from behind a boat under a vault on the river-shore. The painting, as such, is not first-rate; but the purpose of the picture is well-reached, and the moonlight is true and beautiful.
>
> (*Works* 14: 166)

Here Ruskin is doing what the painter himself had not done: provided some sort of narrative context for the painting which explains what is happening in each panel of the triptych. This is the more striking since Egg had attached a text to the image when it was shown at the RA:

> August the 4th – Have just heard that B— has been dead more than a fortnight, so his poor children have now lost both parents. I hear *she* was seen on Friday last near the Strand, evidently without a place to lay her head. What a fall hers has been!

The claim of a recent critic that Ruskin became 'a kind of docent in print' tells only part of the truth (Garrigan 1989: 148). What he is doing is supplying the kind of data which the Victorian gallery going public were accustomed to being told in a verbal passage which accompanied an illustration, either in a novel or in apparently factual reportage. That Martineau's painting was so successful shows that, like Fildes, he had successfully realised that very explicit clues indeed were needed when the dual discourse of word and image was not available to aid in the presentation of narrative. That Hunt and Egg failed – despite, in the latter's case, the insertion of a fragment of a diary – shows that they had underestimated the essential role of the narrative and descriptive verbal text in contemporary cultural production. This might well be one reason for the relative success or failure of individual paintings of this period.

Fildes' illustration to *The Graphic* reveals two key points about the unified verbal-visual discourse in the second half of the nineteenth century. First, the unified discourse of the illustrated novel had become such a powerful way of assimilating narrative that it was used as a way of making actual contemporary events seem more real, by placing them in a structure that resembled the familiar 'sharing' of a contemporary novel. Secondly, it spread over into fashionable painting, to the degree that those paintings which were most successful often used a simplified form of the unified discourse by providing very direct literary semiotic systems to provide a narrative context, and those which failed often did so because a public, used to taking in narrative images only as part of a dual discourse, were unable to read purely visual semiotic structures. The world of the Victorian illustrated novel, it would seem, was one whose boundaries spread very wide indeed, colouring in its special unified discourse the whole system of absorbing and responding to contemporary reality and its moral ills.

3

FAIRY PALACES

Identification and ideology in children's fiction

A few months after the first number of *The Graphic* appeared at the end of 1869, Royal Assent was given to Forster's Education Act of 1870. Its provisions were fairly limited: higher grants were given to church schools, and local boards were set up to oversee education – yet it set clear the path for state development of education as a right for all children. Further acts in 1880 and 1902 extended its provisions: they were part of a larger movement which acknowledged, for the first time, the importance of childhood as a separate state of being which needed nurture, support and encouragement. Legislation against cruelty to children, changes to the law on poor relief, the inception of nursery schools, and the range of provisions of the Children's Act of 1908 all combined to ensure that childhood was now a condition with its own rights: not for nothing was the new century hailed as 'the century of the child'.

For the middle classes, increasing standards of health and housing, and the beginnings of contraception to limit the size of families, meant that children were something that could now be enjoyed rather than endured. Legislation earlier in the century had limited the employment of children; even before the education acts, church schools had spread an education which was moral as well as literal. The Victorian notion of self-improvement enhanced the desire for education, which in turn created a need for books aimed especially at young readers.

There had been books for children since the beginning of printing; what made the childrens' books of the last quarter of the century so different was the way in which they approached the child readers – as individuals with tastes and attitudes different from those of adults, which had to be satisfied in different ways.

The Sunday School prize-books of the earlier years of the century were heavy and didactic in their ideas and presentation: a glance at the work of Esther Copley, a popular writer in this field in mid-century, will reveal acres of moralistic print with little concern for pleasure or involvement.

At the turn of the century – roughly, in the years between Forster's Education Act and the Children's Act – a change took place in children's books which affected the style of writing, the moral direction, and the presentation of the book as a physical object. Crucial in this is the use of illustration: from being decorative patterns and scaled-down versions of the wood engravings used in adult fiction, they changed to something flexible and intimate, allowing the child to become involved in the story as a form of fiction to encourage and develop imaginative fantasy – an essential part of the newly recognised condition of childhood. At the same time, they provide a mirror of the adult's ideas of the place of children, and often reveal elements of an ideology far from the carefree, attractive idyll we might expect. Nowhere is this more important than in the growth of children's books concerned with fairies and magical happenings. By studying the different styles and approaches used in significant children's stories of this period, we may see not only subtle and by no means straightforward changes in the use of illustrations as part of an enveloping imaginative experience of the book, but also reveal shifts in the social, moral and intellectual standing of children within the ideological circumstance of the period.

II

Kate Greenaway, Walter Crane and Andrew Lang are usually regarded as important figures in the liberation of the children's book from its most grimly Victorian restraints. Up to a point this is true; but in many ways their works are just as distant from their readers as the most austere Victorian morality. Greenaway's achievement in *Under the Window* is well, but confusingly, summed up by Ruskin: 'the fairy land she creates for you is not beyond the sky nor beneath the sea, but nigh you, even at your doors' (*Works* 33: 348). Ruskin is referring to the real world, not that of faerie: Greenaway does not illustrate supernatural kingdoms. He seems to be commenting on the way in which Greenaway's illustrations use children, in an outwardly 'real' context, to create an atmosphere which is magical in its visual delights. The world Greenaway creates is certainly familiar, with its bright-red houses, blooming borders, delicate china and floral-smocked girls. This is something that a child can feel part of; the unknowable, distant figures of the earlier moral tales have been replaced by familiar children in a world which, in the paradox noted by Ruskin, seems exotic and exciting because it is so fresh. The children who read this book are both onlookers and participants; they are given the eyes of a Wordsworthian child, seeing all afresh, all new. The intensity of this makes them part of what they see, because it has become part of them. This exchange is a step towards the involvement in the world of text and illustration so important for the Edwardians: if children can be part of the real world in stories, they stand more chance of entering the world of the fairies.

Yet this involvement is not all it seems. Greenaway's children dance along in neatly ordered lines and circles, always in elegant profile, arranged in a pattern as decorative as a line of Laura Ashley offspring at a Hampstead tea-party. The impersonal, decorative air is enhanced by their blank faces: these are ciphers incapable of good or evil, not real children capable of both, let alone the psychologically astute children of James Barrie's *Peter Pan*. They are ornaments, fashion accessories: it is tempting to say that they reflect an arts-and-craftsy Victorianism in which children knew their place, were never heard, and seen only when arranged in pleasing patterns. Greenaway's idea of childhood is firmly controlled by her exquisite visual sense; yet the sense of involvement which we find in later children's books, and the concomitant sense of pleasure and psychological release in play, is clearly lacking. Greenaway seems here to be creating an image of childhood which is acceptable to adults – a frequent component of children's illustrations, seen perhaps most clearly in the lavish gift-books of the later Edwardian years with their sumptuous illustrations by Edmund Dulac, Kay Nielsen and others.

Unlike Greenaway, Walter Crane frequently depicts the fairy world in his illustrations; yet here too the artist's sense of decoration invariably cancels the child reader's sense of involvement. This is particularly true of *The First of May; A Fairy Masque* (1881), 'Presented in a series of 52 designs', photo-engraved by the new Goupil process. Crane's child-fairies are real children, anatomically accurate, with genitalia as well as wings, and the mature fairies are all women, in the nude tradition of Joseph Noel Paton and other

Victorian fairy painters. There are evil shapes, too, in the forms of animals and spirits who balance and offset the otherwise cosy world of fairies and animals, reminding us that the folk tradition of fairies is by no means uniform and secure. Perhaps most important, real children take part in the story. Yet, despite this, the images do not offer the child reader a genuine involvement.

Plate XIII shows well the duality of the book's illustrations. Here, the children are singing to welcome the spring. The text is presented in manuscript while, in the left-hand third of the page, a group of children stand in elegant poses. The whole is a design of the kind developed by Burne-Jones where there is no recession and instead the figures are presented almost as one above the other in an airy, graceful ascent. The children have been organised into a decorative pattern which puts them outside both the real world and the fairy kingdom. As a result we do not enter the world of the book; we are held at a distance outside it. The remoteness continues in the text:

> Merrily, merrily let us sing
> This is the daybreak of the spring
> Primroses on the hill-sides born,
> Break with a golden flower-dawn;
> Whilst the cuckoo-buds and broom
> Race the furze which next shall bloom;
> Merrily, merrily let us sing,
> This is the daybreak of the spring.

This is clearly a late-Victorian adult's view of childhood, full of sweetness, light and elegant dance steps: the expression of a tolerant and slightly sentimental Victorian ideal. There is no Edwardian reality here: Edith Nesbit's Bastable family, heroes of *The Wouldbegoods* (1901) and *The New Treasure-Seekers* (1904), would never sing like this. That the children of Crane's fairy masque are a creation of aesthetic adulthood, with little connection to the real demands of child readers, should come as no surprise: the elaborate presentation of the book, with its expensive plates and open-weave paper, holds it far away from the average child and places it instead in the rather curious convention of the time, the children's book aimed at the aesthetic adult reader.

This is not always true of Crane's work. His much earlier *Toy Books* (1874), produced by Kate Greenaway's printer Edmund Evans, give an occasional hint of involvement derived from the skilful use of illustration, and so suggest the engagement found in later children's illustration. In 'The Yellow Dwarf', for example, we are allowed, in an illustration, to see from mid-air a flying chariot, glimpsing events as they are seen by the tale's characters. We do not stand in the chariot alongside the main characters, but are flying just behind it, so that we see the swans which draw the chariot, the two characters who drive it and, most important, the princess lying on a bank outside a fairy palace beneath. It is a moment which offers us what the protagonists see and something of their sensations of flight, while still allowing us to see them as separate fictional creations. In this way, Crane allows us to have the best of both worlds, sharing their experience as something magical, yet allowing us to experience the nature of the story as a story, so that the awareness of the magical nature of the story is matched with an awareness of the magical nature of story-telling – a metafictional awareness which reveals not only a subtlety in the image, but a grasp of a childlike delight in being told a story as well as in the story itself.

This subtlety is, however, not shared by the text which accompanies the illustration, which soon removes our sense of belonging in the action:

> She made him enter her chariot, to which she had now harnessed swans, and fled with him from one pole to the other. Whilst thus travelling through the air, he beheld his dear Princess in a castle all of steel, the walls of which, reflecting the rays of the sun, became like burning-glasses, and scorched to death all who ventured to approach them. She was reclining on the bank of a stream. As she lifted her eyes, she saw the King pass by with the Fairy of the Desert, who, through her magic arts, seemed to be very beautiful; and this made her more unhappy than ever, as she thought the King was untrue to her. She thus became jealous, and was offended with the poor King, while he was in great grief at being so rapidly borne away from her.
>
> (1875: pages unnumbered)

This is stiff and formal: any sense of taking part which we might have had from the illustration is quickly cancelled by the text, with its clumsy narrative devices such as the dragging subordinate clauses and the repeated use of 'thus' and 'while', an idiolect of adult order rather than childlike experience.

The generation of writing after Crane's 'Yellow Dwarf' was dominated by a series of anthologies produced by Andrew Lang. Beginning with *The Blue Fairy Book* in 1889, they continued with volumes named after the colours of their bindings until 1910. Most have illustrations by H.J. Ford, the later ones including colour plates; some also have plates by Lancelot Speed.

Lang's fairy books are collections of stories from many sources. Several are from Grimm or Andersen, but others are folk tales from Spain, Germany, Japan, Finland, Hungary and other countries: in this they represent the scholarly interest in folk mythology that had been developing since the middle of the century. Yet despite this, Lang's tales are clearly intended to be read and enjoyed by the children themselves. The desire to engage and involve the child reader is evident, for example, in the opening of the preface to *The Pink Fairy Book* (1897): 'A child who has read the Blue and Red and Yellow Fairy Books will find some old friends with new faces in the Pink Fairy Book, if he examines and compares' (1897: vii). The reader–writer relationship here is much closer than anything Greenaway or Crane achieved; it hints that the first steps are being taken towards an enclosed fairy world which includes the child reader, but it is as if the child, though present, is being discussed by a pair of well-meaning adults – doctors, perhaps, or schoolmasters. Yet the degree to which this is made possible by the texts and illustrations is often less even than this limited involvement.

This is apparent, for example, in Lang's version of Grimm's 'The House in the Wood', from *The Pink Fairy Book*. The story deals with a 'maiden' who releases a prince who has been condemned to live as an old man deep in a wood, accompanied only by his servants who are transformed into a cow, a cockerel and a hen. In feeding the three beasts, the maiden undoes the spell; the prince regains his royal stature and the house becomes a palace again.

> When the beasts were satisfied, the maiden sat down beside the old man at the table and ate what was left for her. Soon the cock and hen began to tuck their heads under their wings, and the brindled cow blinked its eyes, so the maiden said, 'Shall we not go to rest now?'
>
> (1897: 22)

This is simple and direct, and the writing is far more fluent than Crane's 'Yellow Dwarf', say. But there is still a formality which

57

keeps the reader outside the action. Nor do we learn anything of the feelings of the characters; they are the literary equivalent of Greenaway's ciphers. Ford's illustrations match this formalism. That which accompanies this passage (see Plate 8) shows the maiden feeding the animals – the action which has freed the young prince. The maiden is kneeling at the right, giving straw to a large cow lying on the floor with its head turned towards her. A hen and cockerel peck at some straw in the foreground; against the heavy black background, the legend 'The Maiden Feeds the Three Beasts' is presented on a flowing scroll. It is heavy and naturalistic: there is no hint in the style or treatment that this action is the turning point of the story, or that the maiden's actions will have magical results.

The illustration has the detail and intensity of the 'sixties style': like almost all of its kind, it is contained in a thick frame, and its composition is four-square and static. The distance is enhanced by the elaborate caption, which places it in the context of a mediaeval illumination rather than an illustration designed for children to engage with. Even though the main lines are curves – the maiden's back, the head of the cow and the bodies of the chickens – the overall effect is one of formality and restraint, to match the writing. The result of this is to suggest distance and separation: the rhetoric of this image is a constant reminder that it is an aesthetic construct, and no effort is made to engender imaginative involvement in the child reader.

Not all Ford's illustrations in the Lang series of books have the same formality; some move towards the greater freedom of later illustrated fiction which works more directly to satisfy the child's imagination. Ford's illustration of the hobgoblin, in 'The Snow Queen', again from *The Pink Fairy Book*, is an important example. It shows the episode where the mirror which magnifies evil and minimises beauty is smashed into fragments. The goblin is recognisably human despite having wings, pointed ears, horns and a scaly skin: his arms are tightly crossed, and he is rubbing his right foot against his left knee. Tiny fragments of glass scatter all around him, and a cartouche beneath has the caption 'The hobgoblin laughed till his sides ached' (1897: 77). This image succeeds because of its concentration – we see nothing except the hobgoblin – and also because it has no heavy frame to separate it from the text and keep us from becoming involved with it. It is also presented alongside an account of the episode it depicts – a rare happening in Lang's volumes – so that we have the sense of an integrated narrative of verbal and visual elements. In its vitality and its direct presentation, as well as in the convincing figure of a goblin that it creates, it enables the child reader to share and experience the fiction far more directly than does the heavy and remote illustration to 'The House in the Wood'.

Other illustrations by Ford continue this greater freedom, which is reflected in the more relaxed text to be found in some of the stories. Important in this regard is a story called 'The Master Thief' translated from a Norwegian folk-tale collected by the folklorist Peter Christian Asbjornsen – further indication of the eclectic and scholarly approach taken by Lang – which appeared in *The Red Fairy Book* (1890).

The story takes the form of a series of challenges which are issued to a young man who falls in with a group of thieves. The first is to steal three oxen belonging to a traveller. In the course of this the thief ties a rope beneath his arms and pretends to hang himself in the path of the traveller. This he does three times, bewildering the traveller so that he goes back to look for what he thinks are the two other suicides, to convince himself that he is not being bewitched. Ford's illustration shows the traveller staring up at the hanging thief from the rear: this means that whereas he cannot see that the rope passes beneath the young man's arms, we can. The choice of this moment, rather than the completion of the act of theft, shows illustration being used to help the reader's grasp of the dynamic growth of the narrative; and the selection of a viewpoint from which we see something that the traveller cannot makes us accomplices in the crime, stressing our involvement in the story to the degree of giving us knowledge which a key character, the traveller, lacks. This is a subtle and complex use of the selection of moment and viewpoint to engage the reader as we share the joke at the traveller's expense. That we can see it in this light is significant: the whole of the text concerns the skill of a young man who is part thief and part confidence-trickster, and this suspension of the normal rules of social morality reveals the structure of the folk-tale as something festive and ludic, a reversal of order of the sort seen in the folk rituals of carnivals and feast days. But it is more than this: in the context of a volume for children, it is an awareness of the subversive nature of childhood in which the rejection of normal, adult rules is central. That illustration and text work together in this way shows a direct grasp

59

of this subversive quality which is not seen in the work of Crane or Greenaway and is almost a complete reversal of the moral tales of earlier Sunday-school moralities.

The same quality of subversion is seen in the illustration showing the thief dressed up as an angel appearing to a priest (see Plate 9). The parody Pre-Raphaelite angel perches in a tree while the priest kneels before him. In the background stands a church of roughly Early English style. That we look at the scene from the usual eyeline of an adult means that we look down on the priest as he kneels; the bunched, balding figure is clearly intended to look ridiculous, and once again the subversive note of the text is strongly echoed in the image. Children in 1890 had few opportunities to ridicule priests: the engagement of the readers must surely have been considerable.

A third illustration shows a group of people chasing a hare in a courtyard, while the thief steals a joint of meat that is cooking in the kitchen, to fulfil another challenge posed him. What is striking here is not the subversive nature of the image: it is the depiction of the hare leaping out of the frame which surrounds the drawing. This gives great dynamism to the image: the action spreads beyond the territory of the illustration into that of the text – a rejection of the usual order of the book which both adds to the reader's involvement and subverts the usual structure of the book, breaking down adult divisions shown in other illustrations' rigid framing.

Taken together, these show a freshness and diversity of approach which suggests that Lang and Ford are moving towards a more dynamic, integrated use of text and illustration, in which the child's rejection of adult forms is balanced by a visual structure which ensures his or her involvement not only in the text but in the conspiracy against order which it represents. Such a discourse is not common in fairy books; but its mere existence is a significant departure from orthodoxy.

The process of integration, involvement and subversion is also seen in a book published several years before Lang's fairy books: *The Princess and the Goblin* (1871) by George MacDonald. The story alternates between the world of the princess and that of the mines in which the hero Curdie is battling against the evil, plotting demons. There is much from the stories of Grimm and the other writers translated by the Victorians: the tower in the castle, the old fairy, the sinister goblins and animal monsters. But MacDonald takes these elements and gives them new life by making them part of a whole new story in which the reader is personally caught up. It may be that it offers a Christian parable, as has been suggested; certainly it follows an archetypal pattern of good struggling to overcome evil in a wider, more accessible fashion than any of the 'improving' fiction of the day.

Here for the first time the child reader can feel part of the world that is created. The dialogue is lively and convincing; we are allowed to share the characters' feelings; there is genuine suspense; and we feel horror at the goblins and delight at the princess. There is also a dialogue with the reader; the child is not lectured, but brought into the conversation. Typical of this is the passage where MacDonald describes the princess in her nursery (1871: 7–9; see Plate 10).

This is a princess that children reading the novel can identify with – in her unexplained boredom with her toys, in her perverse longing to catch 'a particularly nice cold', in the sudden change of mood, and in her desire to go up the 'curious old stair' which she has already partly explored and forgotten. Because we identify, we are involved: we want to see what is up the curious old stair, and this is a great breakthrough in the growth of the fairy story. MacDonald's tone, too, draws us into the novel. We are involved not only in the shared attitudes of childhood – the boredom and perversity – but also by the way we are made part of the writer's discussions about what the artist can and cannot do when illustrating the scene.

This passage is important for several reasons. To begin with, the writer is speaking directly to the reader, something earlier fairy writers did only to hector and moralise. Then there is the rejection of the ordered world of the narrative the novel itself seeks to create, with the writer stepping out of the fictive world to remind us that it is all a literary construct. Only a writer of great confidence can create a fictional world and then destroy it, yet MacDonald does this successfully, showing again the close relationship he has with his reader and the control he has over it. It is an early and exciting example of a self-conscious deconstructive process: the fiction of fiction is directly confronted, perfectly matching the child's burgeoning awareness of the nature of fiction. Subversion of genre and structure is here used both to involve the reader and, paradoxically, to reinforce the idea of the reading process.

The Princess and the Goblin has illustrations by Arthur Hughes, whose work and influence as an illustrator is unjustly undervalued. These are close, dark wood-engravings of true sixties style, yet they do much to bring us into the action and mood of the book. Almost all are drawn from a child's viewpoint, with a lowered eyeline that directly involves the child reader. Although they are all framed, they have a freedom of composition which Ford's drawings, though later, never achieve. They also have a darkness which conveys exactly the story's mixture of mystery and evil. There are some fine moments of tension, as for example on the pages where the knights see for the first time the 'hideous and ludicrous' animals which the goblins keep 'in the regions of darkness' (see Plate 11). The knights' fixed stare and the outstretched arm of the central figure force us to look across at the strange shapes presented in another frame on the facing page. Not only is folklore adapted and developed to suit new readers, but those readers are drawn into the confrontation to experience it directly themselves.

All of this suggests an awareness of the reader which is of quite a different order from those of any other fairy writers of the age. There is much that is still Victorian here – the identification is with the princess, after all, not with the fairies, and the princess is still a long way from the reader socially, geographically and temporally. The magic story involving contemporary children is still some way off; but MacDonald comes closer to it than any other Victorian, and in many ways he is the creator of the modern fairy story. His view of childhood is witty and psychologically acute: even if the unity between illustration and verbal text does not achieve the level of single discourse achieved by Lang and Ford in 'The Master Thief', his dialogues with the illustrator and the rejection of the closed model of narrative it heralds introduce an element of subversive deconstruction quite fitting to the world of the child, and make *The Princess and the Goblin* an important departure.

III

A superficial approach might suggest that, once the more integrated approach to text and illustrations had been employed in a discourse of greater ideological freedom by Lang and MacDonald, it would continue to grow and develop, especially as the idea of childhood as a separate state, freed from the constraints of adult responsibility and moral sense, expanded in the first years of the new century. Yet this is by no means the case. Certainly, the new freedoms suggested by Hughes, MacDonald and, in places, Lang are employed by writers and illustrators of the next generation, yet often the ideological significance of the texts they produce is far from what one might expect. This can be seen by looking at two children's stories which were popular in the early years of the new century: Edith Nesbit's 'The Psammead', with illustrations by H.R. Millar, and Rudyard Kipling's *Puck of Pook's Hill* (1906), with illustrations by Claude A. Shepperson.

Both appeared first in serial form in *The Strand Magazine*, a circumstance which perhaps influenced their form in the presentation of a series of largely self-contained stories. The nature of these magazines and the place of children's stories within them is something to be explored in Chapter 4: here, my concern is instead with the way that illustrations are part of a discourse which has an ideological bias markedly different from that of MacDonald and Lang.

Edith Nesbit's 'The Psammead' was serialised in the *Strand* in 1902, later appearing in book form as *Five Children and It* in 1905. It marks a significant advance in children's fiction to do with the supernatural world in that the children who are involved in the action are recognisable contemporary figures with whom the reader can readily identify. The Psammead of the title – a strange being with the body of a hairy spider and the limbs of a monkey – appears in their world and grants them a series of wishes, so that the world of faerie comes to the children rather than vice versa. This immediately makes the world of the story accessible, and this is aided by the illustrations.

Here there is a crucial difference between this story and its predecessors. While the illustrations of Ford, Hughes and their contemporaries were, with very few exceptions, presented as rectangular, framed images isolated from the text, those by H.R. Millar which accompany Nesbit's tale have no frames, and are often irregular in outline. Here the format of the magazine is important: its larger pages, arranged as two columns of text, makes possible the insertion of illustrations in a range of positions within the page – something not possible in the smaller format of the separate volume in which the story later appeared. The arrangement of the text around the illustrations, in longer and shorter lines according to the available space, further enhances the link between word and image, and the greater freedom made possible by the larger format also makes possible the appearance of the illustrations close to the text to which they refer – something not often the case with Ford's illustrations to Lang's anthologies.

The greater physical involvement resulting from the lack of borders and irregularity of shape is enhanced by skilful use of viewpoint, the general style of Millar's drawing and the presentation of the children in strictly contemporary clothes of the kind worn by the original readers. Yet the illustrations stop short of drawing us completely into the action: like the text, they retain an awareness of the nature of the tale as a story, in something of the kind of metafictional awareness seen in the passage of MacDonald's *The Princess and the Goblin* discussed above, with something of that book's awareness of the subversive nature of its child readers.

All of these elements are shown clearly in the fourth episode of the story which, like all the others, is effectively a self-contained story in which the Psammead grants a wish for the children and an appropriate adventure follows (see Plate 12). Here, the wish is for wings, which the children are duly granted. They fly over their home county of Kent, alight briefly to take plums from an orchard, and then, still hungry, take food from the larder of a clergyman's house before landing on the top of a church tower. By this time it is near evening and the children sleep. When they awake, they find that their wings have disappeared, each wish lasting only for a day; they have to shout for help, and are released by a puzzled vicar and an angry gamekeeper, a circumstance which is used by Nesbit to draw a moral about the children's behaviour in taking food.

Nesbit's text is aimed at educated child readers who are a touch disbelieving of the traditional fairy story: some of their doubts are assumed into the text in the form of very down-to-earth details about how the children manage to fly. Robert, for example, is described as looking 'very awkward in his knickerbocker suit' with the addition of wings; the children have to fly 'quite a long way apart' so as not to knock each other's wings; it is only with difficulty that they manage to perch on the plum tree to take the fruit. This acceptance of practical unlikelihood makes the fact of their flying more believable, and certainly it is enhanced with many convincing details. The countryside is described as 'a beautiful live map', and we are told of the children's delight at flying with 'their great rainbow wings, between green earth and blue sky'.

64

Millar's illustrations maintain this mixture of involvement and distance, seriousness and satire, with which the children are presented. The first illustration shows the children flying over a very realistic representation of Rochester Cathedral and its surroundings, even to the extent of showing the new tower and the railway, river and factory chimneys behind to stress the immediate contemporary setting of the story. This is all shown from an aerial viewpoint, so that we share to some degree what the children themselves see. However, we also see the four children, flying across the scene in the middle distance. They are flying somewhat awkwardly, with arms and legs hanging in a rather gangling manner beneath their large wings. The overall result is that we are drawn into the magic of flight, but remain distant from the fliers: it is a representation of both the magic of the story and an older child's unwillingness to believe it as fact which is constantly present in the text.

The involvement, however, deepens in the other illustrations. We see the irate farmer sitting nonplussed in the orchard while Anthea hovers above him, his hand in his waistcoat pocket to touch the threepenny bit the girl has just given him to pay for the fruit they have taken. Here we are drawn into the children's world by seeing the events from the viewpoint of one of their number, hovering above ground on a level with Anthea so that we effectively become one of the children. The same involvement is shown in the image depicting Cyril handing food out of the vicarage window to Robert and Anthea who hover outside: as Jane, the youngest, is not shown, it is almost as if we see things from her viewpoint as she hovers to keep watch.

Nesbit's awareness of the children as real people, not those who figure in a conventional story, is shown when she points out that their hunger appears, 'curiously enough', when they fly low over the plum orchard. Here and elsewehere, the children are in a sense being mildly satirised to maintain the interest of sceptical, modern child readers. We might also think that the references to whether or not taking the plums is stealing, and how much money should be left for the vicar's food, is a satiric attack on earlier stories which are concerned with teaching morals rather than offering entertainment: yet the moral voice is still there, and the structure of the story tends to support this reading rather than one which stresses the subversive freedom of the children from normal rules of adult behaviour.

At the close of the story, the children, stranded on the top of the tower, are released by Andrew the manservant who warns them 'I've got my gun handy – so you'd best not try any tricks.' This is comic, of course, as is the reference to his astonishment when his torch reveals the 'group of desperadoes' and he gasps 'So help me . . . if they ain't a pack of kiddies.' The denouement is held off by the introduction of an illustration which shows the vicar, Andrew and the gamekeeper on the steps to the tower about to go in and seize the intruders, a delaying use of illustration to heighten the tension before the climax and also to add to the comedy by revealing the incongruity between the defenceless children and the rather alarmed adults.

Yet it is not all comic. The vicar's wife tells them 'You ought to be ashamed of yourselves' and, after Andrew is told by the vicar to take the children home, we are told by Nesbit: 'So you see they got off better than they deserved', even though Martha, their nurse, 'swept them to bed in a whirlwind of reproaches'. In one sense, this is a parody of a Victorian moral tale, showing what happens when children break essential laws of trespass and theft: and in this, of course, it continues the appreciation of children's awareness of the conventions of genre and pleasure at their satiric rejection which we see, for example, in MacDonald's direct address to the illustrator in *The Princess and the Goblin*. Yet, in another sense, the moral is real enough, helped by the final shift of viewpoint in the last illustration: it is a comic parody of the arrival of their just deserts, but nevertheless it does change our view from that of the children to that of observers outside the action. Nesbit has been called both the inventor of the modern children's story and a disguised Victorian moralist. 'The Psammead' certainly uses text and illustration subtly to involve us in the action, and the kind of integration that Millar's illustrations achieve is continued in his treatment of Nesbit's later work. Yet it is worth remembering that, as we are drawn to identify with the children, we are also drawn to identify with the moral comments that are made about their actions. The idiolect remains ambiguous, but the moral statement is still part of its significance: involvement has been used as a way of continuing adult moral values, not subverting them, and ultimately Nesbit's scheme is more conservative and authoritarian than what we might have expected had the subversive child world of George MacDonald been developed more fully in her writing.

Kipling's story is significant in bringing two directly contemporary children into the narrative. Una and Dan act as the representatives of the child readers within the story, and follow the technique begun by Scott in being close to the model readers at which the story is aimed, to increase involvement by apparently adding a sense of realism. When we first meet them they are acting out a play based on *A Midsummer Night's Dream* which their father has adapted for them from Shakespeare, with the aid of a cardboard ass's head from a Christmas cracker; they eat a picnic supper of hard-boiled eggs and Bath Oliver biscuits, with salt in an envelope; and their frequent asides – as will become clear shortly – show their knowledge of English history. In Shepperson's first illustration they are shown in contemporary dress, Una in a short pinafore dress, Dan in shorts and pullover. In short, the two are presented in verbal and visual terms as model middle-class children of exactly the sort who would read the story on its first appearance, in serial form in the *Strand* in 1906. Yet the kind of awareness of the difference of the state of childhood, in particular the subversion of both narrative and social order, that is found in MacDonald's discourse is almost completely absent, despite this apparently explicit direction towards the contemporary child and his or her apparent involvement.

The acting of a version of *A Midsummer Night's Dream* does more than establish the class identity of the two children, however, it also enables the appearance of Puck himself, released from his home in the hills by the incantations of the children '*on* Midsummer Eve, *in* the middle of a ring, and under – *right* under one of the oldest hills in England' (1906: 48). This establishes the pattern of the story: in each episode, Puck either tells the children a tale from his experiences as 'the oldest thing in England' who has been within the hills for 1,000 years, or brings a character with him to tell of an episode from the distant past. This leads to an involvement of a particular kind between reader, children and narrative, which is considerably enhanced by the illustrations.

In the first illustration (see Plate 13), as already noted, the children wear contemporary clothes, so that we – as contemporary readers – are involved because we see them as one of a group to which we belong. From the lowered viewpoint of a child, we see Una and Dan looking at the figure of Puck, a short, wizened figure with pointed ears and a long pointed cap, dressed in what seems to be a version of the traditional jester's motley. The composition draws us strongly to Puck, through the shadows of Una and Dan which lead towards him, and their lowered heads which aim directly at his face. This is the beginning of an involvement which continues in the text and the subsequent illustrations, when we become part of the group to which Puck tells the story. The second illustration shows the children watching while Puck carves out a piece of turf which he gives to the children to show that they are properly seized of the land – an image which becomes of increasingly greater importance as the story progresses.

From the third illustration onwards, the children's figures are omitted and the images show episodes from Puck's story. This is an important omission since it shows that we, the readers, have become one with the child listeners in the story. We see, or imagine that we see, what Una and Dan see while Puck's narrative continues, and hence we are directly involved. The degree of involvement that this offers appears to be considerable, largely because of the nature and style of the illustrations. This is most evident in the first episode, which tells the story of Weland, an anglicised version of Volundr of Teutonic myth, who is released from servitude as a way-side blacksmith with the name Wayland-Smith when a farmer whose horse he has shod is forced to thank him, by Hugh, a novice in a monastery. In gratitude Weland makes Hugh a magic sword and he leaves the order, in so doing laying the ground for the second story.

After the initial 'establishing shots' of the first two images, which show Una and Dan listening, we move directly into the events told by Puck. The third illustration shows Puck looking intently at the recumbent form of Weland, a dark, hairy figure with icicles on his lips, who is lying in a galley belonging to ancient pirates. The viewpoint is again the low one of a child, who is standing within the boat; the line drawing is light, with considerable variation in density of hatching, with a sketch-like quality which aids our involvement by avoiding the heavy rhetoric and formality of H.J. Ford. Like all of the illustrations, it has a frame, but this is a single, thin line only, so that the feeling of involvement is not lessened appreciably. Technical considerations account for some of the difference here, the Edwardian photographic plate allowing reproduction of a much looser style of pencil drawing; but we should not assume that the heaviness of Ford's images was the only style available to the artist working in wood engraving, as a quick glance at collections such as Forrest Reid (1928) will make abundantly clear. Here, as so often, the style is connotative as well as denotative; but the freedom is not all it seems, as will shortly become clear.

The remaining images continue this mood of involvement. The second shows Hugh the novice in the act of pitching the ungrateful farmer from his horse, while Wayland-Smith dances in jubilation in the background (see Plate 14). Again the use of a rich variation of line and density involves us, as does the dynamic movement of the image, with Hugh's hands under the farmer's feet producing a strong diagonal which is developed in the neck of the horse and the flying body of the farmer. The image uses a good deal of white space to suggest sky and background, and this openness again furthers our involvement. The third illustration shows us Weland with the magical sword he has made for Hugh, with a lowered viewpoint which places us close to the mysterious hooded figure, again enhancing our sense of being part of the events.

Subsequent episodes of the narrative continue this style of illustration, and make a similar approach to the narrative. In the first illustration of each part, we see the children looking at Puck or the figure he has brought with him to tell the story; in the second and subsequent images, we see an image from the tale itself. Yet this involvement is not quite what it seems. With MacDonald and with Lang, the degree to which we are involved depends on the nature of the illustration and the way in which the narrative supports the needs of the child readers. With Kipling, despite the sense of involvement added by the illustration's placing of the reader alongside Una and Dan, we are excluded from the action simply because they are excluded from it. Instead of its being a story which happens to the children, as is the case with Nesbit's stories, *Puck of Pook's Hill* is one which is told to them. This is reinforced by the formal way in which the narrative unfolds, and the absence of any of the subversive comments about the nature of narrative or the idea of a children's story that we find respectively in MacDonald and Nesbit. The role of Una and Dan is essentially passive, making clear that any element of subversion and rejection of order – in the process of maturation through experiment which often runs counter to the accepted pattern of adult behaviour - is rigidly denied and replaced by a far more authoritarian view of the child's place in the adult's world. As readers, we subconsciously come to adopt the submissiveness of Una and Dan when we become involved with the illustrations: as the two children play no part in the story, instead accepting it passively and being 'shown' what happens, so do we become accepting of the events and how they are related: as they sit obediently listening, making no comment except an occasional one to clarify a historical reference – to show their grasp of history and their good education – so, in essence, do we.

The illustrations offer us an identity with a model of childhood far removed from that offered by MacDonald, one which stresses passivity and respect in both the ordered presentation of the narrative and in certain elements of the narrative itself. This is part of a larger ideological envelope. I have already stressed the fact that the children are well educated in literature and history: as the story progresses, it becomes apparent that it is a very specific view of English history, which is being presented to stress the ancient roots of English society, law and custom. This is shown not only in the appearance of figures from the past, but also in the idea of the landscape enduring from Saxon times to the present, and the continuity of certain place names from earliest times until today – Puck says, for example, that the ancient Brunanburgh is the modern Beacon Hill. The importance of gratitude is stressed in the way Hugh punishes the farmer; ideals of chivalric conduct are stressed not only by Hugh's actions but by the exhortation from the Abbot when he leaves the monastery that he should 'be as gentle as you are strong and courteous' (*Strand* 31 1906: 55) – aims which he certainly fulfils in the second episode of the story.

This is part of a larger movement of the time concerned with the purity of the English people and the perfection of English values, seen in its origins in Saxon times and often emblematised in the beauty of the landscape – stressed here not only in the frequent references in the text, but by the depiction of the landscape in the overwhelming majority of the illustrations. Add to this the ideology of passivity and educational success of the children, and it seems clear that Kipling's notion of an ideal people is strongly apparent – an ideology that is revealed as markedly right-wing in the Indian tales which assert the racial superiority of the English. What appears to be a sense of involvement and freedom in the illustrations becomes, within the context of the text, a discourse which offers only limitation and constraint in the authoritarian structures it offers. That the children are touched with 'oak, ash and thorn' at the end of each episode to prevent their speaking of what they have seen to their parents is almost an invitation to conspiracy, which involves changing the view of the nation. It is going too far to suggest the kind of right-wing social engineering seen later in the children's division of the thought police in Orwell's *Nineteen Eighty-Four*: but the structures of text and illustration and the ideology they reveal are clearly far removed from the apparent freedom and involvement they suggest at first glance.

IV

Any attempt to construct a linear account of the changes within a literary or visual convention is fraught with temptation and danger. The conventional wisdom about children's literature is that it follows a pleasing exponential curve from oppression to liberation, as the high Victorian notion of the concealment of children and their inculcation with the wages of original sin gives way to Edwardian freedoms and delight in the subversiveness of the state of mind which had been invented along with the concept of 'the century of the child'.

The foregoing pages should sound a clear warning against the seductiveness of such views. Not only do they suggest that the ideology of childhood to be found in Nesbit and Kipling is just as repressive as that of many earlier writers: they also imply that the apparent freedom of the illustrations which seemingly contribute so much to juvenile sweetness and light can in fact be part of a much darker world view. Only in George MacDonald, and his illustrations by Arthur Hughes, can we see a freedom of approach which extends to the idea of childhood and the notion of the illustrated book – a kind of metafictional awareness that works on a number of levels which, for an adult, are hard to quantify, even though for a child they make up a delightfully ridiculous and immediate whole.

It would, of course, be possible to construct a wholly different history of children's illustrated books during the rough half-century covered in this essay, by looking at different works and approaching them in different ways. But what is striking in the works that have been discussed here is that the complex dual discourse of illustrated fiction has a structural and ideological basis which goes far beyond the realm of literary or linguistic studies, and can thus be located within a notional history of ideas in which the social and political construction of childhood has an important, and too long neglected, place.

4

ILLUSTRATED MAGAZINES

By the turn of the century, the great success stories of the Victorian periodical publishing explosion were reaching their final stages, if they had not folded completely. Among the monthly journals, *Bentley's Miscellany* had folded in 1868, incorporated in *Temple Bar*; it was followed in the 1870s and 1880s by *Broadway*, *Fraser's* and *St. James's*. *Argosy* and *Temple Bar* carried on until 1901 and 1906 respectively; *The Gentleman's Magazine* kept on until 1922, though with a circulation far lower than the 10,000 it had boasted in 1870 (Ellegård 1957: 32). All suffered falls in circulation: *The Cornhill*, launched in 1860 with an early circulation estimated at 80,000, had fallen to a mere 12,000 in 1882 (33). All of these were magazines largely concerned with fiction, with various proportions of factual articles and reviews, generally referred to as 'padding'. Mostly available through Mudie's Circulating Library alongside the novels for borrowing, they appealed to a range of readers from upper-middle to lower-middle class, with a diversity of educational levels. The reasons for the decline in readership are not my primary concern; yet it is clear that one was the competition they faced from a new type of magazine in which visual interest was prominent.

Of these, one of the earliest was *Cassell's Magazine*. Launched in 1867, this was in effect a new version of *Cassell's Illustrated Family Paper*; in 1870 its circulation was estimated at 200,000 and an advertisement in the *Newspaper Press Directory* of 1871 claimed that it 'circulates largely amongst the Upper and Middle Classes' (Ellegård: 36). This was probably optimistic: its general approach suggests a rather lower educational level. Other illustrated monthlies followed. *The English Illustrated Magazine* appeared in 1889 and the most famous of all, *The Strand Magazine*, was launched in 1891, its editor's insistence on a picture on every page earning it a circulation of 300,000 for the first number. At the peak of the popularity of its Sherlock Holmes stories, the *Strand*'s sales remained around half a million for several years. *The Windsor Magazine* appeared in 1895, and *Pearson's Magazine* two years later. That these magazines were launched and administered by a new breed of proprietors is significant. *Cassell's* was part of the large popular publishing house of that name, and *The Windsor* belonged to the similar organisation, Ward, Lock and Co.; the *Strand* was part of the empire of George Newnes, which had begun with the 'family magazine' *Tit-Bits* in 1881; *Pearson's* was the product of A.C. Pearson, who went on to found the *Daily Express* in 1900.

Mechanical advances also helped in the production of these cheap, large-circulation magazines. Even in the 1840s, Richard Hoe's revolving press could produce 20,000 copies of a newspaper in an hour: the development of the stereotype printing plate in the 1870s meant that copies could be made of the original typeset page, to facilitate multiple printing from several copies of the same page. The newsprint roll, up to $3\frac{1}{2}$ miles in length, came into use in the 1860s; the use of wood-pulp as the main ingredient of paper instead of the more expensive cotton rag followed in the next two decades. These changes made possible popular newspapers; the new magazines not only used their production facilities, but also adopted their more populist tone and approach. Influences from America were strong in what became known as the 'new journalism', and again, what is true of popular newspapers is true, to a slightly less degree, in the new monthly magazines, which borrowed style, content and presentation from American examples such as *Harper's*, *Scribner's* and the *Century* which, produced in New York, was also available through T. Fisher Unwin in London.

Whereas the older magazines of the 1850s and 1860s had contained episodes of serial fiction, usually with one or at the most two wood-engraved illustrations for each part, the new magazines were largely composed of self-contained short stories, each of which had three, four or more illustrations, often in half-tone. Those serials which were carried were often in the form of self-contained stories discussing the adventures of a single character or group of characters; and while, like the older magazines, big 'names' were offered to lure readers from the competition, illustrative material was also an important draw. Colour plates for special numbers, and supplements of paintings, were designed to appeal to the tastes of each magazine's particular group of readers and the sheer quantity of illustrations was often held up as an additional feature. The availability of cheap photographic process-plates helped greatly in this, and photographs of exotic locations, railway disasters, well-known personalities and any other objects judged likely to appeal to the readers were prominent. Format, too, differed. Instead of the close letterpress of the older magazines, the new ones were set in two columns, often of larger, more widely leaded type. Instead of the plates being printed on separate pages, now they were 'cuts' – illustrations included within the text itself, often without borders, and with the text shaped around them to give the appearance of integration of text and image. All of this made the new magazines much more attractive and accessible to the new class of urban readers who wanted something more immediate and less off-putting than the styles accepted by an older generation. As the numbers of graduates of the new board schools established by the 1870 Education Act grew, so the stress on an attractive, illustrated style and a format which avoided unrelieved acres of print became more pronounced.

The shift towards short stories was one of the most obvious changes in the new fiction magazines; clearly it was a popular one, since the circulations of the new periodicals were way in excess of those of their predecessors, and many remained in production well into the inter-war years. The success of the *Strand* magazine was increased by the presence of the Sherlock Holmes stories, but this should not be allowed to overshadow the other periodicals, or be seen as the only reason for the *Strand*'s high circulation. Despite the complaints of devotees of the older periodicals, the new monthlies clearly had much to offer the new generations of print-hungry urban middle classes. Exactly what this was, and how the illustrations participated in the narrative styles and structures they offered, may be seen by examining in close detail one monthly issue which, in the stories it contains, represents something of the range of material, both verbal and visual, to be found in such publications: the *Windsor* magazine of November 1905 (22 (131)).

II

The *Windsor Magazine* for November 1905 is a thick paperback measuring 9½ " x 6½ ". It contains 122 pages of editorial material, with a further 60 pages of advertisements, along with bound-in full-page cards advertising The Times Book Club and Henessey's brandy, and a smaller card offering men's and boys' overcoats from 'Edward Grove, The Great Outfitter' with an address at the back of Waterloo Station. Other advertisements, for Ward Lock's latest fiction list, including *Ayeshi*, the sequel to H. Rider Haggard's bestseller *She*, and for the *International Library of Fiction*, biography and a range of other kinds of writing – 2s 6d down and 5s a month, complete with 'Handsome oak Bookcase' – suggest clearly that this is aimed at a middle-class, middlebrow readership very much of the kind developed by the educational changes of the last quarter of the old century. Advertisements for furniture, foodstuffs and patent medicines confirm the appeal to middle-class readers who have no servants – in short, the new army of suburb-dwelling clerical and administrative workers so often dismissed by intellectuals as 'the clerks'.[1] The range of the advertisements – for bust development cream as well as cures for baldness, cigars as well as bread – makes clear that the magazine is read by both men and women; that it is also directed in part towards children is indicated by the inclusion of a story by Edith Nesbit, then one of the most fashionable children's writers, in this number.

All of this makes clear that the magazine is read widely by families of lower-middle-class readers, and although details of its circulation are not available, it would seem reasonable to regard it as a major element of reading among this significant and growing social group. It thus represents an important example of the kind of popular fiction being consumed by such readers, and of the place of illustrations within the narrative structures of such fiction. That the fiction is placed within a context of such advertising would suggest that it is clearly materialist fiction. This, of course, should come as little surprise; but my point is simply that the fiction itself is reinforced in its social and material nature by the advertising context in which it is found, to a degree not present – if it be present at all – in the single-volume novel of the same period. The presence of illustrations within the magazine largely performs the function of reinforcing this materialist stance and context; thus the elements of the magazine combine to create a single statement that is ideologically quite harmonious, even allowing for minor differences in style and theme.

This issue of the *Windsor* has four factual articles of general interest: 'The Art of Mr G.A. Storey, A.R.A.' by Adrian Margaux, illustrated with photographs of the artist's work; 'My Friends in Feather and Fur' by Lady Ingram, with photographs and drawings; 'Localised Eatables' by Leonard W. Lillingstone, with photographs and drawings of places where the 'eatables' may be found; and 'Woodcraft III – Playing "Injun"' by Ernest Thompson Seton, with drawings and diagrams by the author. Short poems, reproductions of paintings, and a section of short pieces called 'The Editor's Scrap-Book' make up the remainder of the 'padding'. The main contents are seven items of fiction, of which one is a contribution to a larger series of adventures occurring to the same central character, and the remaining six quite self-contained. They range in length between five and fourteen pages; the majority contain four illustrations, though the shortest has three and one of the longer, five, in a combination of half-tones, usually wash-drawings reproduced photographically, and line drawings.

From this, it is clear that the fictional material makes up the bulk of the number – around sixty-eight pages as opposed to forty-eight of 'padding' – and that illustrations are of considerable importance; there are only seven page openings which do not contain some visual image, and of these one has a whole page advertising the next number of the magazine and another is the last page before the index to the volume which this number concludes. What, then, is the relationship of these illustrations to the verbal text of the magazine stories? How may we define their contribution to the experience of reading, and to the ideological structures of the stories? Are they, as has been suggested,[2] a mere cosmetic addition to the fiction they punctuate, a superficially attractive lure to the barely literate, or is there a function of more considerable insight in their contribution to a genuinely shared discourse of word and image? Detailed study reveals that, far from being separate images added hastily after the completion of the stories with no awareness of character, narrative or development, the images all perform important functions in expanding the reader's awareness, so that they work with the verbal text to produce a single mixed discourse which in some cases is of not inconsiderable complexity in ideology and social or moral function.

The first story in the magazine is 'Private Bell, Signaller' by

O. Crow, with illustrations by G. Montbard (1905: 628–33). The narrative records a small incident in the fighting in Afghanistan, where at the time of writing British forces were deployed to maintain the frontiers against feared Russian aggression and in consequence were under attack from Afghan tribes. Private Bell is one of a group of scouts who advance into a pass, his role being to signal back to the camp about what they have discovered. He is ordered to report that nothing has been found but, because the clouds are obscuring the sun, he cannot use his heliograph – a large signalling mirror which focuses and reflects sunlight – for transmitting messages in Morse Code. Bell is told to remain where he is until the clouds pass and he can signal to base, while Corporal Stubbins and Private Holden return, sneering at his inefficiency. Bell then sees a large party of Afghans advancing, but remains at his post until the clouds clear and he can make his signal. By the time he has done this the Afghans are close by, and he has to fight them off by using his heliograph as a club (see Plate 15). He then sees a column of troops approaching, and is rescued and fêted in camp that evening, to the chagrin of Corporal Stubbins.

Montbard's three illustrations – one on each of the story's page openings – concentrate on stages of Bell's adventure. The first shows him standing alone while the two other soldiers scramble down the steep hill before him. It is an image which follows closely the geography of the location constructed in the story – Bell is on the 'rocky promontory, that jutted out into the valley' – but it goes further than this. In showing Bell standing against the sky the illustration reveals his dangerously vulnerable position, suggesting a sense of danger without specifically indicating later events; and by showing the two other soldiers in the foreground, it parallels the feeling we are given of their unjustified desertion of Bell in the story – their contempt for him encourages us to take his side, and their abrupt departure as shown in the illustration draws us further to sympathise with Bell, the clear underdog in this situation. Thus the illustration presents the scene, a bare and exotic location for the readers of 1905; implies a hint of suspense about future action; and draws us into the human relations established in the story by drawing our sympathies to the single figure set against the sky. In so doing it considerably reinforces the content of the text and, by presenting us with visual details of the scene, forces us to slow our reading of the text, encouraging greater concentration on character, theme and action.

The second illustration selects another of the story's nodal points, the moment where Bell repels attacking Afghans. Once again, the written text is carefully incorporated into the visual. We are presented with the same scene as in the first illustration, but from a reversed viewpoint: instead of looking up past the two soldiers, we are looking down from close to Bell on his promontory. In the foreground, an Afghan falls theatrically backward, a rifle clutched in his hand; this is Bell's rifle, which the tribesman has clutched to save himself from falling when Bell strikes him with its butt. Another Afghan is shown about to climb up on to Bell's platform, a dagger in his hand: Bell faces him with the heliograph held aloft, about to bring it down on his assailant. Here, the illustrator has again compressed elements of narrative and character, linking the two moments of attack to make clear why Bell is using the helio as a weapon, and showing his bravery in repelling the raiders. The fact that Bell uses the helio, the instrument of a craft which earlier Corporal Stubbins has doubted, shows Bell's courage and his resourcefulness: in seizing on this moment, the illustrator has stressed both a turning point in the narrative and a key episode in the revelation of Bell's character as he proves his worth. It is, in Barthesian terms, both a cardinal function and an index proper in the roles it performs.

The final image shows Bell scrambling down the cliff, the promontory behind him. Movement is accentuated by the figure apparently sliding towards us amid the column of text: the illustration shows Bell, having performed his duty, returning to camp as instructed. It is an image of duty completed: only now can Bell think of himself and return to camp, and the selection of the moment for visual treatment is again subtle and secure, stressing the individual and the sense of duty rather than the fêted hero in camp later that night.

All of the illustrations are unframed, spreading irregularly across both columns of text: the first two are washes, the last a line-drawing. Detail of uniforms and landscape is precise and, as far as can be discerned, accurate. These elements and the closeness to key parts of text, which extend both narrative and character, reveal that the illustrations are an integral part of a single discourse.

This takes on a greater importance when the ideological significance of the story is considered. The Afghan fighting reached its peak in the 1890s, so that the story is largely historic. Yet the Boer War of 1899–1902 was much more recent and, although the British ultimately overcame the Boers, the easy victory of a great imperial power was far from inevitable. Crow's story focuses on an individual act of heroism from a despised private soldier – it is as much his victory over the sneering Corporal Stubbins as the Lancers' over the Afghan tribesmen that is recorded. Alone on his promontory, Bell resolves to stick at his post: 'Bell was done for, but he'd save Fisher's party. It's one private agin a 'arf section.' Duty and sacrifice is linked to an idea of personal triumph over the bullying Stubbins. To this is added a further dimension - Bell is proving himself in his actions since, early in the tale, we are told that 'Bell was certainly not brilliant, but he was a "tryer".'

Owen's story is thus a chronicle of personal growth, duty to the cause and a statement that the real worth of the empire is to be found in its lowly private soldiers, not its jumped-up corporals. In this ideological complex, the illustrations have a major function to perform, by selecting key points of the action, conveying a sense of suspense and progress, and in drawing our sympathies towards the central character, and are thus a central part of the unified discourse of the story. There is, of course, one further significance: the central character and the private soldiers of whom he is a representative are drawn at least in part from the clerk class who would be reading the *Windsor Magazine*.

An ideology of quite a different sort is presented in Florence Warden's story 'Lady Anne's Trustee' (1905: 653–67). This is the first person narrative of 'Miss Jeannette Purley', who is taken on by Lady Anne Smeeth as companion and secretary. When Lady Anne discusses her own unconventional nature, and says that a room in her house is kept ready for 'Mr Mossop', one of her trustees, Purley accepts her story, and rejects the disapproval of the other servants. An extravagant shopping trip, and an episode in which Lady Anne dresses Miss Purley in Spanish costume, along with scenes where Lady Anne's guests make incomplete insinuations, add to the mystery of her identity and nature. After a visit to Sir Harry Rolveden and his uncle, Miss Purley is dismissed by Lady Anne's relations, and subsequently visited by a Scotland Yard detective who questions her about jewellery missing from Sir Harry's house. Sir Harry then appears, and it is revealed that Lady Anne is a kleptomaniac. The love interest and the plot are completed when Sir Harry proposes to Miss Purley, and the two return to Lady Anne's house to begin the task of returning the contents of 'Mr Mossop's room' to their rightful owners and 'making plans for taking care of this most harmless of involuntary criminals' (1905: 667).

The story is a mystery-romance which works by a series of false leads, but which nevertheless has significant ideas beneath its apparently conventional surface. In developing these ideas John Cameron's illustrations play a significant role. The first shows Lady Grace and another unnamed visitor to Lady Anne's soirée sitting talking before a table with a silver coffee pot and an elegant coffee-service. The two are expensively dressed in furs and lace-trimmed hats; the elder figure of Lady Grace looks down with aristocratic hauteur while her companion looks her attentively straight in the face. The image is captioned 'I don't like that girl' (see Plate 16); yet the words do little to construct the significance of the illustration in the manner of Barthes' 'anchorage',[3] since – as is the case with the great majority of captions to this kind of magazine illustrations – without a knowledge of the larger context of the story we cannot locate the scene depicted either within the narrative or within its larger ideological structure. The words are taken from an episode a couple of pages later in the story where the two are discussing Lady Anne and her servants. The verbal text presents these words as being overheard by Miss Purley, and the illustration shows the two guests talking as she would have seen them. Thus we are identified with the narrator by seeing what she sees: added to the use of the first person voice, this presents a unity of reader and writer which involves us to a very large degree in the action. Involvement of this sort is not frequent in popular illustration: its significance here is considerable, in that it helps in the identification of the reader with the mythic movement of the story.

Jeanette Purley is 23, with one French grandmother, and by implication comes from a respectable middle-class family; she has two elderly aunts with whom she stays when she is dismissed by Lady Anne; she is delighted to be involved with the 'ease and luxury and the refinement of a cultivated taste' that she finds in her new employment (1905: 654). Her timidity is shown when she rushes from the room when she is dressed as a Spanish lady and Sir Harry Rolveden visits; yet she is by no means without spirit. She stands up to Lady Grace when the latter voices her disquiet, demands to see Mr Mossop's room, argues with Greening, Lady Anne's maid, and writes a forceful letter to Sir Harry when she assumes he suspects her of stealing. At the end, when she is drawn into the aristocratic world she has experienced only as a servant, by becoming Lady Rolveden, the identification is complete: Miss Jeanette Purley is a distillation of the ideal reader of this kind of fiction, young, socially insecure, yet with spirit and independence, who is delightedly elevated into high society through love and marriage. It is almost a type of the new independent young woman, earning her living by being a companion or 'lady type-writer', who would buy the *Windsor* or similar magazine to pass the time on the Metropolitan line while journeying to the city – independent, yet with enough awareness of the older view of woman's role to welcome the idea of being an aristocratic wife and hostess. The text establishes this identification by the use of the first person narrative; the illustration furthers this by placing us in the narrator's position, and letting us see what she sees.

The second illustration apparently moves away from this identification, since it presents an image of Jeanette Purley herself. However, the circumstances in which she is placed make clear that the larger movement of the story is being advanced: she is presented sitting in an open brougham with Lady Anne, with two uniformed footmen on the box at the front, and a single rider just visible in the background (see Plate 17). The image illustrates the passage where the two women are out for a drive in Hyde Park, showing them to all intents as equals in a pursuit popular in society circles: the transformation from secretary into society lady is prefigured here, and the presentation of the scene in the frozen time of the illustration forces the reader to linger on it. The result is the anticipation of Jeanette's – and the reader's – inclusion into the charmed ranks of society.

The illustration is also significant in terms of the mechanical movement of the plot. Its caption, 'Supposing we do some shop-ping' (1905: 660), is taken from Lady Anne's words to Jeannette in the park. Greening has already warned Jeannette that Lady Anne must not be allowed to go shopping, supposedly because her health will not stand it, but Jeannette rejects this as absurd. The shopping expedition results, as we are to learn at the end of the story, in a further outburst of kleptomania. In selecting this moment for illustration, Cameron has thus both advanced the social elevation of Jeannette and presented a crucially decisive moment in the growth of the narrative.

The two remaining illustrations have similar functions. That on page 663 shows a man kneeling to look beneath a bureau, while the two elderly aunts look on, one on either side. A comic, almost parodic, element is added by the presence of a large cat and tiny kitten looking on in the foreground; the placing of the aunts, shown in rigid profile on either side of the composition, is echoed in the placing of two candlesticks on top of the desk. Once more, we see what Jeannette sees: the aunts are comic, but not ridiculous, and the tone of the illustration extends and develops the mood of the writing, as well as adding suspense in holding back the denouement which comes with Sir Harry's arrival and his explanation of Lady Anne's 'illness'.

The final illustration is roughly analogous to the second in function. It shows Lady Anne reclining on a delicate sofa, holding Jeannette's hands as she stoops over her. Sir Harry stands, hat in hand, in the background, while Greening kneels weeping before her mistress. The two last figures direct our response to the image, suggesting its emotional depth and significance; the caption, Lady Anne's words 'Oh Child, I thought you'd run away from me!', reinforces the emotional nature of the reunion. At the end of the story, Jeannette returns, as friend rather than paid companion, now that she has agreed to marry Sir Harry: but the significance is greater than this. As well as her friend, she is also Lady Anne's moral saviour, since it is she who will sort out the future, not only in caring for Lady Anne but in 'finding the real owners of the accumulations of Lady Anne's trustee', an allusion to the fictitious Mr Mossop's room where the proceeds of the kleptomania are stored. Jeannette is not only admitted into the social elite; with her independence and resilience, she is the only one who can resolve its confusions and provide a 'cure' for Lady Anne. The final image, in showing her in this function, confirms the dual role which is the fulfilment of both the social movement and the plot of the story.

This is, however, evidence of more than a unified discourse of image and text: it also reveals the tale as being essentially lawless and open, moving to a human conclusion which rejects the formal justice of Scotland Yard – indeed, ridicules it in the presentation of the comically kneeling detective – and replaces it with an idea of care and compassion for the 'involuntary criminal'. In this, it offers a structure which avoids a formal, male closure, instead offering an open ending stressing compassion and care which might perhaps be seen as more female in nature, even though the ending is achieved with the qualification of independence in Jeannette's marriage. Within the standards of the time, however, this is not a limitation; along with the assumption into society that comes with it, Jeannette's marriage is an appropriately triumphal resolution. The reader's identification with the central character, created by the use of the first person narrative and the skilful, dual perspective of the illustrations, which alternate between Jeannette's own viewpoint and a view which presents Jeannete as an equal to Lady Anne, constitute an essential part of the ideological structure of the story: the unification of illustration and text is once more essential to the story.

After Florence Warden's tale comes a story for children by Edith Nesbit, 'Molly, the Measles and the Missing Will' (1905: 668–77). The first paragraph of this reveals its nature and main theme: it stresses that 'the inside part, the part that we feel and suffer with, is pretty much alike in all of us' (1905: 668). Molly goes to stay with her dour Aunt Maria, and discovers that the appearance of a long lost relative is endangering the inheritance of her aunt and her parents unless the missing will of Molly's grandfather can be found. Molly has a dream which involves going inside a secret compartment in a bedroom cabinet and, following consultation with the cabinet-maker, the will is found and all is saved. Yet what is more important is what is revealed about Aunt Maria: her fiancé killed in a hunting accident, she has lived alone and bitter, the butt of the children's jokes. With the will is discovered an ancient rose: Mr Sheldon, Aunt's fiancé, had apparently placed will and flower in the cabinet, but had been killed before he could deliver the rose to Maria or the will to the solicitor.

The main thrust of the story lies in the discovery of Aunt Maria's life of feeling, as revealed in her love for Mr Sheldon and her distress at the thought of having to sell her house – in which she had been born, and in which she had met Sheldon. The stress on shared feeling shown in the first paragraph is thus embodied in the tale as a whole; and this is true also of the illustrations. The third of these – the only full-page illustration in the whole magazine – is captioned with the line 'Molly embraced the tall, gaunt figure' and shows Aunt Maria sitting on a rustic seat amid trees while the small figure of Molly holds her arms around her neck (see Plate 18). The contrast is heightened by the difference in tonalities between the figures, the almost solid black of the Aunt's coat being strongly offset against the thinly sketched white of Molly's dress; the former's young, open face also contrasts strongly with the heavily lined face of Aunt Maria. It is a turning point in the story, showing the young girl embracing a relation whom hitherto she has disliked and resented; as such, it opens the way for Molly's hunt for the will which takes up a major part of the story. In addition, it is a reinforcement of the story's main concern – that, however different people may be in age or circumstances, they all share feelings. The contrast between the figures paradoxically emphasises this; the prominence of the image parallels the importance of the moral message in the tale.

The final image of the story shows Aunt Maria holding in her hands the rose which Molly found with the will (see Plate 19). The caption 'It fell into dust in her hands' locates the moment precisely in the narrative, and the cameo-portrait of Mr Sheldon on the wall behind makes clear the origin of the rose and Aunt Maria's thoughts, the link made stronger because, like the cameo, Aunt Maria is shown in profile. Here, we see what Molly sees; the moment of realisation that the aunt, too, once felt strong emotions is emphasised and again the main theme is stressed. In this the illustration considerably enhances the text, which says that the rose 'dropped to dust when it was moved': the caption and the image present the rose – the symbol of Aunt Maria's lost love and lost youth – actually falling apart in her hands, so that the emotional intensity is greatly heightened.

Both of these illustrations show clearly a development of the story's main idea – a sentimental and moralistic one, perhaps, but nevertheless a genuine point which the writer seeks to convey to her child readers. The two earlier illustrations show Molly's mother peering through the gates of her house, from which Molly is excluded when it is thought that the other children have measles, and Molly sitting in bed writing a note to her mother. While these lack the intensity of the other images, they are by no means merely incidental. The former establishes a key device of the narrative, since without the exclusion Molly would not have to stay with her aunt; and the latter shows Molly behaving dutifully at a time when she is far from happy at being with her aunt, to make the reconciliation with Aunt Maria even more poignant when it comes on the next page.

In a sense, to explicate these relationships is to destroy them, since the story works at a very light and delicate level – and, to a modern reader, the level of sentimentality and the moral message is perhaps not easy to accept. Yet within contemporary notions of childhood and its rights and obligations, the story is valid enough in its exploration of feeling, and this exploration is one that is shared between verbal and visual text.

III

Robert Barr's 'The Speculations of Jack Steele', which ran for several months in the *Windsor* from June 1905, is a serial composed of separate stories which have no link except in their presentation by the fictional storyteller, 'Jack Steele'. In itself this is an indication of the shift in the contents of the magazines, from being composed wholly of episodes of longer stories to being virtually restricted to short stories. The story in the November 1905 issue, 'The Richest Woman in the World', is significant in revealing another ideological context in the presentation of an adventure story which seems to be aimed at both men and women readers, and yet which includes certain features often found in women's romance fiction.

The story concerns the relationship between the wealthy Constance Berrington and Mr John Steele, a man who, swindled out of $10 million by one of her agents, confronts her when she is out riding from her retreat near Lake Superior. The two return to her lodge, where he is lent evening dress and given a haircut by her servant; the next morning he returns and, refusing her cheque for the lost money, offers marriage instead and is accepted. It is not in the events of the story that its main force lies, but in the relationship itself, with its alternations between aggression and tenderness, and the taming of Steele and the blossoming of Berrington in each other's company.

This is apparent in the first illustration (see Plate 20). Captioned by a line of the text, 'The horse reared and for a brief second lifted the man off his feet', it illustrates a passage which occurs a page or two after the appearance of the image. Having sprung into the saddle and attacked her horse with her whip when the groom has not held it properly for her, Constance Berrington has ridden off into the woods. John Steele, having tracked her progress, leaps out and grabs the horse's bridle. The moment illustrated shows the struggle between the two which, in the text, is forceful and threatening: it is a moment of dramatic confrontation in which, trying to escape from Steele's sudden attack, the woman beats the horse wildly with her whip and then tries to strike Steele. The illustration shows the horse rearing, with Berrington thrown back and Steele lifted clear of the ground: in the selection of the moment with no clear suggestion of the outcome, the illustrator has shown a fine dramatic sense of the narrative's progression, leading the reader into the story in an immediate and vigorous way. This dynamic effect is increased by the placing of the image a page before the episode is described, which makes us want to read on to see not only the outcome but the reason for the violent encounter. By starting in the middle of events, the illustrator has used a common technique of fiction, in which a striking incident is used as the start of a story with no explanation, to be followed by an account of preceding events and a narrative of the resolution to follow.

This intensity of action is countered by the relaxation and stillness of the next image. This shows Steel standing before Berrington in a clearing in the forest, with the horse just visible running off in the background, so denying its rider the chance of escape. Tension is continued, however, in the strong diagonal created between the faces of the two figures: Steele stands with his back to us looking down at Berrington seated on a fallen tree, and we are led by the angle of his head to her face. On the way we take in the horse bolting in the distance; and the face, when we reach it, is controlled and smiling. The incident and its mood is completed by the caption: 'Now, Mr John Steele, of Chicago, what is the next move?'

Again this image is taken from a page further ahead in the story, so that once more we are led into the verbal narrative by a desire to see what has occurred. What is striking here, though, is that the woman's smiling face and relaxed posture suggests that it is she who is in control, despite the fact that her horse has bolted and she is apparently at the mercy of her attacker: it appears that this is a confrontation of equals, which the woman seems to be enjoying as an intellectual challenge and battle of wills. This in turn advances and develops the relationship between the two, moving us from threat towards a kind of respect – and, once more, we are drawn into the tale and wish to know how it is resolved.

The next page opening is one of a very small number in the magazine which have no illustrations – an unusual occurrence in a publication of this kind, which perhaps indicates the sureness of touch in the placing of illustrations to make us read on. The third image, on the next page, shows a transformed male figure in evening dress raising to his lips the hand of a Constance

Plate 1 George Cattermole, The Death of Little Nell, *The Old Curiosity Shop*
Source: Dickens 1951: 539

Plate 2 Phiz, The Emigrants, *David Copperfield*
Source: Dickens 1948: 832

Plate 3 Phiz, Coming Home from Church, *Dombey and Son*
Source: Dickens 1950: 447

Plate 4 W.M. Thackeray, final illustration from *Vanity Fair*
Source: Thackeray 1878: II, 373

Plate 5 Luke Fildes, 'Houseless and Hungry'
Source: *The Graphic*, 4 December 1869: 10, reproduced by kind permission of the Syndics of Cambridge University Library

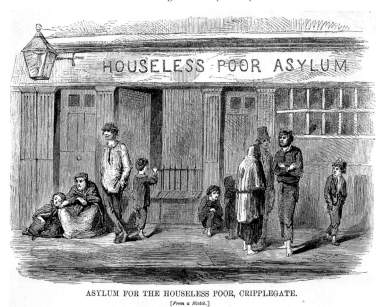

ASYLUM FOR THE HOUSELESS POOR, CRIPPLEGATE.
[*From a Sketch.*]

Plate 6 Anonymous engraving from *The London Street Folk*
Source: Mayhew 1851: 419, reproduced by kind permission of the Syndics of Cambridge University Library

Plate 7 Phiz, 'The Asylum for the Houseless', illustration from *Paved with Gold*
Source: Mayhew 1858: 9, reproduced by kind permission of the Syndics of Cambridge
University Library

Plate 8 H.J. Ford, *The Pink Fairy Book*
Source: Lang, ed., 1897: 22, reproduced by kind permission of the Syndics of Cambridge University Library

FATHER LAWRENCE, CONCEIVING HIMSELF TO BE ADDRESSED BY AN ANGEL, FALLS ON HIS KNEES BEFORE HIM.

Plate 9 H.J. Ford, *The Red Fairy Book*
Source: Lang, ed. 1890: 77

selves, and that makes all the difference: you can't get tired of a thing before you have it. It was a picture, though, worth seeing—the princess sitting

in the nursery with the sky-ceiling over her head, at a great table covered with her toys. If the artist would like to draw this, I should advise him not to meddle with the toys. I am afraid of attempting

Plate 10 Arthur Hughes, Text and illustration from *The Princess and the Goblin* Source: MacDonald 1871: 8

another came over to their side, until at last there was only one left to laugh at all his companions. Two nights more passed, and he saw nothing; but

on the third, he came rushing from the garden to the other two before the house, in such an agitation that they declared—for it was their turn now—that the band of his helmet was cracking under his

chin with the rising of his hair inside it. Running with him into that part of the garden which I have already described, they saw a score of

creatures, to not one of which they could give a name, and not one of which was like another, hideous and ludicrous at once, gambolling on the lawn in the moonlight. The supernatural or rather

Plate 11 Arthur Hughes, Text and illustrations from *The Princess and the Goblin* Source: MacDonald 1871: 128–9

All the words in the English dictionary and in the Greek lexicon as well are, I find, of no use at all to tell you exactly what it feels like to be flying, so I will not try; but I will say that to look down on the fields and woods instead of along at them is something like looking at a beautiful live map, where, instead of silly colours on paper, you have real moving sunny fields and woods laid out one after the other. As Cyril said, and I can't think where he got hold of such a strange expression, "It does you a fair treat." It was most wonderful and more like real magic than anything the children had yet. They flapped and flew and sailed on in their great rainbow wings, between green earth and blue sky, and they flew right over Rochester and then swerved round towards Maidstone, and presently they all began to feel extremely hungry. Curiously enough this happened when they were flying rather low, and just as they were crossing an orchard where early plums shone red and ripe.

They paused on their wings—I cannot explain to you how this is done, but it is something like treading water when you are swimming, and hawks do it extremely well.

"Yes, I dare say," said Cyril, though no one had spoken. "But stealing is stealing even if you've got wings."

"Do you really think so?" said Jane, briskly. "If you've got wings you're a bird, and no one thinks it stealing for a bird to take things, and they eat worms and slugs, and even chickens, so it's quite the opposite of cruelty to them," said Anthea.

"THEY FLEW RIGHT OVER ROCHESTER."

the birds always do it, and no one scolds them or sends them to prison."

It was not so easy to perch on a plum-tree as you might think, because the rainbow wings were so very large; but somehow they all managed to do it, and the plums were certainly very sweet and juicy.

Fortunately, it was not till they had all had quite as many plums as were good for them that they saw a stout man, who looked exactly as though he owned the plum-trees, come hurrying through the orchard with a thick stick, and with one hand over his eyes, and distracted their wings from the plum-laden branches and began to fly.

The man stopped short, with his mouth open. For he had seen the boughs of his trees moving and twitching, and he had said to himself, "Them young varmint—at it again!" And he had come out at once.

her pocket for a threepenny-bit with a hole in it, which she had meant to hang on a ribbon round her neck for luck. She hovered round the unfortunate plum corner, and said:

"We have had some of your plums—we thought it wasn't stealing, but now I am not so sure. So here's some money to pay for them."

She swooped down towards the terror-stricken grower of plums and slipped the coin into the pocket of his jacket, and in a few flaps she had re-joined the others.

The farmer sat down on the grass, suddenly and heavily.

"THE FARMER SAT DOWN ON THE GRASS, SUDDENLY."

glad it was only wings, though. I'd rather see birds as aren't there and couldn't be, even if they pretend to talk, than some things as I could name."

He got up slowly and heavily and went indoors, and he was so nice to his wife that day that she was quite happy, and said to herself, "Law, whatever have a-come to the man!" and smartened herself up and put a blue ribbon bow at the place where her collar fastened on, and looked so pretty that he was kinder than ever.

So perhaps the winged children really did do one good thing that day. If so, it was the only one—for really there is nothing like wings for getting you into trouble. But, if you are in trouble, there is nothing like wings for getting you out of it.

This was the case in the matter of the fierce dog who sprang out at them when they had folded up their wings as small as possible and were going up to a farm door to ask for a crust of bread and cheese, for, in spite of the plums, they were soon just as hungry as ever again.

Now, there is no doubt whatever that if the four had been ordinary wingless children that black and fierce dog would have had a good bite out of the brown-stockinged leg of Robert, who was the nearest. But at its first growl there was a flutter of wings, and the dog was left to strain at his chain and stand on his hind legs as if he were trying to fly too.

They tried several other farms, but at those where there were no dogs the people were far too frightened to do anything but scream; and at last, when it was nearly four o'clock, and their wings were getting miserably stiff and tired, they alighted on a church tower and held a council of war.

"We can't possibly fly all the way home without dinner or tea," said Robert, with desperate decision.

"And nobody will give us any dinner or even lunch, let alone tea," said Cyril.

"Perhaps the clergyman here might," suggested Anthea. "He must know all about angels——"

"Anybody could see we're not that," said

Plate 12 H.R. Millar, Text and illustrations from 'The Psammead'

Source: *Strand Magazine* 1902: 106–7, reproduced by kind permission of the Syndics of Cambridge University Library

"AT LAST HE BEGAN TO LAUGH."

"THEN HUGH THE NOVICE LOST HIS TEMPER."

Plate 13 Claude Shepperson, illustration
from 'Puck of Pook's Hill'
Source: *Strand Magazine* 1906: 49

Plate 14 Claude Shepperson,
illustration from 'Puck of Pook's Hill'
Source: *Strand Magazine* 1906: 54

"The helio flashed in the sun as it swung round."

Plate 15 G. Montbard, illustration from 'Private Bell, Signaller'
Source: *Windsor* 1905: 631

" ' I don't like that girl.' "

Plate 16 John Cameron, illustration from 'Lady Anne's Trustee'
Source: Windsor 1905: 655

LADY ANNE'S TRUSTEE.   659

" ' Supposing we do some shopping?' "

Plate 17 John Cameron, illustration from 'Lady Anne's Trustee'
Source: Windsor 1905: 659

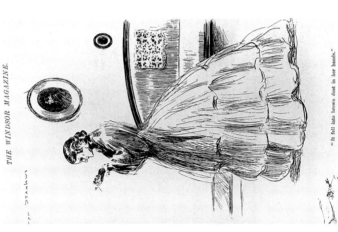

"It fell into brown dust in her hands."

Plate 19 Penrhyn Stanlaws, illustration from 'Molly, the Measles and the Missing Will'
Source: Windsor 1905: 676

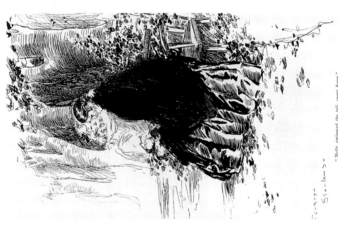

"Molly embraced the tall, gaunt figure."

Plate 18 Penrhyn Stanlaws, illustration from 'Molly, the Measles and the Missing Will'
Source: Windsor 1905: 673

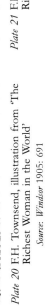

Plate 21 F.H. Townsend, illustration from 'The Richest Woman in the World'

Source: Windsor 1905: 699

Plate 20 F.H. Townsend, illustration from 'The Richest Woman in the World'

Source: Windsor 1905: 691

"'God be merciful!' she whispered.

Plate 22 Fred Pegram, illustration from
'The Cardinal's Comedy'
Source: *Windsor* 1905: 726

"She was not sure; no,
she was not sure."

Plate 23 Fred Pegram, illustration from
'The Cardinal's Comedy'
Source: *Windsor* 1905: 727

Plate 24 Fred Pegram, illustration
from 'The Cardinal's Comedy'
Source: *Windsor* 1905: 729

Plate 25 Norman Hepple, frontispiece to *Gone to Earth*

Source: Webb 1930, reproduced with kind permission of the Syndics of Cambridge University Library

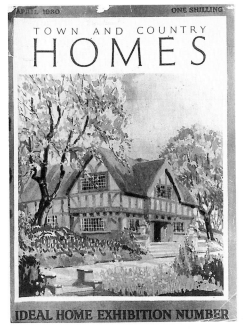

Plate 26 Town and Country Homes (April 1930)

Plate 27 Norman Hepple, illustration from *Gone to Earth*

Source: Webb 1930: 185, reproduced by kind permission of the Syndics of Cambridge University Library

Plate 28 Norman Hepple, illustration from *Gone to Earth*

Source: Webb 1930: 39, reproduced by kind permission of the Syndics of Cambridge University Library

Plate 29 Norman Hepple, illustration from *Gone to Earth*

Source: Webb 1930: 215, reproduced by kind permission of the Syndics of Cambridge University Library

THE KENTISH DOWNS.

Plate 30 Edric Holmes, illustration to *London's Countryside*

Source: Holmes 1922: xii

Plate 31 Alan Stranks and John Worsley, page from 'PC 49'

Source: Stranks and Worsley 1994: 8, reprinted by kind permission of Hawk Books, Fleetway Publications

Berrington wearing a sweeping, diaphanous gown. The relationship is transformed along with the characters' costumes; now they are behaving, if not as friends, then certainly as social acquaintances. Once more, the illustration is used to engage us with the changing relationship and lead us forward to the point in the verbal narrative where the encounter is described.

The final image comes on the penultimate page of the story, and again anticipates the action it presents (see Plate 21). Steele is standing, feet apart and hands on hips, before a Berrington who looks quizzically up to him from her perch on the edge of a table. The caption reads 'I'll not accept your cheque, but I ask you to accept me.' From this, the reader will deduce that a proposal has been made, and perhaps that Berrington's offer of repayment has been refused – there is a slip of paper visible on the edge of the table which, when the caption is read, is revealed as a cheque. Once again we do not know what will happen; the artist has chosen a moment of decision in the story, without suggesting which way events will turn. Like the other illustrations, this image selects a key moment which is yet to occur, without suggesting what is to happen afterwards, at the same time indicating a further change in the relationship between the two protagonists.

Overall, the selection of moments for the illustrations and their placing in the text reveals a firm grasp of the tale's progression as both narrative and human relationship, in a way which subtly encourages the reader to move on to the account of the events shown when it appears in the text. The use of illustration here is thus a way of controlling the reader's progress through the text, showing a subtle and measured relationship between the verbal and the visual which works to create a complex reading experience of anticipation and fulfilment. Text and illustration work as a single unit in arousing and fulfilling the reader, as well as presenting a shared awareness of the growth of the characters and their relationship which, whether the reader is aware of it or not, is a subtle and significant pairing.

The illustrations are also significant in a further way. In selecting the moment of open confrontation between Steel and Berrington as the first image, the illustrator has presented us with a visual equivalent of the moment of what Roland Barthes refers to as 'inoculation':[4] the presentation of an element of violence or threat as a way of protecting the reader from the real appearance of that violence. This phenomenon, it has been noted, is not infrequent in fiction intended to be read by women: it raises the reader's awareness, and also increases the sense of pleasure and release when the violence does not develop, just as a small dose of serum can protect against illness in a medical immunisation. The presence of this in both text and illustration reveals again the complex interaction of the two forms. This subtlety is perhaps not surprising when the identity of the illustrator is considered: F.H. Townsend was a leading illustrator for the journals of his day, contributing cartoons and sketches to *Punch* which show an astringent and enquiring intelligence which is perfectly stated in visual form.

The final story differs slightly in narrative form from the others: whereas they are concerned with action, this is concerned with a single moral dilemma presented to a central character. The Countess de Castro is offered a choice between giving a list of names to her inquisitors, or allowing her husband to die at dawn. The story is extended and developed with several techniques of suspense: the opening sequence discusses at length the condition of the prison, the building of the gallows, and the moving of the Countess to a cell overlooking the courtyard where the execution will take place: there are dialogues between the Countess and the Cardinal de Valdiva, her interrogator; and, finally, a lengthy account of the Countess's anguish as the night passes and dawn brings with it her moment of decision. The moral anguish of the Countess derives from the fact that, if she saves her husband, she will betray a group of others, whereas if she keeps silent her husband will die.

The first illustration establishes the setting by showing the Cardinal and his assistant being admitted to the prison by the jailer. The threatening, enclosed atmosphere is suggested by the low, rounded ceiling and the extreme contrast of the dark shadows and the light coming from the jailer's lantern. The caption, 'If ghosts could speak, Excellency', adds a temporal dimension to this darkness, concentrating the idea of suffering through the ages which is presented in the first two pages of the story in its general account of the prison. The dark, swirling nature of the illustration – a wash drawing in which the robes of the Cardinal and the other figures merge with the surrounding gloom – is suitably imprecise and sinister; the illustrator has presented both the physical setting and the moral atmosphere of the tale, while introducing an element of suspense, since the image appears before we are told the purpose of the visit. The location and nature of the image thus add greatly to the foreboding of the story at this stage.

The remaining four illustrations focus on the Countess, an emphasis which, simply by repetition, adds concentration to the character's dilemma and also emphasises repeatedly her isolation in the prison. The first of this group shows her kneeling before the Cardinal and his assistant, hands clasped beseechingly, with the caption 'Not such a choice as that!' making explicit her suffering. Again the chiaroscuro is intense: the light comes from behind the interrogators, throwing their features into sharp relief, and falling on the Countess's face turned upwards towards them while her back, turned to us, remains in shadow. The use of a line-drawing technique makes the image far sharper than the first illustration, fittingly reflecting the shift to a more specific situation. What is more striking is the presentation of the figures in complete stillness: they stand as if in a frozen tableau vivant, stressing the moral nature of the dilemma rather than the detail of the interrogation. The extreme contrast of light serves both to remind us of the physical constraint of the situation and to heighten the emotional atmosphere. Once again, the action is suspended so that, for a moment, we can appreciate the Countess's dilemma more acutely.

The third illustration (see Plate 22) shows the Countess framed in an arch of the prison, while the Cardinal's assistant turns towards her. Here she is being led from her cell to the one overlooking the gallows: the selection of this moment shows the progression of the narrative as well as stressing her anguish in the very elongated presentation of her figure, with head bowed and long dress trailing on the stone floor. She is presented almost as a saint in a niche; once again presentation achieves a kind of stillness to stress her suffering. By the next illustration, we have reached the stage in the narrative where the Countess is alone in her new cell. She is shown standing before a heavy wooden door, head in hands and frowning with anguish. The caption makes her dilemma explicit: 'She was not sure; no, she was not sure' (see Plate 23). This ties the image directly to the part of the text where the Countess rises and goes to the door, resolved on saving her husband, and then changes her mind before calling for the jailer. The illustration catches this moment of doubt and, once again, halts the narrative so that we can experience more fully her suffering.

The final illustration is a full-page wash-drawing (see Plate 24). It shows the Countess with arms outstretched to the window, through which dawn is breaking; as she reaches out she falls backward in a swoon. The caption reads 'For not all the bolts and bars in Los Perdidos could hold Inez de Castro prisoner.' It thus draws together key elements of the inner and outer progression of the story: the dawn light shows that the Count is executed; the swooning Countess with outstretched arms shows her devotion to her husband; the caption, and her refusal to give the list and so release her husband, shows her moral courage and truth to her principles. This moment of concentration is given due importance by the full page of the image and by the dramatic lighting, which maintains the use of light as a means of emphasising both setting and moral theme throughout the illustrations.

Fred Pegram's five illustrations to the story perform a number of functions. At the level of narrative, they proceed in a series of stages, separating the events of the story into tableaux – the entrance of the inquisitor, the first response to his offer, the move to the new cell, the moment of doubt, and the final resolution. This technique both adds suspense by slowing the narrative in presenting a series of cross-sections through its continuum, and enables the reader to share both the Countess's anguish and her final triumph: the illustrations thus play a crucial part in the development of narrative and moral struggle.

Within this context, a particular ideology is revealed. The Countess is shown as intensely loyal to her husband, and one might raise doubts about this being a particularly male view of suffering womanhood: the elegant elongation of the Countess in the illustration might be said to add to this. In addition, the presentation of the Spanish figures and the overall setting might be seen as a reflection of a xenophobia common in the Edwardian period. Yet for all this there are strengths in the tale: the woman does, after all, remain true to a principle instead of saving herself and her husband, and she is one of a persecuted sect – so that we sympathise not with the figures of authority but with the imprisoned and persecuted rebels. Whatever one's reading of the ideological strengths and weaknesses shown here, it is clear that the illustrations play a major part in exploring moral dilemma and conveying suspense: again the visual text is a key part of the discourse.

IV

The range of relationships between written and visual elements in the stories of the *Windsor* magazine for November 1905 is subtle and various. Montbard's illustrations for 'Private Bell, Signaller' explore stages in narrative and the personal moral growth of a key character; Cameron's treatment of 'Lady Anne's Trustee' involves the reader in both the story and the aristocratic world of the first person narrator, deepening the identification which the intended reader will feel with this figure. F.H. Townsend's illustrations control the pace of narrative and relationship in Robert Barr's story, while adding suspense through their careful placing; and an inner moral struggle is linked with narrative progress through a series of tableaux in Fred Pegram's visualisations of Hamilton Drummond's story of the inquisition. All show quite clearly that the illustration is a subtle, supple partner to a written text.

The two remaining stories in the issue are 'The Last of the Dorias' by Eden Phillpotts (1905: 634–42) and 'A Lost Opportunity' by E.E. Kellett (1905: 701–7). The former, a tale of lost inheritance and revenge, has illustrations by Cyrus Cuneo which reveal character, motive and narrative; the latter, a story about the 'ragging' of a new master at a public school, has illustrations by L. Raven-Hill which are largely concerned with exploring character. If neither has the complexity of the other stories discussed here, both use illustrations as part of the reading structure of the narrative, and thus share the unity of word and image found throughout the magazine.

The remaining articles use illustrations in different ways. The factual ones employ diagrams and descriptive images to amplify a written text; more interesting is the article by Adrian Margaux which discusses the paintings of G.A. Storey. The painter and his work are now forgotten; at the time, he enjoyed no little success as a painter of historical narratives. All of these demand careful 'reading' to establish circumstance, character and event – a kind of reading that would have been acquired by contemporary readers trained by practice through reading illustrated narratives of the sort represented by the stories discussed in this chapter. The presence of reproductions of further narrative paintings as separate items in the magazine confirms this. Arthur J. Elsley's *Divided Affection* shows a girl playing with a dog and a cat; Eva Roos's *Home Lessons* shows a group of children gathered around a sofa table in a contemporary drawing room giving their attention to schoolbooks. That these, like the paintings of Storey, are fairly undemanding, sentimental narratives, should not surprise us. As well as revealing the taste and ideology of the urban middle-class readers of the magazine, they recall the circumstance explored in Chapter 2, which made clear the fact that, as far as reading images is concerned, the Victorians were adept at reading combined narratives of both verbal and visual content, and often needed verbal contexts for a full understanding of more complex emblematic works: visual texts alone must make their narrative points far more simply and directly, as Chapter 2 has demonstrated.

That the dual text of word and image works together in establishing narrative and exploring character in the popular illustrated fiction of the day, and that both reflect the ideology of the clerkly class in a range of facets, is quite clear from the fictions examined in this chapter. Edwardian illustrated magazines are far from being insubstantial, unthinking pulp: they represent collections of fictions in which word and image create a dual discourse of not inconsiderable sophistication, and deserve more critical attention than they have as yet received.

5

GONE TO EARTH AND 1920s LANDSCAPE IDEOLOGY

Norman Hepple's colour frontispiece to Mary Webb's *Gone to Earth* shows the rakish figure of a man standing, one foot resting on a tombstone, before a picturesquely crooked half-timbered house with leaded lights and bottle-glass windows (see Plate 25). The scene is bathed in rich, warm light from the moon at the top left-hand corner; the whole suggests a degree of uncertainty which is mitigated by the softness of the tones and the soft rhythms and organic textures of the old building and natural surroundings.

This is the first visual image with which the reader of the illustrated edition is presented, and as such it is of considerable importance in suggesting not only the nature of illustration within the volume but also its role in the amplification of the text. A clear direction to the place in the action that is presented is given in a quotation and reference beneath the image: 'She was made for me' (1930: 144; 1978: 125).[1] The scene illustrated occurs in Chapter 14 of the novel. The figure outside the house is Jack Reddin, the squire who has earlier seduced the central figure, Hazel Woodus; the house is that of the novel's local minister, Edward Marston, who has just proposed marriage to Hazel and been accepted. As a frozen statement of the two male forces between whose tension the life of Hazel is manipulated, the illustration is a fitting way of beginning the novel; yet in other ways it offers a less valid reading of the text in setting, theme and circumstance.

The illustration's antithesis between the security of the moon-drenched building and the figure posed Sir Jasper-like outside suggests a simple clash between good and evil which is far from the situation explored in the novel. Rather than stating such an opposition, the passage illustrated is concerned with creating a direct parallel between the two men in their desire for Hazel.

93

Edward Manston lies in bed thinking to himself 'She was made for a minister's wife' (1930: 144; 1978: 124); Reddin stands outside thinking 'She was made for me' (1930: 144; 1978: 125). The narrator goes on to make the point explicitly: 'Both men saw her as what they wanted her to be, not as she was,' a single sentence which probably sums up the novel's fundamental concern more than any other statement. That the illustration ignores this tension, instead suggesting the conflict more in terms of unqualified extremes, shows how it significantly modifies the thrust of the book's verbal text.

This larger shift is matched by other apparently more superficial, but ultimately deeply significant, alterations. The house in the illustration is a large Tudor construction, with tiled roofs sweeping low at the left beneath a tall, square brick chimney while at the right there is a gable end, half-timbered, with walls out of true. On the first floor, golden light shines through a leaded casement, while beneath is a recessed wall with a full bow window with small panes of bottle-glass. This is markedly different from the edifice described in the novel: 'The chapel and minister's house at God's Little Mountain were all in one – a long, low building of grey stone surrounded by the graveyard, where stones, flat, erect and askew, took the place of a flower-garden' (1930: 70; 1978: 56). Only the graveyard is retained in the illustration; the building is quite different in design, material and stature, two-storey half-timbering replacing the low 'grey stone' building, to install variation and warmth in the place of monotony and cold. A similar difference may be seen in the building's surroundings. Instead of the text's 'woods . . . like heathen creatures under the night' whose 'small soft leaves hung limply in the frost' (1930: 70; 1978: 56) we see large, full trees behind the house; and the two trees in the foreground have leaves which are clear and crisp in the moonlight. The light, too, is used for different effect. The text has the house as 'moon-silvered', but any suggestion that this is an effect of richness or warmth is negated by the references to the rime which whitens Reddin's shoulders and the light which reveals white hairs at his temples to 'mock this young passion' he feels for Hazel. Nor is there any hint in the image that, at the end of the night, Reddin is 'chilled through and through'.

What has happened is that a prose passage which stresses the wish of both men to change Hazel's nature in different ways, presented in a setting of architectural austerity and chill of atmosphere, has become a hazily romantic picture of a raffish figure standing outside a picturesquely antique cottage in a rich glow of moonlight. These changes are not, I think, the result of simple impercipience on the part of the illustrator: they are part of a subtle and complex network of related circumstances of the illustrations and the period which show how the book and its themes have been relocated within a quite different ideology from that of Webb's text. For this reason, the illustrated edition is of much interest as an example of how a visual text may redirect and reconstruct the nature of the purely verbal novel.

II

Mary Webb's *Gone to Earth* first appeared in 1917, published by Constable. It was issued in *The Collected Works of Mary Webb* by Jonathan Cape in 1928, with an introduction by John Buchan. By March 1932 this edition had gone through twelve separate impressions and in that year was reissued in Cape's Florin Books series, a list of reprints of popular novels and essays at the price of 2s. This made it widely available at a reasonable price, though not as cheaply as the sixpenny novels of the Nelson's Library or The Reader's Library. The Florin edition of Mary Webb that I have before me as I write is a properly casebound volume of crown octavo size – roughly equal to a standard paperback volume – instead of the smaller Nelson's Library volumes which used poorer quality wood-pulp paper and cheap paper-covered boards. The difference is important: Mary Webb's books were popular with a group of the reading public other than that seeking the cheapest books, and this difference is significant in any consideration of the illustrations and their functions, as I shall make clear later.

The edition of *Gone to Earth* with illustrations by Norman Hepple is part of an illustrated edition of the works of Mary Webb which was produced by Jonathan Cape – alongside its *Collected Works* and the Florin Edition – beginning in 1928 with *Precious Bane*. These are lavish productions in large crown octavo with a green cloth binding heavily gold-blocked. *Gone to Earth* is perhaps the most lavishly illustrated, with four tipped-in colour illustrations on art paper and thirty full-page black and white drawings reproduced photo-lithographically. In addition, a further fifty-one vignettes are added to the text, generally as headpieces or endpieces to chapters, a title-page drawing and pictorial endpapers.

All of this makes the book of importance as an aesthetic object: it is far more than a simple reading edition of the novel, offering a very different reading experience from that provided by either of the editions offered simultaneously by Cape or the first Constable edition. Its cost, as well as the format and general appearance, would put it beyond the reach of the general run of bestseller buyers: while it would be wrong to dismiss it as a coffee-table book or a volume for the gift-book market, it is probably true to say that this was a volume for those who treasured books as objects as well as those who followed Mary Webb's writings.

It is pertinent to ask why *Gone to Earth* became so popular in the later 1920s after its relatively quiet reception at its first publication, since this has a bearing not only on the very existence of the illustrated edition but also on the nature of the illustrations and their presentation of the text. The first appearance of the novel attracted little interest – in 1917, perhaps, the concerns of readers and reviewers were elsewhere, and the novel certainly has little explicit connection with the war. Twelve years later, Stanley Baldwin, then Prime Minister, made a speech at the Royal Literary Fund Dinner in which he praised Webb's work (Wrenn 1964: 1). In the same year he wrote an introduction to Cape's reissue of *Precious Bane*. Baldwin's introduction is more sensitive than one might have supposed: he seems to get as close as many other critics to the special identity of Webb's writing when he talks of her being 'more alive to the changing moods of nature than of man' (1978: 5) and continues: 'Almost any page at random will furnish an illustration of the blending of human passion with the fields and skies.'

Yet within Baldwin's introduction are elements which give the clue to the change of approach evident in Norman Hepple's *Gone to Earth* illustrations. Speaking of the Shropshire mereland in which the novel is set, he says that 'There are of course the old castles and timbered black and white houses for the motoring visitors' (1978: 4), but goes on to describe the deeper richness of the land which Webb 'saw and felt as a girl and remembered with lyrical intensity as a woman'. The main thrust of Baldwin's praise for the novel is concerned with this latter quality, the intense feeling for human-kind – perhaps more particularly womankind, though Baldwin is not specific on this – and the magical landscape. Yet the opening of the passage quoted above shows another response to the country-side – one which rests on its new accessibility through popular motoring for the more affluent middle classes after the First World War.[2]

This is part of a much larger and more complex reinvention of the countryside which had been taking place in England at least since the 1860s.[3] It is a fabric composed of many different strands, which have to be carefully separated if we are fully to appreciate the significance of the illustrations to *Gone to Earth*. The chivalric myths and mock-mediaevalism of the Victorians most celebrated in Tennyson,[4] are one dimension of a desire to return to an ideal Englishness rooted in a village life seen as natural and self-sustaining, in the face of a contemporary reality in which the nation's energies were being sapped by colonial expansion and its true identity distorted by urban industrialism. William Morris's *News from Nowhere* (1890) and Richard Jefferies' *After London* (1885) both celebrate the creation of new, post-industrial communities which have grown up after the decay of the city; significancrly, Richard Jefferies was one of Mary Webb's favourite writers. The *Georgian Poetry* anthologies,[5] collections of poems which celebrated rural life, were edited by a metropolitan civil servant; their concern with rural manners suggests a return to the ideal relationship between humankind and nature celebrated by Wordsworth in 'Tintern Abbey' and the early passages of *The Prelude*.

This concern for the countryside as an intellectual and moral system is broadened and blunted by an interest in the country as a place for recreation which burgeons from the beginning of the century in more popular culture. The growth of the outer London suburbs, with posters of the new underground railways offering rural paradise in Golders Green and the further outposts of the Northern Line, is one dimension of this; another is the growth of charabanc trips and railway excursions into the country. E.M. Forster's Leonard Bast is a representative of the new class of clerks which yearns for its roots in the countryside when, in *Howards End* (1910), he takes a bus to the outskirts of London and spends the night walking through the Surrey woods and fields. In the 1920s, open charabancs offered days in the countryside to dwellers in working-class industrial centres; more sensitive tastes were satisfied by enclosed motor-coaches providing trips at about a penny-halfpenny a mile. And, as Baldwin's preface shows, for those with slightly more money, the cheap, mass-produced motor car offered the possibility of rural escape. This was a social

97

phenomenon so well known that advertisers made thorough use of it. A brochure of the 1920s shows an open four-seater passing a group of cottages – half-timbered, roses round the door, and ivy-clad with low, sweeping eaves – with the legend 'Through Surrey lanes on a 10 hp Old Mill'.

It is precisely to this clutch of ideas and images, and its way of seeing the countryside as a means of escape from urban realities, that Stanley Baldwin refers when he mentions the 'black and white houses for the motoring visitors' in his introduction to *Precious Bane* (1924: 4). His point is that Mary Webb's Shropshire is far more than this superficially attractive image; yet, since this was an image which had great appeal at the time, it is that which came to dominate in the reader's response to the novel and which, inevitably, is one reason for the great upsurge in popularity in the writer's novels in the 1920s and early 1930s. Instead of a concern for the relationship between humanity and nature which the writing explores, it is as an exploration of picturesque scenery and delightful cottages that the novels appeal to readers of those decades; the text has been subtly reconstructed in the reader's mind, and the elements of threat which are presented by the instinctive freedom – and perhaps the sexual hunger – of the main women characters become instead an approach to the idea-lised freedom and picture-book thatch of the perfect English village.

A further dimension of this longing for the rural ideal is seen in domestic architecture. The return to what was seen as the strong vernacular of the Saxons seen in the work of Norman Shaw and C.F.A. Voysey in the later nineteenth and early twentieth centuries respectively is scaled down to become the half-timbered mock-Tudor semis that dominate 1920s and 1930s speculative ribbon-development. Middle-class town dwellers are offered the fiction of living in a country cottage, as any number of popular magazines and journals about homes and gardens will testify. The 'Ideal Homes Exhibition Number' of *Town and Country Homes* (April 1930; see Plate 26) shows this well. Its front cover shows a large, mock-Tudor thatched house surrounded by spring flowers and trees in blossom: a comparison between this and Norman Hepple's account of the house on God's Little Mountain – both images which appeared in the same year – will show exactly how the illustrations relocate the novel into this middle-class idyll of stockbroker Tudor.

Webb's country is idyllic in a very different way; its magic depends on a grasp of the place of human feeling and female sexuality within the larger patterns of the natural world, that the male characters of *Gone to Earth* cannot fathom. That world is deeply destructive because of the collision of these two forces: the world of pretty cottages seen in the popular escape culture of the late 1920s is infinitely safer and tamer. Yet it is to this world of idealised, sub-Voysey cottages and motor-trips to picturesque Shropshire that Norman Hepple's illustrations move Mary Webb's text, in a major act of ideological relocation.

Norman Hepple was born in 1908 and studied at the Royal Academy Schools, the Royal College of Art and Goldsmiths' College. He exhibited at the Royal Academy from 1928 onwards, first producing etchings and later portraits and figure studies at the rate of four or five a year. It is his earliest work which is of relevance here, however, since *Gone to Earth* was one of his first commissions. Before it, Hepple had produced etchings, exhibiting three at the Royal Academy: *Gethsemane* in 1928 and *All Hallows* and *Hoo Marsh* in 1929. These are important in revealing in subject matter and treatment the influence of an artist who had died in 1881 but whose work was to have considerable impact on a much later generation of artists: Samuel Palmer. Palmer's work was the subject of a large-scale exhibition at the Victoria and Albert Museum in 1926. It had a powerful effect on the generation of young artists of which Hepple was a part: figures such as Paul Drury, F.L. Griggs and Graham Sutherland began to produce images of rolling hills, deeply ploughed fields, sheepfolds in the hills and thatched cottages enfolded in the landscape with warm light shining from small, leaded casements. Palmer's work is far more than a town-based idealisation of the country; so, at its best, is Sutherland's. Yet, taken in conjunction with the landscape ideology of the mass market in the 1920s, its influence becomes in the work of Norman Hepple a way of diffusing Webb's text into something popular and anodyne; the subversive nature of the writing – its exploration of female freedom and female sexuality – is made respectable in what we might call an act of superversion in which the illustrations subsume the text into the safe dominant ideology of countryside-as-safe-retreat.

The influence of Palmer seems to merge with another force in Hepple's work: the large number of illustrated books on the English countryside which appeared in the 1920s. Often illustrated with line-drawings, such volumes became increasingly popular in the 1930s with the series produced both by A. and C. Black[6] and by Harry Batsford,[7] celebrating aspects of Englishness such as traditional crafts and buildings as well as the nature of the landscape and the particular characteristics of individual counties. Hepple's work needs to be seen as part of this burgeoning tradition: he is clearly responsible in part for the way in which a generation of middle-class readers looked at the English countryside, its buildings and communities, and it is into this tradition that the illustrations for *Gone to Earth* fall, with significant consequences on the view of the text that they present.

How this works in practice has already been shown with regard to the frontispiece of *Gone to Earth*. That it continues throughout the illustrated edition can be seen by studying further illustrations and their treatment of the text.

III

To match Stanley Baldwin's introduction to *Precious Bane*, Cape commissioned John Buchan to write a prefatory note for *Gone to Earth*. Buchan was then famous not only for his spy thrillers including *The Thirty-Nine Steps* (1915), but also for his work as an intelligence officer – which included writing the semi-official account *The Battle of the Somme* – and as head of the Department of Information from February 1917 to its transformation into a Ministry a year later, when he became Director of Intelligence. In 1927 he was elected Tory MP for the Scottish Universities: when the introduction to *Gone to Earth* appeared in 1930, Buchan, like his party's leader, Stanley Baldwin, was in opposition during Ramsay Macdonald's Labour administration, but he nevertheless spoke with an establishment voice because of his background and current parliamentary position, and once again the espousal of Webb's writing by the political right wing is striking. Like Hepple's illustrations, Buchan's introduction provides further evidence of the way the novel is subtly changed as it is subsumed into a larger ideology of rural retreat. A key part of this is Buchan's claim that the novel is set 'perhaps fifty years ago' (Webb 1930: 9). This does more than suggest that the novel happens in the past; it adds the final necessary dimension for the ideal view of the countryside, that of temporal remoteness.

Close examination of the novel itself, however, reveals that Buchan's assertion about the novel's setting is simply not true, since two explicit references contradict it. When Hazel goes into town with Mrs Marston to buy clothes for the wedding, they go by 'the traction trailer' (1978: 93) which belongs to the stone quarry: 'At last the traction engine appeared, and Mrs Marston was hoisted into the trailer – a large truck with scarlet painted sides, and about half full of stone' (1978: 95-6). Buchan's claim would place the events in about 1867, whereas steam traction engines were not in regular use until about twenty-five years later and had their heyday in the years before the First World War. That this later period is the setting of the novel is confirmed by the statement in the description of the county fair that the prize-giving was held on a platform made of 'a lorry with chairs on it' (1978: 115). There is no mention of the events of the war; it is thus reasonable to suppose that the novel is set somewhere between ten and fifteen years before the date of its publication, a distancing that, since the middle of the nineteenth century, has been the accepted temporal location for many popular novels.

The difference between fifteen and fifty years ago is more than a matter of mere figures. It is the difference between being within close memory, a way of reinforcing the validity of the omniscient narrator as storyteller, and being at least a generation before, negating this immediacy and placing the story almost within the category of folk-legend or 'historical novel'. That the novel itself is set within recent time is important, since it allows us to share the feelings of its participants, instead of seeing them within an imagined, distant rural past. For Buchan to place it in a different convention hints again at the ideal of the lost golden age of country life, but goes further: it moves the story from the disordered years before the First World War, riddled with industrial and political strife, to an imagined, perfect past. This is, of course, a frequent right-wing manoeuvre: 'all contemporary conservatives are displaced in the sense that they live in exile from the historical community they celebrate' (North, 1991: 110). Not only is the past another country: the country is another past.

The rural ideal is amplified in one of the full-page illustrations which Hepple provides for Buchan's introduction. It shows a man ploughing a hilly field behind a single horse, with a low-eaved thatched cottage nestling between the field and a group of tall, lush trees, while to the left further fields and trees enfold farm buildings. The cottage is loosely reminiscent of one in a Samuel Palmer image – that in *A Rustic Scene* (1825: sepia mixed with gum, $6\frac{7}{16}$ x $9\frac{3}{16}$; Ashmolean Museum, Oxford), perhaps, or even *The Gleaning Field* (1833: oil and tempera, 13 x 18; Tate Gallery) – and the motifs of deeply textured ploughed land and stylised, rounded trees certainly continue Palmer's technique of exaggerating and deforming natural structures to stress their symbolic rather than naturalistic significance, although there is no hint of such mystical purpose in Hepple's work. The whole creates an image of timeless rural continuity, a version of country life as idealised in any number of Georgian poems and illustrated books on the country from the preceding two decades. This is a view of the country that is quite distinct from that of Mary Webb's novel: it is a picturesque retreat, not a locus of passionate feeling between human and animal experience.

The mere fact that Hepple has illustrated the introduction is remarkable in itself and supplies further evidence of a shift away from the site of the novel and its concerns. It is as if we are being presented with an alternative, visual text, which colours and distorts our reading even before the verbal one is presented. This is true not only of the full-page image but also of the three other drawings which accompany the introduction, although these work in a slightly different way, to relocate the text not in the perpetual timeless past, but by referring to imagery of more recent years which, in its turn, is an attempt to recreate a long-lost rural ideal. The vignette at the head of the first page shows a group of cottages clustered around a church with a square tower, with a pair of trees to the right. This is an idealised village community of the kind which has no place at all in *Gone to Earth*, which deals instead with isolated houses – Reddin's Uddin House, the minister's church and home at God's Little Mountain, Abel Woodus's cottage – and the natural locations of the woods, spinney and quarry. The vignette asks us instead to think back to the imagined perfections of an organic, corporative community of the middle ages or earlier, couched in the terms of illustrated books on English villages which were popular in the 1920s and 1930s both as guide books for middle-class motorists and as a way of selectively celebrating the rural community of England.

The other two drawings – those which come on the verso page facing the start of the Introduction, and at its conclusion – are of a different order. The first shows a cottage with low eaves and square chimneys, very much in the style of Voysey's vernacular

102

architecture of the turn of the century. The second shows what seems, from the sign that is suggested at the right, to be a village inn, again steeply pitched and low eaved, with square chimneys and a dormer window – another favourite and much illustrated emblem of rural life in the countryside literature of the 1920s. Neither is representative of the houses central to the novel's action; both relocate it firmly within the contemporary ideal and again skew our reading of the text.

Time is important in these images. In the full-page drawing, a timeless past is suggested, but it is in the imagery of the 1920s which is a reinvention of the style of Samuel Palmer. In the others, the style of a contemporary travel or countryside book and the kind of architecture which aims to recreate ancient English home-steads are jointly employed to present a view of the ideal past seen through the filter of a contemporary view of earlier ages. The result of this is clear: it separates the reality of the novel from the direct reality being experienced by the reader, and so moves us subtly away from an immediate involvement with the novel and its concerns. Even before we begin reading the novel, the way we construct it has been directed towards a safe, mythic and in many ways male countryside which is a long, long way from the timeless, intuitive and innately female locus of Webb's writing.

IV

Locating the action of *Gone to Earth* in a different time is a technique which is used in a markedly contrasting way in the illustrations to the novel itself. Instead of the timeless English pastoral suggested in the full-page drawing to the introduction, an England which is strictly contemporary is presented. This brings the action into the experience of the reader, but also distorts it. Instead of the remote qualities of much of the description of the novel we are offered views of a countryside and a rural way of life, which seem to come straight from a manual of 1920s architecture and interior design in the fashionable cottage style. Once again, the novel has been appropriated by the contemporary ethic of the countryside as picturesque retreat, instead of being allowed to maintain its own very specific approach to the nature of rural life and the place of woman within it.

This can be seen in one of the earliest full-page drawings, which shows Hazel and her father, Abel Woodus, in their home, a single-storey building roofed with corrugated iron. The illustration shows Hazel reaching down a jug from a shelf above the open fire. She wears clothes contemporary with the illustration, a simple jumper and mid-calf length skirt; Abel, too, is dressed in a jacket which, while it cannot be dated too precisely, is clearly post-war and suggests a 1920s sports coat instead of the 'black cut-away coat and snuff-coloured trousers and high-crowned felt hat' (1930: 66; 1978: 54) which are described a little later – clothes which, fashionable at the end of the century, are still worn by Abel Woodus several years later.

The illustration is distortive of the text for several reasons. It gives the pair an appearance of affluence which is far from the circumstances of the novel. More important, it goes against a major narrative impulse of the scene. When Hazel reaches up, not to get a jug but to cut some bacon off a flitch that is hanging by the fire, we are told that 'her dress, already torn, ripped from shoulder to waist' (1930: 22; 1978: 15). The need to replace this dress leads Hazel to go into town, where she meets Jack Reddin; it is thus a major narrative departure. The illustration ignores this, showing Hazel instead quite well dressed and subsuming her into a fashionable middle-class world. This shift is aided by the fireplace which is shown. Instead of a squat open fire or the Kitchener stove which it is likely that a family of this sort would have used for both heating and cooking – or even a much older open ingle-nook – the fireplace is a large, brick structure with a hood extending outwards over the burning logs. This sort of fireplace descends directly from the large open grates designed by Philip Webb, most particularly that of the Red House, Chorleywood,[8] and much imitated in middle-class housing in the 1920s and 1930s. Once again, the setting and the main characters are subsumed into a different view of the countryside, and not only the spiritual relation with the country, but also a major narrative thread, are lost as a result.

The relocation of the text continues in different ways and to different degrees with almost all of the succeeding illustrations. On page 39, we are shown the figure of Andrew Vessons, Jack Reddin's manservant and factotum, striding across the courtyard at Undern, carring a bucket; at his feet stand a cockerel and a hen (see Plate 27). It is a sturdy image of a countryman going about his work, the figure given greater strength and impact by the very low viewpoint, so that we see him almost from the eye-level of the chickens. The text makes no mention of such a specific image, but does refer to

Vessons moving around the grounds 'with pig buckets or ash buckets or barrows full of manure' (1930: 40; 1978: 31). Nothing as sordid is shown in the illustration; instead of pigs, we have chickens, a much more acceptable icon of country life. Eighteenth-century watercolours which idealise rural existence frequently show a group of hens clustered cosmetically around a cottage door: here, Hepple has perhaps subconsciously developed that tradition and once again shown an image which moves us away from the dark severity of the text, here embodied in the surly and insular Andrew Vessons, towards a rural ideal made acceptable in the noble figure striding past the hens against a background of an ancient stone mansion.

Cosmetic changes which bring the novel into the realm of a 1920s motor-tourist guide can be seen in the illustration showing the scene where Reddin stops outside a public house in which Abel and Hazel are drinking. Reddin is enquiring of the landlord where Hazel lives: at this stage he does not know her name but knows that her father is a musician. Abel goes to the door to talk with Reddin who remains outside on his horse. It is a scene compounded of menace and desire, as Hazel sits inside recognising Reddin's voice but unwilling to show herself, and Abel offers his services as a musician, while the publican and Reddin exchange bawdy comments which increase the erotic tension. Hepple shows Reddin on horseback from behind, while a figure at the left leans rather effetely – hand on hips, arm raised to rest on the door-frame – against the Tudor inn. Both figures are dressed in contemporary clothes, that at the left in jacket and trousers and what appears to be a rather elaborately embroidered waistcoat. If this is the publican, he is adopting a very leisurely pose and is uncharacteristically rich in dress; if Abel, then his dress differs once more from his black coat and snuff-coloured trousers, and the posture is far too elegant and affected for his down-to-earth nature. The whole is much more suggestive of a pair of undergraduates out on a drinking trip to an inn in the Cotswolds – the kind of excursion popular from Evelyn Waugh's Oxford – than of the erotic tautness of the novel. Further distance from this is provided by the inn sign at the right, which announces it as 'Ye Captain's Biscuit', a name not mentioned in the text and, again, redolent of 1920s archaism in its use of 'ye' as a mis-reading of the Middle English þ or thorn seen in countless roadside 'Ye Olde Teashoppes'.

It is not the only scene where narrative elements are erased and erotic tensions slackened by a shift towards a softer view of a notional countryside. A parallel relocation into the land of the motor-tourist is apparent in the illustration on page 117 which shows Hazel and Mrs Marston on their shopping trip to Silverton before the wedding. They are shown standing in a cobbled street outside the bottle-glass bay-window of a Tudor shop, outside which hangs a sign on which can be discerned: 'nsor & Ne' 'Artists Colourm'. These we take to mean 'Winsor and Newton' – the leading manufacturer of artists' materials – and 'Artists' Colourman'. That Mrs Marston is looking into the window of this shop significantly changes our idea of her character. In the novel she is a devoted and somewhat fussy mother, whose dominant concern is Edward's well-being, physical and moral. Her religious faith is intense, her moral sense conventional; she is outraged at Hazel's forthright language and lack of faith. In the episode shown, the two women are looking at a shop displaying religious pictures, especially those of 'that particularly seedy and emasculated type which modern religion seems to produce' (1930: 114; 1978: 98). Hazel is outraged at the anguish shown in one depiction of the Crucifixion over which Mrs Marston lingers, and this provokes a discussion about man's brutality and the redemptive nature of Christ's death. Hazel sees it as savage and literal, Mrs Marston as part of a mythic pattern and thus unrelated to real pain. The quarrel is used to reveal a genuine difference between the characters and, most particularly, to stress Hazel's sensitivity to the animal kingdom and suffering within it. Not only is this character delineation quite lost in the illustration, which presents instead a conventional scene of two women window-shopping; there is in addition the suggestion that Mrs Marston is an amateur artist, placing her in the convention of well brought up young ladies producing tame watercolours. The hint of the Picturesque is aided by the presentation of the two figures in something like eighteenth-century costume, with long dresses and, for Mrs Marston, a shawl and bonnet. Once more a key element in the narrative has been skewed by an attractive image which belongs to quite a different register.

A little later on, at the fair, Hazel and Edward go into the barn where produce and fruit are displayed. The exhibits, though described as being presented with 'stern simplicity' (1930: 128; 1978: 110), are themselves described with great sensuality: 'There were rolls of golden butter, nut-brown eggs, snowy bouquets of broccoli, daffodils with the sun striking through their aery petals, masses of dark wallflower where a stray bee revelled.' It is almost a garden of earthly delights, yet not in the negative mediaeval reading: this is a banquet of the senses which again stresses Hazel's instinctive oneness with the natural world of which she is a part, and the sensuality central to her nature. Edward gives her a jar of honey, sealed in a box edged with lace which is 'provocative as the reserve of a fair woman' (1930: 128; 1978: 111), telling her to open it on her wedding day. We are then told 'the symbolism, so apparent to him, was lost on Hazel'. It is a scene of no little complexity, stressing that for Hazel the sensuality of the honey is real, not symbolic, and revealing the gulf between her and Edward. Yet the illustration shows only a few small boxes of produce and two large jugs, in the lower right-hand quarter; the rest of the page is taken up with an exquisitely rendered view of the interior of the old barn, its irregular beams and rafters shown with great richness and skill, much in the style of the barn paintings of George Clausen which were popular at this time. The figures of Edward and Hazel, at the left, are more those of town tourists at a country fair, in the scene but not of it: once again, the thrust of the novel is lost by the illustration's subtle redirection.

One of the most significant relocations occurs in the passage where Hazel goes to pick mushrooms. In the novel, the land is overlaid with 'soft, woolly and intensely white' mist (1930: 184; 1978: 162) so that the rose-briars 'looked elvish against the wintry scene'. The richness captivates Hazel and she runs and dances through the mist, 'wild as a fairy' and 'like a tightly-swathed nymph . . . with her slim legs and arms shining in the fresh cold dew', calling to the cuckoos and talking to a young one she finds in the grass. In itself this is an image of female sensuality which reveals much about Hazel's nature, showing it as a valid alternative to the extremes of predatory eroticism and self-debasing celibacy she is offered by Reddin and Marston respectively. Yet it is given further significance by the fact that she has with her to collect the mushrooms a small bag which Marston uses to take communion to another chapel at which he ministers. While she dances, 'In her hand, and in that of the shadow, bobbed the little black Lord's Supper bag' (1930: 184; 1978: 163). The symbolism is clear; this dance of Hazel's is an instinctive equivalent for the communion, allowing her to become symbolically one with the natural world of which she is part. The sacramental nature of the episode is made quite explicit when we are told that, 'In her eyes nothing could be more magical and holy than silken, pink-lined mushrooms.' This is an image of natural, sacramental sensuality which goes against both the organised religion of the church and its authority – a heavily male authority – in the freedom and the innately female nature of Hazel's actions.

Nothing of this is shown in the illustration (see Plate 28). Hazel is shown standing quite still, with the house and its trees – another view of the building shown in the frontispiece – in the near distance. In her hand Hazel carries not the communion pouch but a sturdy wicker basket; there is no hint of mist, dew or young cuckoo. That this should be simply the result of a superficial reading of the text seems unlikely, since Hazel's skirt is shown hitched up at the side with what we can just discern to be the butterfly-shaped pin mentioned in the text. Yet the absence of any of the other key features which make this scene both powerfully literal and intensely sacramental very clearly changes its significance. The effect is to remove the threat which its sacramental sensuality poses to established order in translating the scene into a town-dweller's idyll of fictive country life.

One further example of this redirection will suffice to show its extent. Hazel leaves the house while Edward and his mother are at chapel and walks out through the woods to keep an appointment with Reddin. Reaching a hill-top she sits down to look at the scene before her, and hears Reddin singing as he leaves his house to meet her. This introduces a paragraph which discusses Reddin's prurient views on sex – something that he approaches with a mixture of fear and appetite, refusing to talk of it or to accept 'the grave, the majestic significance of the meeting of the sexes – holding as it does the fate of the golden pageantry of life, sacrificially spending as it does the present for the future' (1930: 214; 1978: 189). When Reddin nears her, Hazel rises, in fear both of the place and of 'the death-pack', the ghostly pack of hounds which by legend haunt the area and which are, in this context, a further foretaste of Hazel's death in her efforts to protect Foxy from the pursuing hounds. Thus the whole of the meditation on the nature of sexuality, with the suggestion that the attempts to deny it can be fatal not only spiritually but literally, takes place within the setting of Hazel's looking down over the valley. It is a further example of the unity of the central character and the natural world, and a further statement of how the male characters are excluded from this magical oneness.

The illustration (see Plate 29) changes the scene considerably. It does show Hazel sitting above a valley, and there is a suggestion of one of the 'gnarled may-trees' (1930: 213; 1978: 188) mentioned in the text: yet little else is there which extends the mood or symbolic significance of the writing. The 'sleek farm-horses' and flying swifts of the text are not shown; nor is the cawing of rooks or the 'aggressively male' neighing of a horse suggested even by the presence of the creatures. Reddin is not shown; indeed, the farm buildings shown bear no resemblance to Undern as it is depicted in other illustrations. Instead, we look over Hazel's shoulder at a valley with a field of sheep, old farm buildings and lush trees, at the centre of which an ancient, square-towered church nestles. The scene is turned into an idealisation of an English village, complete with ancient church which represents not only picturesque antiquity but also the social system of the Church of England, very different from the freethinking ideology of the chapel of which Edward is a minister. It is a view familiar from countless drawings of villages in valleys found in countryside books of the time (e.g., Pakington 1934: 28, 94; see Plate 30): the sexual tension and sense of unity of the novel has been diffused by visual and ideological transfer to the inoffensive notion of a sleepy countryside under the ideological restraint of a placid Anglican church.

V

Important though the process of relocation is in the illustrations, it is not the only approach that is employed, nor does the visual text always go against the thrust of the verbal. One important additional technique, for example, is the portrayal of individual characters in the novel as a series of rural types at intervals throughout the novel. Hazel Woodus, the central figure, is not explored in any psychological depth in the illustrations, and neither are any of the other figures. Yet they are presented with a kind of surface interest which is again suggestive of an outsider's view of the countryside. In Baldwin's introduction to *Precious Bane*, just before the reference to the black-and-white houses and castles familiar to the tourist, there is mention of 'an uncommunicative population' (1928: 4). The idea of the distant, and at times surly, countryman had been celebrated before in work such as Jerome's *Three Men in a Boat*. Just as *Howards End* contains an archetypal urban explorer of the countryside in Leonard Bast, it has too a remote, slightly magical character in the form of Miss Avery, who strangely takes control of Howards End as the novel reaches its conclusion. Portraits of country characters had been popular since the end of the century in the work of artists such as Stanhope Forbes and George Clausen: strong, unnamed figures who pursued rural crafts for the unspecified fulfilment of the urban audience at the Academy and elsewhere.

Examples of such images are frequent in *Gone to Earth*. I have already referred to the image of Andrew Vessons feeding chickens, which falls in part into this category: others show the figures more directly, with less detail of background but enough to show the characters' nature. Abel Woodus is presented playing the harp (1930: 27), revealing the instinctive, joyful quality repeatedly stressed in him; Mrs Marston is shown sitting primly on a kitchen chair waiting for the traction engine (1930: 111), showing herself ill at ease with the natural world around her. A further full-page drawing shows an old man walking across the field where the fair is taking place, leaning heavily on a twisted stick (1930: 131). The text refers to his 'gazing into her [Hazel's] mouth with the steadfast curiosity of a dog at a gramophone' – incidentally a further reference to the time of the novel which places it firmly after the patenting of the HMV trademark in the early years of the century. Yet Hazel is not shown, the illustrator instead presenting only the old man almost as a rural curiosity on display at the fair. Almost immediately after (1930: 134) we are shown a woman sitting in front of a Romany caravan, selling daffodils to Edward Marston from the large baskets she has before her. The scene as such is not mentioned in the novel; instead, we are told that Edward approaches Hazel 'tying up some daffodils' (1930: 114) as she talks to Reddin. Edward has not overheard their conversation and is serenely unaware of the tension between Hazel and the other man; instead of this dramatic irony, the illustration presents a man buying flowers from a rural 'character', the Romany flower-seller. Like all the other character drawings, this serves further to move us away from the text into the imaginary countryside of the urban visitor.

A similar function is performed by the large number of headpieces and tailpieces. Every chapter begins with a small drawing, the majority of which show a rural building or group of buildings, or an ideal landscape scene, in the manner of scenes shown in greater detail in the larger illustrations. There are some exceptions, most notably the headpiece to chapter 36 (1930: 307), which shows a fox, presumably Hazel's pet Foxy, standing apparently exhausted, her curved back echoed in the rolling form of the land on which she stands and sharing its dark texture. These links suggest that the fox has somehow grown organically out of the land, a relationship totally appropriate to the fundamental theme of the novel as it affects both Foxy and Hazel.

This image is, however, an exception: the remaining vignettes in their repeated presentation of stylised villages, fields, trees and scenes of rural activity constantly reinforce the work of the larger images in moving the text firmly towards a strictly contemporary, strictly conventional rural ideal.

One area of the illustrations' reinterpretation of the text is, however, less straightforward, containing at least a suggestion of an awareness of the novel's conclusion and the movement towards it. At the end of chapter 7, Hazel and her father stand at the edge of the quarry, a 'precipitous place' (1930: 67; 1978: 54) which Hazel finds 'so drodsome'. Her father's comment that a cow who fell over the cliff was found 'all of a jelly' (1930: 67; 1978: 55) is greeted by Hazel with passionate sobbing; the pre-vision of her own death is hinted at clearly here. Hepple's illustration shows the two figures reduced to tiny forms at the top of a cliff which is steep and jagged. If there is no suggestion of Hazel's sobs, there is a clear stress on the danger of the place and its remoteness: is there, perhaps, a hint of the novel's darker elements here?

A similar ambiguity is present in the very last full-page image (1930: 318). Hazel is shown from the back, carrying Foxy in her arms, hurrying to the gable end of a building which we recognise from the frontispiece as Hepple's version of Edward's house at God's Little Mountain. Rich and full trees still rise behind it; yet the composition is given concentration by the uneven land in the foreground which moves towards the farmhouse in broad, dark perspective swathes, which have the effect of pushing Hazel further to the farmhouse which is the composition's focal point. Is this a visual suggestion of the novel's inevitable conclusion? Certainly, the darkness and intensity of the composition would suggest so. Yet, ultimately, the image does not match the novel's conclusion. It is to the house that Hazel is drawn, not to the edge of the quarry: the move to the house – which is not the original squat building, but the same reinvention of it in fashionable 1920s Tudor style shown in the frontispiece – suggests that, once again, the novel has been redirected into a safe, contemporary view of landscape and away from the dark, if melodramatic, catastrophe of Hazel's fall, with Foxy, 'into everlasting silence' (1930: 319; 1978: 287).

VI

Mary Webb's novel has been much satirised, most notably in Stella Gibbons's *Cold Comfort Farm* (1932), and it is easy to dismiss it as melodramatic and over-written, its central character unconvincingly innocent for someone apparently at one with the natural world of which she is a part. Yet, for all that, it does attempt to explore a relationship between a young woman and the natural world, and the way in which two men's refusal to see her except as they wish her to be leads – because of their own refusal to accept the sexual in their own natures, and the place for it in Hazel's – to their own suffering and Hazel's death. Webb shows a directness and honesty in approaching sexuality rare in writing of the time, albeit through an elaborate network of symbolic references in which the land is fundamental: it is, as Webb openly states, 'a countryside teeming with sex' (1930: 40; 1978: 31). Hazel's own nature, in its innocent delight in the country, is a powerful statement of female freedom and the self-destructive power of female sexuality when it unwittingly opposes itself to the bleakness of male authority. That Hepple's illustrations move it into a world of 1920s images of an idealised country, full of Tudor farmhouses and Anglican churches suggestive of a male-dominated structure, is an act of superversion which relocates the novel firmly within a mainstream, middle-class ideology, moving it far away from the dangerous and turbulent currents which the verbal text itself generates.

6

THE ROMANTIC CONTINUUM
Rebecca and internal visualisation

All the texts so far considered have been concerned with the
creation of a dual discourse of word and image caused by the
use of illustrations within fictions of different sorts. These
illustrations may offer us involvement of a variety of kinds in
the fictive discourse and hence its 'action'; yet they always have
two elements in common. By being synchronic rather than
diachronic, they serve – however effectively they are integrated
into the fiction's diachrony – as frozen moments in the action.
Secondly, however closely they integrate us into the action of the
scene, perhaps by manipulation of viewpoint so that we share that
of the protagonist, they place us outside the events, since the very
externalisation of the seen image is an act of distancing. Of their
nature, these illustrations function best in that kind of narrative
fiction where there is the constant presence of a central directing
consciousness, an omniscient narrator who presents the action,
selecting, commenting and drawing moral points from it. Just as
we are presented with the action in the verbal continuum from this
figure's viewpoint, so we see what he or she wishes us to see, in the
manner he or she chooses, in the illustrations. We are thus offered
a compound of word and image sharing a common origin and
control of view which has the effect of controlling our
involvement in the action in terms of both pausing the continuum
of experience at key moments, and of establishing the viewpoint
from which we see it, in the mere fact of presenting it ensuring our
partial exclusion from it.

There is, of course, another convention of the novel, in which
illustrations do not appear at all, yet in which the visual sense is still
more acute in importance. This is the tradition in which the reader
directly shares the experiences of the narrator who is an invention

of the writer, and who experiences the events, feelings and attitudes – essentially, a whole continuum of being and response – with which the reader comes to identify during the reading process through the writer's use of the first person voice. There is no intermediary to comment or direct; the central character relates events and feelings in a single, continuous experience, so that essentially we become this character when we make the act of reading: the 'I' of the narrator becomes the 'I' of the reader.

It is this identification which has led generations of critics to condemn novel reading as a kind of literary day-dream which is morally corrosive. Coleridge refers to the process as 'a kind of beggarly day-dreaming, during which the mind of the dreamer furnishes for itself nothing but laziness and a little mawkish sensibility' (Shawcross: I, 34n). More recent writers have found the manner of writing just as alarming. Q.D. Leavis diagnoses a condition of mind called 'Living at the novelist's expense'[1] which results from the reading of such fiction, refers to it as a 'form of self-indulgence' (1932: 53) and warns 'a habit of fantasying will lead to maladjustment in actual life' (1932: 54). One may wonder about the degree to which the reader quite suspends his or her sense of any reality outside that of the novel, or how far the experience created in the novel comes to colour and distort that of his or her actual life. To counter such accusations, one might also suggest that the process of what is often called 'losing yourself in a book' will offer a cathartic escape, or some sort of moral journey, which will better enable one to face daily reality.[2] And one might also, of course, question the right of literary critics to make judgements about how or why people read novels.

The moral significance of this kind of novel is not my direct concern here: yet it is of relevance for one particular reason which also involves the special nature and place of the visual sense within such writing. Ian Watt points out that the epistolary novel of Richardson is the progenitor not only of the modern 'romance' – 'a popular purveyor of vicarious sexual experience and adolescent wish-fulfilment' (1963: 229) – but also of the novel of 'unrivalled subtlety in the exploration of personality and personal relationships' (ibid.). The difference between these extremes, I would argue, lies as much in the method of reading as in the method of writing. For the former - the popular romance or thriller – the arrangement of words as a linguistic structure is for most readers of almost complete insignificance: it is instead an instrument for conveying impressions so that the reader can get on with the business of experiencing what the language records. For the latter – the serious novel of the inner life – the structure of language is dominant. Works such as *Mrs Dalloway* (Woolf 1925), for instance, operate by challenging the reader to see experience afresh through the linguistic defamiliarisation that they offer, and by setting up a series of patterns of language and idea which work at a symbolic and mythic level to formalise and contextualise that experience. Thus, in the 'art' novel, the process of identification between reader and narrator paradoxically calls attention to itself and its language, demanding a metalanguage of critical address in the reader; whilst in the 'popular' novel, the process aims to render the language of text invisible and the experience concrete within the mind of the reader. Thus one could argue that the retreat from reality is greater in the art novel than in the popular, since the former encourages literary analysis where the latter can engage – though it does not necessarily have to – with social, moral and pseudo-ethical issues in the experience it generates. The place of the visual sense within this, I will argue, can be of central significance in the operation of the continuum of experience on which the popular novel rests, and also to its larger psychological effects and functions.

II

It is in this context that we need to read Daphne du Maurier's bestseller *Rebecca*. Just how the visual sense works in this novel – in distinction from the visualisations discussed in the preceding chapters, can be seen by looking closely at the novel's opening.

> Last night I dreamed I went to Manderley again. It seemed to me I stood by the iron gate leading to the drive, and for a while I could not enter, for the way was barred to me. There was a padlock and a chain upon the gate. I called in my dream to the lodge-keeper, and had no answer, and peering closer through the rusted spokes of the gate I saw that the lodge was uninhabited.
>
> No smoke came from the chimney, and the little lattice windows gaped forlorn. Then, like all dreamers, I was possessed of a sudden with supernatural powers and passed like a spirit through the barrier before me. The drive wound

away in front of me, twisting and turning as it had always done, but as it advanced I was aware that a change had come upon it; it was narrow and unkept, not the drive that we had known. At first I was puzzled and did not understand, and it was only when I bent my head to avoid the low swinging branch of a tree that I realized what had happened. Nature had come into her own again and, little by little, in her stealthy, insidious way had encroached upon the drive with long, tenacious fingers. The woods, always a menace even in the past, had triumphed in the end. They crowded, dark and uncontrolled, to the borders of the drive. The beeches with white, naked limbs leant close to one another, their branches intermingled in a strange embrace, making a vault above my head like the archway of a church. And there were other trees as well. Trees that I did not recognize, squat oaks and tortured elms that straggled cheek by jowl with the beeches, and had thrust themselves out of the quiet earth, along with monster shrubs and plants, none of which I remembered.

(1975: 5)

Here the identity between reader and writer, and the way in which the narrative orders events, are both established in the first sentence. As we read we become the 'I'; and at the same time as sharing the dream, we share the narrator's relationship to the events – that of a reliving of the past which places it in a continuous present. The fact that the narrator 'dreamt I went to Manderley again' makes clear that he or she has been there before, but offers no other clue as to subsequent events. From the very start, then, we experience events directly, apparently with no clarification from hindsight. This reveals one of the clearest and most essential conventions of the genre: although the narrator figure knows of all the events subsequent to the time of which she writes, and writes of this time in the past tense, she does not reveal the outcome, instead relaying them as if living through them for the first time.

This has many advantages, principally at the start of the novel the creation of suspense and a desire to know 'what happened next'. It is essential to the reader's involvement that she or he does not know the key elements of the plot that the narrator clearly does know: that Maxim de Winter did not love Rebecca, and is not constantly comparing the unnamed narrator unfavourably to her;

or that he shot her in the boathouse, but will not stand trial because she was suffering from cancer so that Colonel Julyan, the magistrate, assumes that she killed herself by sinking the boat in which her body is found. In terms of the visual sense, however, the significance of this concealment is that it presents the events as a constantly evolving psychological continuum in which we, the readers, live through the events being experienced. In this continuum, visualisation has a central and pervasive function.

External visual reality is essential to such a technique, but it is presented as seen by the 'I', not the 'eye': in other words, we are offered the scene as experienced with a complex of emotions, fears, recollections and forebodings of the character living through it, instead of being given an ostensibly objective visual account. This is clearly apparent in the novel's opening passage. Visual details are important – the viewpoint is defined as 'by the iron gate', and the 'padlock and chain' are noted - but they are selected by the speaker, and involve a series of developing emotional and intellectual responses. The narrator is 'puzzled and did not understand', but this soon gives way to comprehension when she bent to 'avoid the low swinging branch of a tree'. As the viewpoint changes, so does the narrator's mood and her grasp of events; the visual and the psychological, the outer and inner, are united in the continuum of the experience as lived in the writing. This continues as we are told of the scene in language which reveals the narrator's response and similarly colours ours, rather than merely presenting a visual reality: nature is 'stealthy' and 'insidious', and the woods have 'triumphed' after being a 'menace'. Already nature has been personified by being given 'long, tenacious fingers'; the anthropo-morphism continues with the 'naked limbs' of the elms in a 'strange embrace', but changes to an architectural metaphor when the vegetation is shown to be 'like the vault of a church'. At the climax of this paragraph the elms and beeches are straggling 'cheek by jowl', 'along with monster shrubs and plants'. The very inconsistency of this, shifting from anthropomorphism to architecture and vague hints of vegetative aberrations, enhances the feeling that we are sharing the speaker's experience as we read, through the analogical process implicit within the response. As well as seeing what she sees and feeling what she feels, we also come to understand the metaphoric processes of the narrator's mind.

Producing a visual equivalent of this in a separate textual illustration would not be impossible; but it would be very difficult. The mood of stealth and menace is simple enough to convey through light and shade, but how might a single, synchronous image convey the threat and menace of the trees in the past? The exact anthropomorphic thrust of 'fingers' and 'embrace', which gives 'naked limbs' its hint of twisted human relations, is linguistic rather than visual; so, too, is the way that the cliché 'cheek by jowl' is given a literal twist by the words that come before it. 'Monster shrubs' are easy enough – but they are monsters because they are not recognised, and owe their strangeness to their incongruity in an otherwise familiar scene, giving them a quality which a single illustration could not convey. And, of course, an illustration would be inescapably synchronous, denying the gradual unfolding of the scene in the burgeoning awareness of the dreaming narrator which is responsible for pacing the scene's unfolding as we read – at a speed which is, as has often been remarked, considerably slowed by the rhythms of the novel's very first sentence.

Another element must be added to this list of difficulties for a would-be illustrator: the fact that the experience is a dream. No illustration can convey the narrator's change to being 'possessed of a sudden with supernatural powers' to pass through the barrier, since this demands an awareness of the preceding state of being. The only possibility would be to present the figure in the act of passing through the barrier and, leaving aside the risks of absurdity in depicting some odd ectoplasmic structure in an otherwise naturalistic landscape, this would break the convention of the writing by moving right outside the narrator's mind and body, suspending the identification with the reader which is fundamental to the text.

By now it should be clear that this passage employs an extremely subtle blending of the visual sense with symbolic language, emotion, memory and a continuing, changing state of dream which incorporates fragments of memory and earlier experience. In assimilating the passage, the visual sense in the reader becomes an important concomitant to the skill of reading; when we take in these paragraphs we see as the narrator sees, experience as she experiences, and place within context as she orders her memory. This is very different from the use of actual illustrations at nodal points – Barthes' 'functions' – of the narrative; and a grasp of its working is fundamental to any understanding of how the novel works.

Having established the special nature of the visual sense in the novel, now we need to consider the larger frame of the discourse within which it operates. The speaker who within the convention of the book narrates the action, and with whom the reader identifies, is presented only through her own recollections. Even the comments of other characters to and about her are presented through the filter of her own personality, so that the identification is apparently complete. This is central to the working of the book. The narrator figure is never named - conventionally she is referred to as 'the Girl' – nor is she given any objective physical description: all we learn of her comes from the comments of other characters which she herself reports. These comments are not from impartial observers. In the early pages they come from Mrs van Hopper, the wealthy woman with whom the girl travels as companion: later, we hear her described by Maxim de Winter, whom she marries, and by Mrs Danvers, the housekeeper at Manderley. Mrs van Hopper seems dedicated to making the girl feel inferior, gauche and inadequate; de Winter is successively distant, dismissive and protective towards her as the plot develops; and Mrs Danvers is constantly comparing the Girl to Rebecca, 'my Mrs de Winter, the real Mrs de Winter' (1975: 253). These are the extremes of responses within which the Girl's character is presented: experiencing them is part of the continuum, conveyed largely in literary-visual terms, which the reader shares by identifying with her.

The absence of name and detailed description is a key element in this identification. The Girl is young, has no money of her own, dresses dowdily, lacks sophistication and, when we first encounter her, is wholly under the control of the older woman for whom she works. She is, in short, almost an abstract of the key elements of one kind of typical romantic novel reader: a young, impecunious and insecure young woman in a job with no prospects. The insecurity, gaucherie and inexperience make it far easier for the reader to identify with her, since she has none of the assumptions about money and breeding that bedevil pre-war English society. The moral implications of this deliberate setting out to create the copy of the reader in the central character are something to which I shall return: for the moment, it is enough to make clear that in using this technique du Maurier is merely carrying to an extreme the model invented by Scott, and developed by H.G. Wells, of having as a central character a figure with whom the reader can identify in terms of age, social background and general outlook, with the key difference that here the identification is made more complete by the lack of physical description and the intense role played by the visual sense within the psychological continuum of the narrative.

The opening scene of the novel presents, as we have seen, an account of a dream, the key feature of which is the way in which the appearance of Manderley has changed from an earlier past. This gives us two dimensions of time and vision: two more are added by the fact that the dream is being recounted by the Girl looking back on it yet relating it as the present. Subtlety of this sort is not common in the novel; but its use at the very opening should alert us to the fact that the ordering of time and experience, inextricably bound up with the visual sense, is a major concern. Visualisation is used in a number of ways to embody experience and place it within a continuum. These uses may be divided into three main groups.

First are the accounts of events which are taking place in the historic continuum of the novel – that is, are related as occurring in the continuous present though being recollected by the Girl. Secondly, there are complexes of scene, action and feeling that are presented as having happened in the past within the continuum, as a larger narrative equivalent of the past perfect tense. Thirdly, there are visual episodes that are wholly invented where the Girl's imagination works freely in creating settings and the feelings they evoke, often involving speculation about future events.

Within the novel's single scale of unfolding time, there are thus pockets which reach further into the past and others which, through the Girl's inner reality, take us into an imagined future. The visual sense is fundamental to all of these; thus, it is central both to the novel's overall temporal unfolding and to what we might call its diversions into a deeper past or a conjectural future.

As the novel's continuum depends on this sort of visual recall, particularly that of the first major kind discussed above, it is not easily possible to separate passages for discussion. Despite this, some stand out as important examples of the way the narrative progresses. One is the Girl's first sight of de Winter (1975: 18). On seeing him she immediately relates him to fifteenth-century Italy by visualising him in 'narrow cobbled streets' whose inhabitants wear 'pointed shoes and worsted hose'. His face reminds her of a portrait seen in a forgotten gallery, and she thinks how, robbed of his 'English tweeds' and dressed with lace trimmings, he would 'stare down at us . . . from a long-distant past'. The characterisation is thus achieved through visual details of an historical setting and – an image used repeatedly by the Girl as a way of fixing the other characters – the resemblance to a portrait. It is, of course, a vision heavily 'romanticised' in the most popular sense – a vision of a past rich with incident and intrigue, developed from Scott by the popular historical novel of the earlier twentieth century and by the popular cinema until it becomes almost an element of popular thought, and is embodied in the mind of the narrator who, by this time, has already become well established as a mirror of the typical romance-reader. More important emotional and symbolic overtones soon follow. The world of intrigue is given claustrophobic visual form in 'narrow stairways and dim dungeons' and, most particularly, 'shimmering rapier blades' and 'silent, exquisite courtesy'. Visual detail is telling, suggesting sexual violence of a degree which implies the process of 'inoculation' in popular fiction noted by Barthes (1973: 150–1) and discussed in Chapter 4. Yet the vision is inseparable from an emotional response: the 'silent, exquisite courtesy' suggests a human relationship. In a single paragraph, the narrative has provided us with an image that is aristocratic, popularly 'romantic', and links hints of violence with a relationship of conventionally archaic courtesy: in short, it is almost a paradigm of the emotional relationship that can be seen as an ideal in many perceptions of romance in popular fiction and films of the 1930s. Emotional, and sexual too – for the reference to 'shimmering rapier blades' is exactly the sort of barely sublimated sexual symbol frequent in Hollywood images of this heavily censored period. Once again visual details are used to contextualise, deepen and emotionally enrich; the imagined scene *becomes* the experience, which we then share because it is apparently made real both before our eyes and within our minds.

A similar complex of experience may be seen in the episode when de Winter is showing the Girl the grounds at Manderley, and they stand looking down at Happy Valley (1975: 115). Here, as often in the novel, visual experience elides with other sensory impressions: not only do the two look at 'the clear white faces of the flowers closest to us' but, when de Winter picks a petal for the Girl, she rubs it over her hand and 'the scent rose to me, sweet and strong'. In the next paragraph the birds begin to sing and soon 'the still air about us was made turbulent with song': this and the new closeness to de Winter combine to make it 'an enchanted place'. The experience that we are offered thus embraces visual stimuli, sounds, scents and a complex of feeling all within the developing plot. This is typical of the manner in which visual and other sensory impressions are combined within a complex of emotional responses; it would be possible to provide endless examples of this sequential process, were there not more complex uses still of the visual sense to engage our attention.

The second major kind concerns the Girl's recollection of scenes within the continuum of recalled action – a kind of memory within a memory, adding depth to the temporal range of the novel and acting as a device both of unity and of development of theme and action. The most significant episode of this kind comes in the Girl's recollection of the party which, at the time, is given scant discussion since the girl is more concerned with the effects on de Winter of her unwitting impersonation of Rebecca, his first wife, and its implications on their marriage.

The party is recollected in powerfully visual terms. The passage begins with the statement that, when she remembers the party, the Girl recalls 'little isolated things standing alone out of the vast blank canvas of the evening' (1975: 232–3) – a significant reference to painting which, as will become clear, is an important device both of unity and of character extension within the novel. Here, the 'canvas' image is important in stressing the recollection of the party as both a visual and in a sense an artificial entity – something at which the Girl is an onlooker rather than a participant.

This combination of visual intensity and personal distance, as if in dream, is continued in the remainder of the account. The Girl remembers an unknown woman in 'a salmon-coloured gown hooped in crinoline form' (233) who passes repeatedly before her, each time smiling in the same mechanical fashion. Lady Crowan is described as 'monstrous in purple' (233); the 'expression on Frith's face' (233) when Robert drops a tray of ices is similarly clear; and the girl insists 'I can see Beatrice . . . watching me from her partner's arms' (233). In all of these there is some measure of the sensory response which goes alongside visual elements in earlier, more direct accounts, which continues when the Girl sympathises with Robert and hears Lady Crowan's high-pitched voice; but the overall impression is one of distance rather than involvement. This is aided by two references to the dancers as 'marionettes' (233 and 234), continued in a list of visual impressions of couples swirling past later in the evening (235–6), and confirmed when the Girl moves outside her own experience in her recollection: 'I can picture myself once more whirled round the room in a desperate dance with Giles' (234). When the recollection moves on to the Girl's dealings with de Winter, the distance continues: 'We were like two performers in a play, but we were divided, we were not acting with one another' (235). Here the separation has two dimensions: in the party as she recollects it, not only is the Girl separated from the continuum of experience, but she is also prevented from sharing it with de Winter. As this isolation is clear during the party, it continues so in its aftermath: when the Girl walks upstairs to bed she does so, again as in dream, past fallen pieces of music, an upturned chair and full ashtrays. The chapter's end completes the idea of isolation, with the Girl recalling lying alone in bed watching her bedside clock as dawn approaches with an insistent refrain: 'But Maxim did not come' (240).

Overall, the visual sense here is used as a double recollection – within the remembered continuum of action is presented another recollection. This is used to present the isolation of the girl from her own experience and from de Winter. The resultant double dislocation is an important part of the novel's growth, and the progress of its central character, since it reveals the Girl's distress and sense of loss as a result of de Winter's rejection of her after her imitation of Rebecca. The use of the visual sense in this unreal, dislocated fashion is fundamental to the effect, and to our sharing of the Girl's feelings.

The scenes involving the Girl's imaginative inventions perform a different, but equally valuable function. They reveal the Girl's efforts to locate herself within her new surroundings, and her speculations about the future – in neither case with any great success or reassurance. Such scenes expand the temporal range of the novel beyond the usual limits of the Girl's recollections, since those that reach back into an imagined past take us into the world of Manderley as the Girl thought it to have been in the time of Rebecca, and those that speculate on the future open new possible avenues of action. The reader's involvement in the enlarged temporal matrix which results from these new visualisations serves further to deepen the imaginative identification with the Girl.

Imagined narratives of events with Maxim's first wife occur when the Girl first lives at Manderley. Conscious of her lack of sophistication, she compares herself unfavourably with Rebecca when she imagines de Winter's friends talking of her: 'I could picture them saying to one another as they drove away, "My dear, what a dull girl . . . so different from Rebecca"' (1975: 129). This thought is synchronous with the novel's action but, of course, stretches back to before its beginning, so that the visual sense – powerful in presenting the scene of the words being said 'as they drove away' – once again defines and extends the novel's chronology. A more direct reaching back is seen on the next page where the Girl imagines Rebecca writing invitations:

> I thought of the docketed pigeon-hole in the desk in the morning-room, I pictured the stack upon stack of invitation cards, the long list of names, the addresses, and I could see a woman sitting there at the desk and putting a V beside the names she wanted, and reaching for the invitation cards, dipping her pen in the ink, writing upon them swift and sure in that long, slanting hand.
>
> (1975: 130)

The visual detail here is considerable – the pigeon-hole, the invitations and the list of names to give static setting matched by the dynamic visual elements of Rebecca's ticking the names, reaching for the cards, and writing in a specific, visually identified style. This is typical of such imaginings, all of which are used to reveal the Girl's sense of inadequacy in comparison with Rebecca. Their immediacy and continuity of visual detail reveal the constant presence of Rebecca in the Girl's mind: the visual sense here reinforces the deep insecurity she feels and places it within the action as a further strand of experience.

Imaginings also stretch forward, with a sense of foreboding which matches and develops the inadequacy at the root of those which stretch back in time. When the Girl fears that de Winter will be tried for the murder of Rebecca, her imaginings produce a concentrated visual sequence: 'Placards in London. Newsboys shouting in the streets, outside the underground stations. That frightful word of six letters, in the middle of the placard, large and black' (1975: 315). Once again, there are elements of both static setting – the streets, the underground stations – and dynamic action – the shouting newsboys. It is significant that so great is the

Girl's dread that she cannot visualise the word murder, but instead refers to it as 'that frightful word': a melodramatic detail perhaps, but nonetheless a valid and striking use of the visual sense – paradoxically, in withholding the image – to complement and extend its use elsewhere in the scene. A little later (329) the Girl recalls 'a picture on the back of a paper' of crowds outside a prison after a hanging: again visual detail is used to convey her fears and to move the action into the future, performing the structural function of heightening the suspense, as well as furthering our identification with the Girl as we are invited to share her fear both with and through her visual inventions. In this last scene, past and future are united within the continuum of the Girl's psychological 'present', since she is remembering seeing the image of the crowd in a paper: once again the visual sense is fundamental to the novel's unfolding and its control of temporal range.

This control is also shown in a number of passages where the visual sense is used in what may best be decribed as an intentionally proleptic manner. In these sequences, the Girl looks at a scene with the aim of preserving it in her memory for reference later, as a way of perpetuating the experience of which it forms part. This is an intriguing and a bold technique: it acknowledges that the experience the novel chronicles is primarily visual, and involves the reader in the process of gathering material for its future extension. In a more immediate sense, it is a statement of a shared way of ordering and preserving experience: at least since Wordsworth and Constable, a visual image frozen on canvas or in the mind has been a way of perpetuating enjoyed or significant experience. Holiday photographs and, in the last ten years, holiday videos, are the most apparent versions of this: they record and perpetuate a visual image or succession of images for consolation and renewal in subsequent days. In her use of this technique of storing actuality the Girl is once more presented as a type of the ideal reader of the novel, even though she uses the pictures in her mind rather than those from a 1930s Box Brownie camera.

The technique is most apparent towards the novel's close, where the Girl looks at Manderley before leaving for London, at this stage expecting that Dr Baker will provide evidence of the motive for de Winter's murder of Rebecca. Kneeling by the window to look out at the garden, the Girl takes in the events of the new day in complete visual detail. The movements of the birds, the gardeners brushing the paths and watering the lawns, the housemaids opening the curtains, and the cooking of breakfast – all are presented as a visual-sensory continuum which carries on oblivious of 'our troubles' (1975: 371) and hence deserves to be retained in memory as a later source of consolation. The idea of fixing the scene for future remembering is stated most clearly a few pages further on:

> I had a curious, inexplicable feeling that I must go back and look in my room again. I went without reason, and stood a moment looking at the gaping wardrobe and the empty bed, and the tray of tea upon the table. I stared at them, impressing them for ever on my mind, wondering why they had the power to touch me, to sadden me, as though they were children that did not want me to go away.
>
> (1975: 374)

Here the concept of storing up an image is explicit; but so too is the emotional response to it, stressed in the final lines on the images' power to move the Girl. Emotional involvement and visual sense are once more entwined within the psychological continuum.

Here visual details are used as a way of storing experience: within the same chapter they are also used as a way of slowing and controlling the pace of the novel, both adding suspense to the narrative and conveying a moment apparently outside time which the Girl seems to use as a moral restorative. Instead of involving the visual sense within a dynamic continuum, the narrative becomes stative, fixing a moment in its perceived objects, as the Girl becomes aware of the continuity of Manderley regardless of 'whatever trouble there was and strife' (1975: 372). Much of this passage avoids the use of finite verbs, instead employing present participles – 'maids sweeping . . . fresh clean air pouring into the long open windows' – or omitting verbs altogether – 'The peace of Manderley. The quietude and grace.' Language and visual sense are alike frozen in extended deixis.

All these uses of visual elements should make clear the essential point: that *Rebecca* is a text in which visualisation in the central character is of fundamental importance to the creation of the world of the novel, and consequently to the involvement of the reader through her or his identification with the unnamed central character. Any attempt to impose actual illustrations on this would destroy the psychological continuum of which the visualisation is a part: as a discourse, the novel is concerned with recreating a sensory experience relived through the memory by a complex of visual, sensory and associative impressions and responses, and the illusion of an immediate shared experience in which this results is, in this reading, a major reason for the novel's great and continuing popularity.

III

The use of the visual sense to deepen the involvement of the reader in the action brings us back to the question of the moral value of the novel. Since its central character is apparently modelled on the typical popular romance reader, and since the reader is constantly drawn into identification and sharing this character's experiences, which are in essence concerned with an unlikely, 'romantic' marriage and events of a sensational and violent nature, it is legitimate to think that what is going on in the reading process is precisely the kind of self-indulgent 'fantasying' of which both Ian Watt and Queenie Leavis – as well as countless eighteenth-century and subsequent moralists – have disapproved. Since the visual sense is at the foundation of the novel's structure and working, it must be in part responsible for this. Yet there is another way of regarding the novel, and the function of the visual sense within it – as a progression in which a clear degree of moral growth is discernible in the Girl; and, since the reader's identification with the Girl is so complete, the whole process may be read as a moral journey for the reader towards some kind of maturity and understanding.

This is seen in the use of certain recurrent elements within the visual continuum. Most significant in this is the Girl's habit of seeing people as though they were portraits, already discussed in her first sight of de Winter. This heavily unreal, romanticised view is repeated in her approach to the portrait of Rebecca. The painting is first mentioned by Mrs Danvers, with her habitual deference: 'A famous artist did it. The picture hung in the Academy' (1975: 177). When the fancy-dress ball occurs, the Girl seizes upon the idea of imitating one of the pictures which is suggested by Mrs Danvers, and when she selects 'a Raeburn . . . of Caroline de Winter, a sister of Maxim's great-great grandfather' (1975: 212) her tone moves first to one of relief and then to one of enthusiasm. At the ball she appears in the dress copied from the portrait and, when greeted by de Winter's silence – caused by his shock at the Girl's having repeated Rebecca's copying the dress – explains 'It's the picture . . . It's the picture, the one in the gallery' (1975: 223). Here the girl's inability to comprehend what is happening, and her apparent exclusion from the world of Manderley, are both emblematised in her seeing the real world in terms of pictures: not only does she see people and events as portraits and landscapes, but she attempts to present herself as such an image. It is a significant use of the visualisation technique to show the Girl's naïvety and isolation.

A little later, the Girl looks again at the portrait in a changed light: recalling that a bishop's wife had hinted to her that Rebecca had copied it, she thinks 'I ought to have remembered that, I ought to have known' (1975: 231). It is a moment of realisation not only of the nature of her act, but of the difference between picture and reality, past and present, and in this sense it marks the beginning of a new stage in her self-awareness and grasp of her situation. This is confirmed shortly afterwards when, while waiting for de Winter to return from the boat found after the storm, the Girl assesses her current position:

> It was as though I had entered into a new phase of my life and nothing would be quite the same again. The girl who had dressed for the fancy dress ball the night before had been left behind . . . This self who sat on the window-seat was new, was different.

> (1975: 272)

This is a change which is not only temporal: it is signalled by the move from an idea of selfhood formed by the external, visual form – the imitation of the picture – to one which is more complex, less simply defined and largely internal. The visual sense, in particular the portrait, is crucial to this change because of the Girl's movement away from it.

The portrait is, however, only one small part of the use of visualisation in revealing the Girl's growth. More important are other sequences where the presentation of the continuum of experience through a complex of vision and other senses and feelings is broken. In an episode after the party, Mrs Danvers taunts the Girl with her inability to replace Rebecca. At its climax, the Girl stands at the window while Mrs Danvers urges, 'Why don't you jump? It wouldn't hurt, not to break your neck'

(1975: 257). The continuum is at first presented through the Girl's eyes as usual – the terrace, the hydrangeas, the fog, the Girl's feelings of rejection from de Winter. It then changes: for a moment it is as if the Girl has decided to jump; and then comes the sound of the warning rockets exploding. At the end of this sequence the action is given new impetus: de Winter appears below with news of the ship gone ashore, and Mrs Danvers goes down to make arrangements. The important point here is that, when the rockets go off, the Girl has her eyes closed; after the explosion, she opens them. This exclusion from the visual continuum sets her apart from the world of images and presents a moment of change and growth. Similar moments occur later in the novel. When the full impact of the new evidence at the inquest hits her, for example, she faints, and twice we are told 'I could not see' (1975: 323). Lack of sight, then, is a response to aspects of reality which are moments of crisis in her life, when outer reality is less important than the inner moral issues which she faces.

This change does not demand the exclusion of the visual world: the Girl's awareness of visual reality remains as strong in the last third of the book as at its start. Yet it works differently. Instead of enmeshing the visual details with other impressions and feelings, using them almost in the manner of a romantic projection of mood, the Girl notes details which are quite irrelevant to the current of her thoughts and actions.

The first use of this technique is quite striking in its difference from what has gone before. It occurs just after de Winter has told the Girl that he killed Rebecca. Her initial reaction is one of numbness and then, when 'he began to kiss me' (1975: 279) we are told that the Girl shut her eyes – another lack of sight at a key moment, since this marks the declaration of love for which she has longed. When she opens her eyes, she sees 'a little patch of curtain above his head' (1975: 280) and notices that it has been faded by the sun. A little later, she watches 'Jasper's sleeping body on the carpet' (1975: 293). Visual irrelevances continue, when she walks about the town during the inquest and looks at the shops, and when she focuses on the floor of the room in which the inquest is held. External reality is continuing, but her concern is for the moral position of herself and de Winter: instead of seeing things as part of a continuum, she is separated from them, and this is a significant measure of her isolation, as well as showing how far the habit of linking emotion to what is seen has been broken by her moral growth. The climax of this technique occurs in the journey to London (376–7) and again on the return: the details are noted, but are irrelevant to the main concerns of the Girl. It is not quite a change of the degree of *King Lear*'s 'I stumbled when I saw': but it is certainly a major realignment of the outer, perceived and inner, moral universe that we encounter in the Girl. And, of course, because we identify with her, we are drawn into the moral growth as we read.

The final dream sequence, which presents the actions of the novel as the Girl dreams of them during the return to Manderley, has a similar moral role: it presents the action in an effort to draw it together, a little like an apotheosis of themes at the end of a Romantic programme-symphony. The events are presented in visual terms, and she dreams first of Mrs Danvers and then of Rebecca. But on both occasions she breaks out of the dream, refusing the images: she is now in control of what she sees and how she responds to it, and the growth is complete.

The idea that the novel is actually one of moral growth rather than one of self-indulgent day-dreaming is not one that is widely held, and it may be argued that, whatever its use of the visual sense and the stress on inner rather than outer consciousness at the close, the whole fabric of the novel, cast as it is in one large recollection, encourages the corrosive habit of fantasying. There is also one larger structural element which would support this.

It can be argued that the presentation of the action in most of the book, before the changes discussed above, is done in an extremely visual manner to reflect the character of the Girl. She has a habit of seeing people as pictures, and her visual sense is emphasised by her sketching and the delight at being given art books by Beatrice as a wedding present. Such a character would quite naturally recall feelings through the external visual elements which accompanied them – thus making the whole structure convincing in method. Yet on the few occasions when the narration passes to another character, the same technique of visual continuum is powerfully present. When de Winter tells the Girl about Rebecca, he does so in acutely visual terms, using exactly the same continuum of perceived and felt experience that structures the rest of the novel. He talks of 'Rebecca sitting there at the head of the table, looking like an angel' (1975: 288) and compares her to 'a boy in her sailing kit, a boy with a face like a Botticelli angel' (1975: 291). Dr Baker recalls Rebecca's visit in similarly visual terms (1975: 382–3); Mrs Danvers says of Rebecca 'She was lovely then . . . Lovely as a picture' (1975: 254). The ability to see has a larger significance in the plot when Colonel Julyan insists that Favell must find evidence from an eye-witness: 'Produce your witness who saw it happen' (1975: 347). The only person who has seen anything is Ben, who has been threatened with being put in an 'asylum': when he is asked, he wisely edits his memory, but still presents it in visual terms: 'I seen nothing' (1975: 353), not 'I know nothing.'

All of this may show that the whole of the novel is presented in a kind of cinematic daydream, where the technique of visual detail as a reflection of the central character's nature is seriously damaged by its use in a near-identical manner for other characters when they recall action. The counter argument, of course, would be that it is the Girl who is representing these characters' recollections, and so inevitably she will recast them in the manner in which her own memory functions.

Moral growth in any novel which works in the double time-scheme of Rebecca is a fugitive notion. With the additional elements of a plot concerned with romance and murder, and a central character deliberately matched to the typical reader to facilitate complete identification, it becomes even harder to say whether the novel is a piece of genuine catharsis and moral growth, which the reader shares with the central character, or a piece of carefully marketed self-indulgence and wish-fulfilment. The argument will doubtless continue; yet it is at least worth pointing out that the possibility of moral engagement is there, and that it is presented in a discourse which seamlessly unites elements of visual perception within a continuum of psychological experience quite as subtle as any other device for uniting reader and central character.

7

EAGLE AND THE
MORALITY OF VISUAL
NARRATIVES

Horror has crept into the British nursery. Morals of little girls
in plaits and boys with marbles bulging their pockets are being
corrupted by a torrent of indecent coloured magazines that are
flooding bookstalls and newsagents.

Have parents really bothered to study them – these weekly
and fortnightly 'comics' that sons and daughters from seven to
17 years old are devouring?

Not mere 'thrillers' as we used to know them, nor the
once-familiar 'school stories'. These are evil and dangerous –
graphic coloured illustrations of modern city vice and crime.

(Morris 1949: 4)

This protest, by the Revd Marcus Morris, was occasioned by the
return of American horror comics after the Second World War,
along with British imitations such as the *Thrill Comics* issued by
Gerald C. Swan from 1940 onwards. Their stock characters were
bleeding heads, giant worms and skeletons with glaring eyes, who
frequently menaced barely clad women: their illustrations used
lurid colour and crude perspective. They followed the American
comic-book convention in being self-contained, single issues rather
than regular weekly numbers with recurrent strips featuring
familiar characters, like the more traditional British comics of the
twenties and thirties.

Public outcry against American-inspired comics of this sort rose
to such an extent that in 1955 the Children and Young Persons
(Harmful Publications) Act was passed, to be renewed in 1965.
Later critics may suspect that the origins of this disquiet lay in
mistrust of the way in which the intellectually and imaginatively
challenging process of reading had been ousted by the apparently

less demanding act of absorbing simple visual images; yet these
feelings were strong, and by no means recent. Disapproval of
comics and their moral system had been present ever since their
first appearance in England at the end of the nineteenth century.
Neither was the anger peculiar to the outraged Tory middle classes:
at the end of the thirties, in the most famous and probably the first
serious critical study of comics (Orwell 1948 [1940]), George
Orwell studied a range of available publications and found that
all showed a remarkable lack of awareness of contemporary reality,
the presentation of all foreigners in stereotyped and frequently
racist terms and an underlying Tory bias beneath an apparently
apolitical stance.

Important though Orwell's study is, it has little to say about what
is the most apparent aspect of comics – their use of visual narrative
as embodiment of ideological structures. The elements of morality
and visual narrative are not, despite what we might think about
Orwell's article, and, what the outcry against horror comics implies,
easily separable, and for this reason the comic-strip narrative is a
form of visual discourse which must be given serious study. Within
this context, one text stands out for such analysis because of its
concern for moral principles and its use of artwork generally
regarded as amongst the finest of its kind: the comic *Eagle*, which
ran for 991 issues from its launch on Friday 14 April 1950 to its
closure on 26 April 1969. At its peak, in the mid-fifties, its
circulation was over a million copies; sales rarely dropped below
750,000. Clearly it had wide popular appeal alongside its clear
moral sense, and how these two worked together reveals the
subtlety of its use of visual narrative.

II

Eagle was conceived by the Revd Marcus Morris and his art editor
Frank Hampson as a way of embodying religious and moral
principles in a form to appeal to young people and thus combat
the corrosive forces of the horror comics he had railed against in
the *Sunday Dispatch*. The idea was accepted by Hulton Press, who
published the comic until they were taken over by Odhams in
1959. It was an appropriate venture for a company who also
published *Picture Post* and *Lilliput*: the former was a crusading
and intellectually tough journal that had often crossed swords
with the establishment in its investigative writing; the latter

published articles by Shaw, Koestler and V.S. Pritchett and photographs by Bill Brandt alongside nude pin-ups and cartoons by Low, Vicky and Ronald Searle. The mixture of the populist and the serious was shown in Hulton's conditions for publishing the new comic: the moral tone was acceptable, but the overtly Christian elements were to be moderated. This had one very significant result: because the Christian approach now had to be expressed less directly, the ideological nature of the visual structures of the comic is of considerable subtlety.

Fundamental to this is the comic's format and layout. A twenty-page tabloid, it resembled in size a picture paper such as the *Mirror* or *Dispatch* rather than the smaller-sized comics, both British and American, against which it competed. Several of the inner pages, including the inside front and back covers and the centre pages, were in colour, unlike many British comics which were at this time largely monochrome. Its front page is powerfully representative of the subtle ideological mechanisms of the comic.

At the very top of the first issue ran the slogan 'Eagle – the new national strip cartoon weekly'. 'Weekly' stressed its orderly regular appearance, subtly revealing its superiority over the sporadic, fly-by-night publication of the horror comics; 'National' suggested the embodiment of British values, as well as rebutting the overseas elements implicit within the transatlantically influenced comic books. The character of the new comic was set immediately by its masthead – the presentation of the title with accompanying symbol. On the first issue, and for the entire run of the comic under Hulton ownership, this took up the top left-hand quarter panel of the opening page. The eagle is shown with wings spread wide, seen from the side and a little to the rear and below. The undersurface of the nearer wing is black, the upper wing pale yellow; feathers, beak and claws are heavily outlined. It is a powerfully naturalistic image of an eagle, drawn with the meticulous draftsmanship that was the hallmark of the comic. Yet it is also symbolic: the title of the comic was invented by Mrs Hampson to parallel the shape and function of a church lectern, a clear indication of the function of the comic as it was originally conceived. The golden tone reflects this, as do the eagle's wings which are spread as if to receive the Bible. The symbolic significance of the eagle is great: in the Christian church it is both an image of divine grace and an emblem of the power of ascending prayer, and in other cultures it emblematises forcefulness – as, for example, in its use as the symbol of the Roman legions.

The remaining features of the emblem reveal a similar subtlety in uniting moral tone and a strong practical concern to secure the readers' interest, along the way impressing us with what we would now term a clear brand image, a visual summation of the comic's basic tenets. The eagle is shown against a rectangle of pure, deep red, with the word EAGLE reversed out, revealing the white of the paper, underneath it. Price, day of publication, number and date appear in small black print in the panel: except for the date, all the information uses the same typeface, a specially designed italic capital which has small serifs and is still quite formal, but which continues the energetic diagonal of the eagle's wings. As the eagle is shown flying from left to right, it leads the reader naturally across to the first frame of the serial which begins next to it; the nearer wing-tip of the eagle breaks out of the red frame and comes between two words of the masthead slogan, a rejection of linearity which reinforces the bird's dynamic movement. Taken together, these elements reveal the masthead as a masterful piece of design and ideology, establishing a symbolic significance which has a clear moral thrust with a typeface that is authoritative but not old-fashioned, stating a clear 'product identity' while dynamically involving the reader and leading him or her on to the action of the comic's first strip.

All of this is in considerable contrast to the horror comics which *Eagle* was intended to oust. Not appearing regularly, they do not have the possibility of a constant masthead; their titles – *Black Magic, Tales from the Crypt, Eerie Comics*, for example – offer no possibility of symbolic visual statement. Instead of the beginning of a strip they have a single illustration which is either one frame from the action continued, generally in monochrome, inside, or a montage of creatures with little precise narrative import. There is none of the regularity of *Eagle*'s cover: title, details of stories and other information is spread around the page with complete free-dom, an anarchic rejection of graphic order the complete opposite of the dynamically tempered grid-structure of Hampson's front page. In its use of graphics, typography and layout, *Eagle* is an idiolect of dynamic order designed to appeal to modern, youthful readers but still imply a clear moral structure.

The remainder of the front page, and the whole of the second, are taken up with the first episode of the comic's most famous serial, 'Dan Dare: Pilot of the Future'. In layout it is a model of order balanced with powerful movement. Each of its eight frames is rectangular, yet each is of a different size and shows events from a different viewpoint. Order is given by the fact that the whole fits into a regular grid, albeit in a manner so subtle as to go unnoticed by all but the most design-conscious onlookers. All of this conveys at a deep, probably subconscious level, an important visual message merging excitement with order to echo the same combination in the eagle motif. Even without considering the content of the first 'Dan Dare' strip, its idiolect is apparent from its layout.

The strip itself is an embodiment of what we might well consider to be a mid-twentieth-century muscular Christianity. Early suggestions had titled the strip 'Dan Dare: Padre of the Future': the character's name had been taken from the popular hymn 'Dare to be a Daniel'. The Christian foundation, modified in the change of role but remaining in the original name, is matched by a cast of characters who move far away from the limited heroes, villains, monsters and scopophilically drawn women of the transatlantic horror strips and also show a breadth of vision lacking in more conventional British fictional writing of the time. Dan Dare is the holder of the OUN (Order of the United Nations), a clear rejection of contemporary xenophobia; not only is Dare's scientist colleague, Professor Jocelyn Peabody, a woman, but she is presented without a hint of sex or romance. This innovative breadth is tempered by more conventional supporting characters. Dare's assistant, Digby Vane, is a working-class northerner, the kind of supporting figure familiar from Ealing films of the war years; and the controller, Sir Hubert, is a silver-haired elder statesman.

What is most striking in this first issue is the nature and quality of the drawing. Hampson's presentation is of great detail and flexibility, the result of painstaking preparation by a studio team of artists which he led at their headquarters in Epsom. Film-style miniatures were constructed of the most frequently used scenes so that they could be shown convincingly from any angle; models were employed to wear the specially designed uniforms of the Interplanet Space Fleet; and Hampson kept up to date with developments in scientific research so that he could incorporate them into the strip. The result was a vision of the future that was totally convincing in its draughtsmanship. In the opening number, the first frame is a filmic establishing shot showing the space centre with a rocket about to be launched; buildings recognisable from recent British originals like Tecton's Finsbury Health Centre make the scene credible, and above it flies a jet capsule which looks remarkably like the cockpit of a Westland Dragonfly, then the latest British military helicopter. When the scene reappears, seen from almost directly above, in the sixth frame, the buildings are recognisably the same, even though foreshortened: there is none of the rushed draftsmanship and discontinuity between frames so common in cheaper artwork. The sense of order this conveys is matched by the calm presence of Dare and Sir Hubert in the control tower watching the launch of the spacecraft, but given excitement by the fact that we see the take-off from three separate viewpoints as the craft accelerates away. Involvement is matched with security, dynamism with control. Added to this is an emblematic significance which, given the origin of the comic's title, seems hardly coincidental. The spacecraft is called 'Kingfisher', a name redolent with Christian associations (Christ the king, Christ as fisher of men). In the first page, the reader is involved with excitement, but given a sense of moral and Christian security which is largely the result of design, layout and draftsmanship: this is comic-strip narrative at its most ideologically subtle, working on the reader's subconscious mind through the subtlety of its idiolectual structure.

III

Along with 'Dan Dare', in its most successful years *Eagle* included several other features which embodied its moral ideology of practical Christianity in a more direct fashion. Each week the centre-page spread was a cutaway drawing of the latest aeroplanes, trains, cars, space machines and other devices such as airport snow-ploughs, produced by L. Ashwell Wood or John Batchelor and accompanied by detailed keyed captions. That the same kind of educational zeal was present here as in the Dan Dare strip is shown in the fact that occasionally a fictional machine of the future was exposed for analysis in this way.

Factual material was also the basis of comic strips. From the first issue, the back page of *Eagle* was reserved for a strip-cartoon biography of a famous historical or biblical figure. The most ambitious of these was 'The Happy Warrior', a biography of Winston Churchill which ran for almost a year in 1957–8, with a script by Clifford Makins and illustrations by Frank Bellamy. Research was meticulous, illustrations from the Imperial War Museum being used as the basis of many of the images. As well as responding to the recreation of the Second World War in mythic terms that was then in full flood, this presented in authentic terms a contemporary Christian role-model for the comic's readers.

For the concluding episode, Bellamy drew a full-page portrait of Churchill as he then was, against a background of heraldic devices and captioned by lines from Wordsworth which suitably complete the heroic structure. Bellamy then moved on to 'The Shepherd King – The Story of David', treating the story with the visual range and intensity of a modern adventure. When this had concluded he produced 'The Travels of Marco Polo', a strip completed by Peter Jackson after the comic's takeover by Hulton in 1959.

Significant though these strips were in conveying contemporary, biblical and ancient history in a vivid comic-strip form based on thorough historical and visual research, they are not unique in their attempts to use the medium for instructional purposes. Educational comics had been in existence in the USA before *Eagle*: *Dagwood Splits the Atom* had appeared in 1949 with a text by Leslie R. Groves, former head of the team which had developed the atomic bomb. But it was the British comic which incorporated the instructional page into a regular weekly publication, thus implanting an ideology of practical educational instruction within the covers of a fictional publication. Religious texts had been similarly treated in American comic books. *Timeless Topix* was a full-colour sixteen-page comic devoted to Bible stories which appeared in St Paul Minnesota in November 1942; *Picture Stories from the Bible* had been published in quarterly parts, beginning in the same year, by M.C. Gaines in conjunction with ten religious authorities including the American Bible Society. These and their imitators had limited sales in Britain; but *Eagle* was the first mainstream comic to incorporate a Bible story as part of its regular weekly contents. This is important. It reveals an ideology in which an awareness of recent advances in technology is seen as compatible with an interest in and acceptance of biblical stories, and a thirst for adventure and the exotic in line with modern adventure stories for young people. Simply by their presence within a context of adventure, both features made a clear ideological statement, which established the particular nature of *Eagle* in British children's comics.

Important though the biblical strip and the technological cutaways were, they remained a separate element, self-contained parts of the comic which did not embody the fundamentally Christian ideology within a fictional comic strip designed to appeal to contemporary readers. This *Eagle* sought to achieve in its other stories, many of which followed the traditional comic genres of western, detective thriller and adventure set in historical or exotic locations: 'Seth and Shorty, Cowboys'; 'Harris Tweed'; 'Tintin'; 'Riders of the Range'; 'Jack O'Lantern' and 'The Luck of the Legion' were among the titles. An idea of how far the ideological balance was achieved, and the function performed by the visual nature and structure of the comic strip in achieving it, can be gained by a study of an adventure strip appearing in *Eagle* when the comic was at the height of its popularity. This is made easier by the recent republication of stories from one of the most popular Eagle strips: 'PC 49'.

'PC 49' appeared in the comic from its first issue until 1957, a seven-year run which reveals its continuing popularity. It had the advantage of using characters already clearly established in another medium: *The Adventures of PC 49* had been launched as a radio series in 1947 with scripts by Alan Stranks, who had begun his career as a crime reporter in Melbourne but had come to England to write radio and film scripts in the late 1930s. In 1949, twenty-eight half-hour stories were broadcast, and to cater for the growing interest among younger listeners who were unable to listen at 9.30 p.m. they were repeated at 7.00. In October of that year the first PC 49 film was released; another followed in 1950. As well as the comic strip, there were books: *PC 49* appeared in 1951, and *On Duty with PC 49* in 1952. *On the Beat with PC 49* came in 1953, as did *PC 49 Eagle Strip Cartoon Book*.

The adoption of 49 by Morris for the first number of the new comic was a wise move in terms of boosting circulation, and the placing of the strip on page three, immediately after Dan Dare, reveals the importance the character was given. Yet the *Eagle* version of the character is by no means identical with that created by Stranks for the radio programme. Joan Carr, Fortynine's fiancée, appeared only in the first two comic strips, whereas she continued to be important in the radio series and the two films. More important, Fortynine, as he is known in the comic, begins to play a less pivotal role, importance passing to the Boys' Club which was introduced for the third *Eagle* story, 'The Case of the

Terrible Twins', beginning in August 1951. This was a very significant shift; it introduced characters of the age of the comic's readership to heighten the involvement of the reader. It also allowed the furtherance of *Eagle*'s moral objectives in presenting a group of young boys from inner-city homes actively engaged in helping the police in the pursuit of criminals and the rejection of criminal activities. Ideologically, the Boys' Club, established and subsidised by Fortynine, is firmly in the tradition of Christian missionary work in the East End of London, which stretches from Booth and Rowntree at the end of the nineteenth century and embraces activities as wide ranging as the Ockenden venture, the adoption of East End boys' groups by public schools, and the provision of university extension lectures, all of which were well established in the years between the wars. The late forties was a period of public fears about the increase of crime and disorder in the cities, in particular among gangs of boys and young men involved with black-market dealings in the bomb sites of London and other blitzed cities, with frequent use of the term 'juvenile delinquent'. The presence of the club is of considerable significance in the ideological structure of the strip, and consequently in the creation of the blending of adventure and Christian morality that is the keynote of the comic as a whole.

Fully to understand how this moral force functions, we need to consider in some detail the particular kind of tempered realism in which the strip operates. Alan Stranks made clear the circumstances which led to the birth of Fortynine: an encounter with a duty sergeant at New Scotland Yard who scornfully rejected 'all this nonsense about special agents' (1952: 94) and urged him instead to write about the realities of policing:

> It's about time you realised . . . that almost ninety-nine per cent of the crimes committed in this country are solved by the keen observation and the devotion to duty of the ordinary bloke on the beat . . . Give the 'bobby' a break – there's no one deserves it better.
>
> (1952: 95)

The idea of the passage is straightforward enough in its rejection of the '"private eyes" in silk dressing gowns' by the sergeant in favour of the professionalism of the police force, and later in the article Stranks mentions the numbers of the force who 'had been killed or gravely injured in their service to the public'. Yet the tone is self-conscious, with a kind of humorous distancing. The sergeant whose words are quoted has been described earlier as a 'magnificent specimen', and his attitude to Stranks is established as one of comic contempt. The reference to the 'bobby on the beat' suggests that we are entering the world of a privileged group through the use of nicknames, but it is clear that we are not part of this group by the way in which the sergeant is presented. What appears to be a realistic approach is in fact much tempered by language which creates a carefully defined convention of response. The passage is a subtle mingling of realism and literary convention, involvement and distance, which places the reader in a complex but precise relation to the characters and issues, and it is this which is carried over into the strip to produce its characteristic approach to the events it constructs.

A similarly complex approach is present in the illustrations. The first adventures had been drawn by Strom Gould but, from August 1951, the visual text was provided by John Worsley, whose previous experience had been as a war artist with the navy: subsequently, as the only war artist to be a prisoner of war, his drawings of the Marlag O and Milag Nord camps provide one of a very small number of first-hand visual records of conditions in such camps. The Imperial War Museum catalogue lists sixty separate drawings of naval and prison life by Worsley. This is significant in establishing a documentary realism which is a fundamental element in the very special kind of presentation of external reality which, as will emerge, is essential to the ideological location of the *Eagle* PC 49 strips.

This quality of tempered realism is employed in visual and verbal text working together, and is the key to the ideological functioning of the comic strip. This is shown clearly in 'The Case of the Spotted Toad', a twenty-part adventure which began in the Christmas *Eagle* of 1952 (Stranks and Worsley 1990: 8–27). The case begins when Fortynine leaves the Boys' Club Christmas 'beanfeast' and discovers young Dickie Duffle asleep in the door of a warehouse with his dog. As he is about to find him somewhere to stay, Fortynine is knocked down by a group of criminals, who take his uniform. One of them puts it on to get past the watchman at the warehouse and steal furs. Fortynine and Dickie are then taken to hospital, and Dickie is taken in by the Mulligan twins and becomes one of the club.

While they are talking in the street, Dickie recognises one of the men who attacked Fortynine. The boys attack him, and when Chief Inspector Wilson and Sergeant Wright arrive he is taken to the police station. He is released for lack of evidence, but not before Dickie has taken a wax impression of the key he dropped. That night, Dickie takes the key that one of the gang has cast from the impression and goes to the Toad's headquarters, discovering the haul from several robberies. A member of the gang discovers him, locks him up and sets fire to the building; meanwhile, Dickie's dog Rip, shot and wounded by the gangster, runs off to the club.

The Boys' Club, Fortynine and the fire brigade converge on the headquarters, while the gang make their escape on the river. Fortynine climbs up a rope to Dickie, and they both jump into the river to be picked up by a police launch, which then chases the gangsters. Before reinforcements from Scotland Yard can arrive, the boys and Fortynine swim to the gangsters' launch and, after being shot at, succeed in overpowering them with the aid of a mooring-hook thrown by Tiki, the black member of the gang. The story ends with the arrival of Wright and Wilson to congratulate the boys on breaking up 'one of the most dangerous and ruthless gangs on the river' (1990: 27) and with Fortynine speculating on what the next case will be.

All of this is in many ways a conventional boys' adventure story in which the elements of violence and disruption present within the main protagonists are harnessed to socially sanctioned ends in the capture of criminals – an approach used at least since the late Victorian period as a way of accepting and channelling the urge to adventure and social dissolution present within the child into an acceptable form. The fact that the boys' club are largely respon-sible for the capture of the gang, yet work always with the help and guidance of Fortynine, is a careful location of this urge within an acceptable social structure, and the ideological message of *Eagle* is clearly embodied here. In other places, too, the ideology is very clear: when Dickie is left alone in the burning building, he is told by the gangster 'You'd better say your prayers, you little sneak' (1990: 19). Dickie responds 'I could do worse than that', and the next but one frame shows him kneeling, bound and gagged, praying that Rip isn't badly hurt and ending 'please don't let me die here alone'. That this is the last frame of the weekly instalment both adds emphasis to the prayer and neatly leads us on to think of what might happen next – so the ideology is combined with that most traditional aspect of the serial, the cliffhanger.

Several other episodes combine ideology and narrative suspense. When Fortynine has climbed up to rescue Dicky from the burning warehouse in episode fifteen, we are shown the warehouse in flames from above. The next frame suspends the action and presents the reactions of those waiting below arranged in four horizontal pairs of faces. At the top, two firemen say that they will not be able to see in the smoke, and conclude 'There's no hope for them, Chief!' Beneath them, the members of the Boys' Club give their reactions. Toby says to Gigs 'If only we could do something' and receives the reply 'I feel sick': the Mulligan twins say that they can't see what's happening, and Pat concludes that he doesn't want to: Bunny asks Tiki what to do, and receives the reply 'Have faith, little Bunny!' That this is the final statement in the frame, and that it comes from Tiki, the black member of the group, gives it further significance, stressing clearly the need for faith in a practical situation, and also revealing the universality of the faith and the equal acceptance of Tiki amongst the group. The frame is presented between two dramatic images which show the building engulfed in flame at the left and, on the right, the figures of Dickie and Fortynine plunging down to the river. It is thus located at a key point of the narrative, holding up events to add suspense but also to stress an ideological point: that faith is a practical necessity in moments of crisis. Christian morality is thus firmly embedded in the visual structure of the strip in a manner which in no way denies the creation of suspense or adventure.

Important though this ideological unity is, however, the main way in which the strip reveals its moral stance is much more subtle since, relating as it does to conventions of presentation of the whole of the action, it is something which underlies the structure of the entire strip. A key part of the special sort of realism of the story is in the nature of the relationship that is created between the characters and the reader. As in the passage from Stranks' article quoted earlier, it is one in which we are involved as a privileged member, but it is far from a state of complete identification. Indeed, there are some aspects of deliberate separation, a kind of visual 'A-effect', which are used to place us outside the action. How this works can be seen from the first page of the strip. It should be remembered that this appeared in the Christmas number of *Eagle* in 1952 – a time itself slightly dislocated from everyday reality in its traditional nature as an occasion where usual rules of order are relaxed or inverted.

The first weekly part (see Plate 31) has at its centre some lines of doggerel about the Boys' Club Christmas feast, flanked by two frames which show the preparations and the meal itself. Each has features which enhance our involvement with the characters, balanced by others which distance us from them. That on the left of the poem shows the boys bringing food to the table and a number of separate episodes. One of the boys is chasing a cat escaping with some sausages, another is sitting under the table eating jam; while 'Gigs', the club's intellectual, practises his speech, two others are planting a device with caps under his chair. Narrative impulse is added by Tiki asking Toby when Fortynine will arrive and being told 'any minute now'. All of this suggests a kind of humorous intimacy in which we are involved – the jokes, nicknames and confused action suggest that we are present. This is offset by the viewpoint. The action is presented from high above, as if we are looking down from one corner of the ceiling of the room. It is markedly non-naturalistic, and gives both a physical and a psychological distance to the scene: we are privileged observers rather than members of the club. This is enhanced by the temporal nature of the frame. Although there is a rudimentary reading structure, in that we will most likely begin at the top left and work across and down the frame, there is no ordered sequence to the episodes the frame covers. We thus create our own temporal structure for the events and are in control of the scene's progression, increasing the distance between us and what is going on.

This modified involvement is continued in the second frame. This shows the boys sitting round the table, with Fortynine at its head, nearest the onlooker, carving the Christmas turkey. The members of the club make references to earlier 'cases' in which they have been involved. The reader is again a privileged observer, especially if he or she has read the earlier issues of the comic. The effect is to reinforce the reader's involvement with the group through shared experience as a kind of gathering point at the start of a new narrative section. Yet this involvement is moderated, both by the use of the same high, remote viewpoint, and more particularly by the fact that we again control the timing of the episode in that we ourselves order the sequence in which each character's comment is read. Involvement is established, but within a clearly delimited and distanced structure.

This it is which allows the ideological significance of the image to have its full effect on the reader. Seen together, the two frames represent a move from chaos to order, in the shift from unstructured preparations to the discipline of the meal itself. The latter is in itself a symbol of familial structure, to which the presence of Fortynine as a patriarchal figure carving the turkey is fundamental; he is revealed as the group's source of order, something implicit within much of the strip's sequence. Were the reader to be fully identified with one of the group's members, this shift towards order would be lost: the ideology is most precisely apparent in its presentation of a structural shift seen from the outside. Yet the frames are not wholly given over to statements of this sort, as there is a narrative impulse within the second frame: Fortynine sums up the discussion of the earlier cases by praising the club for the 'grand parts' they have played in the adventures, and concluding 'I wonder what the next one will be?' This echoes the reference to the 'Case of the Spotted Toad' mentioned in the verse which separates the two frames, and prepares us for the final frame of the page where two men are shown from behind watching Fortynine as he leaves the clubhouse to go on duty.

The Christian, moral function of the strip is revealed in two further dimensions of this initial part. The penultimate frame shows Fortynine facing straight out of the page towards us speaking these words: 'Happy Days, chaps. Don't be too late out of kip. It's good to know all you blokes are on the side of law and order in these days of dirty doings' (1990: 8). The remarks are addressed to the Boys' Club, but because of the viewpoint, which places us directly in front of Fortynine, as a club member, they are also addressed to us as readers. It is as if, once the statements of order and structure have been made in the idiolect of the preceding, paired frames, we can be allowed in as members. This has the result both of completing the sense of identification presented earlier in more qualified terms, and of making the words appear as addressed directly to us. The advice is tempered by an assumption that we, too, are 'on the side of law and order', a statement wholly in accord with the comic's ideology.

The second ideological reference is one which works at a much deeper level of association. The frame showing Fortynine carving the turkey appears just before he goes out on duty and is run over

by criminals. Within the Christian frame of the comic, the episode
is a sort of Last Supper, the parallel made more telling by the fact
that there are thirteen figures shown around the table. The parallel
does not bear too detailed analysis and should not be stressed too
far; there is no suggestion of a Judas figure in the group, and the
hands of a fourteenth member can be seen in the top left of the
frame. Yet the suggestion of a band of disciples aiding a central
Christ-like figure is one which, given the iconographic subtlety
of the lectern reference within *Eagle*'s symbol, cannot be
altogether discounted.

It is also a significant contribution to the larger, mythic pattern
of the narrative, in which the qualified identification and the
technique of modified realism are also of major importance. In
short, what is happening in the first episode is the creation of a
very carefully defined and limited sense of involvement, which
conveys the ideology of the comic within a context that is lively
and humorous, with a strong narrative thread designed to appeal to
its readers.

The special kind of involvement is aided and balanced by a
special kind of realism within which the story operates. In many
ways, the visual nature of the strip is fundamentally realistic, most
especially in its creation of setting. If it does not have the advantage
of specially built miniature sets of the Dan Dare strip, 'PC 49' is
placed within a clearly delineated setting of London docks, and
each separate locale is created with considerable care for detail.
The tall, isolated warehouse which is the gang's headquarters is
shown first in the sixth episode as a gaunt structure shored up with
baulks of timber at the edge of the river, typical of buildings which
have survived the recent bombing and are surrounded by waste
land. The nature of the warehouse is of fundamental importance to
the plot: it backs on to the river allowing the gang to escape by
boat, and its height makes possible the dramatic dives by which
Fortynine and Dickie escape. The hospital in which the two
characters recover after the raid on the fur warehouse, and the
home of the Mulligan twins, are similarly realistic in depiction, for
reasons which are ideological as much as narrative: both reveal an
ideology of care and nurture which is basic to the strip. The first
provides a location for Fortynine's offer of friendship to Dickie
and his adoption into the gang when the Mulligan twins visit, as
well as providing the obvious restorative function of the hospital:
the second reveals the family nurture which we have already

encountered in the opening scene in the club house, with Mrs Mulligan caring for Dickie and other members of the club as well as for her own sons. Her role reflects a clear gender stereotype; but, given the views of the age, it is not an unusual one, and it is also part of a larger concern for nurture which transcends gender boundaries in the tale and which is, as I shall later make clear more fully, one of the key elements of the ideology of the story.

A further dimension of the apparent realism is in the depiction of vehicles and machines in the tale. Most of the vehicles which appear are instantly identifiable: the police Wolseley is depicted accurately from a range of viewpoints as we might expect, but there are also accurate portraits of a Bedford OB van, an LCC Daimler ambulance and a Leyland fire appliance, the last presented from a dramatically lowered viewpoint. The police launch and the tug and barge on which the spotted toad gang make their escape are drawn with similar detail and accuracy, from a wide range of viewpoints in the last eight episodes, with a complete consistency between depictions that is not surprising when we recall John Worsley's earlier subjects as a war artist. Given the readership of the comic, and the interest in mechanical devices displayed elsewhere – in Dan Dare and the centre-page cutaways – this is a quite fitting concern for accuracy which does much to establish the realism of the setting and hence of the story itself.

This realism is enhanced yet at the same time qualified by the very wide range of viewpoints which is employed. Even in those parts which use only one setting – those at the end, for example, which concentrate on events on the gang's tug – we are never presented with events seen from the same viewpoint twice. This gives the effect of a three-dimensional realism to the tale as it progresses, enhancing the effects of the accurate depiction of scenes already noted. It also does much to enhance the dramatic effect and dynamic progression of the narrative. Yet it also has the effect of imposing distance between the reader and the events shown, since in no way can the constant shifting of viewpoints be described as naturalistic – even though a very few individual frames do show the action from what might be described as a subjective viewpoint of those involved in the tale. It is rather like a film shot with a large number of cameras, giving us the illusion of being placed close to the action but keeping us away from it simply by the sheer diversity and dexterity of the medium. The non-naturalistic nature of the constant shift of viewpoints is matched by the non-naturalistic nature of many of the viewpoints themselves. In particular, Worsley is fond of showing events from a very high, remote angle, exaggerating the perspective to create a very dramatic effect. This is shown most effectively in part fifteen (1990: 22) where the burning warehouse is shown from way above, in a tall, narrow frame which emphasises the height of the building and the intensity of the flames offset against the verticals of the fire brigade's ladders and the jets of water from the fire-launch. Lowered viewpoints are also used powerfully, for example in part fourteen (1990: 21) where we see from the level of the river the police launch and the escaping gang on their barge at extreme ends of a long, narrow frame which has the warehouse engulfed in flame at the centre, with the tiny figure of Dickie at a window from which a speech-bubble cries 'Help!' The frame advances the narrative, combining the escape of the gang with the coming of the police launch, and also stresses the isolation of Dickie: the very low viewpoint enhances all of these effects.

In such frames, dramatic effect is powerful, but related to that sort of drama which does not present the illusion of personal involvement: we do not see as the characters see or feel as they feel. This is most apparent when we consider what is not shown: we do not see what Dickie sees as he looks out of the burning warehouse and, when Fortynine climbs up a rope to rescue Dickie, we see him climbing up from an impossible viewpoint somewhere close above the roof of the building. The next frame provides a suitable cliffhanger in showing the rope almost burnt through while Fortynine's hand reaches out in the foreground; yet this is not what Fortynine himself sees, and again we are offered an image which appears naturalistic but which actually provides a considerable distance from the events.

A further level of distancing is added by the use of humour in the strip. The comic element in the radio programmes, though present in the comic strip, is sharply reduced and changed in emphasis. The comic catch-phrases of the radio series, 'Out you go, Fortynine' and 'Good morning all' disappear, and Fortynine's exclamation, 'My Sunday helmet!' is rare. In 'The Case of the Spotted Toad', comedy is used at its simplest in the scenes in the clubhouse discussed earlier, and in the comments of Fortynine himself, especially when he feels badly treated by Wilson and Wright. But these are largely separate from the main events of the narrative: a more specific use of comedy is the treatment of the members of the gang. This treads a very narrow line between accurate depiction of genuine violence and the presentation of distance through the use of comic stereotypes. The scenes showing Fortynine being run down by the crooks' car in the second episode appear realistic and dynamic, yet we are not shown Fortynine's injuries in anything like the blood-curdling detail of the American horror comics of the late forties: when we next see him, telephoning for help, Fortynine appears to have nothing worse than a black eye. Similarly, we do not see the attack on the nightwatchman – though his backing away from the crook with a cosh is a forceful image of his fear. The crooks themselves are made to look comically ridiculous as well as threatening: the device of calling one 'Smiler' after his permanent grin helps here. Yet the level of aggression in the story is not inconsiderable: to the attempted murder of Fortynine with the car and the assault on the watchman is added the leaving of Dickie bound and gagged in the burning building and the gunfight on the barge at the end of the story. That the crooks are thoroughly evil is shown by the fact that one shoots Rip, Dickie's dog. The two forces, of comedy and serious aggression, are carefully balanced, giving a further level of distance from the strip's fictive world and events.

To these techniques needs to be added the larger presentation of the narrative. Instead of following the progress of one line of action – what happens to Fortynine, the Boys' Club or the Spotted Toad gang – the narrative repeatedly cuts from one to the other. Part six (1990: 6), for instance, begins with Wilson and Wright talking to Fortynine in hospital, and then cuts to the warehouse exterior in what in film would be an establishing shot, and then goes inside to follow the discussions of the gang. We then return to the hospital for two frames, but the next shows Dickie outside the hospital and the rest of the episode shows Smiler by the fur store trying to retrieve the key to the warehouse but being recognised by Dickie. This range is carefully controlled by a mixture of visual and verbal clues. The exterior of the hospital is identified by the Daimler ambulance parked outside, and the shift to the fur store introduced by one of the boys' saying 'Let's walk home past the place where it all happened last night', an index of how closely verbal and visual elements work together in establishing and directing the narrative.

This cross-cutting occurs in most of the weekly parts, with the exception of the early ones which are concerned with establishing character and plot and the closing ones which cover the denouement with considerable concentration of setting and event. We are thus placed in the position of privileged observer to all the layers of action – Boys' Club, gang, Fortynine, even in one very dynamic frame in part seventeen (1990: 24) the Information Room at Scotland Yard sending out a message and four separate groups of policemen rushing to the warehouse in response. It is a visual equivalent of an omniscient narrator controlling and directing what we learn in a very measured manner. This again shows the sophistication of the single discourse for word and image, but it also reveals the key to the dynamic ideology of the strip: by presenting events from a range of viewpoints, many of which are non-naturalistic, and by including events concerning each group of characters, the narrative presents no more than an illusion of involvement which is really a considered distancing of reader from experience. What results is the semblance of an adventure story within the structure of a moral fable: and it is this which allows the Christian morality of the story to make its effect on the reader.

What emerges from this tempered realism is an ideology which stresses key elements of Christian morality. Right and wrong is a fundamental part of this, in the pursuit of the criminals and the maintenance of law and order. Yet there are elements which are more important than this, significant among which is the presentation of the Boys' Club and its values. Dickie Duffle is accepted into the group and becomes a key figure in the story; and the boys work together to protect each other, fight the criminals and support Fortynine. The presence of Fortynine as a guiding and nurturing figure is also important; but it is far from a simple relationship. While the policeman exerts a benevolent and protective influence over the boys – most obviously in saving Dickie, but also in his general interest in the Boys' Club – he is also the subject of such nurturing concern himself, as is shown when the club fight to help him on the barge at the end of the tale, playing the decisive role in the capture of the gang.

This mutuality of nurture is important in several ways. First, it avoids the idea of an invincible and unreal super-hero prevalent in American comic books of the Superman genre. Secondly, it makes clear the presence of what some clinicians refer to as 'concessive vulnerability', the willingness to reveal one's own faults before others, especially within a group or a close relationship. Both of these suggest a grasp of the nature of human relations at a level which goes far beyond the mere surface realism of the adventure story. Overall, the concern for psychological and physical nurture is a subtle and significant part of the strip's ideological structure: it rests on Christian ethics but goes beyond them to suggest a model of nurture of no little depth. Because of the tempered realism of the strip, combining the immediacy of an adventure story with the power of a moral fable, this ideology is convincingly conveyed at a far deeper and more successful level than would be possible in an overtly educative or doctrinal text.

It is not only in the presentation of a nurturing ethic that the strip reveals its ideology. Important too are the presentation of the intellect and of multi-culturalism, as shown in the treatment respectively of Giglamps and of Tiki. Giglamps is the intellectual of the group, preparing his speech in the opening episode, knowing that 'bufo' is Latin for toad and natterjack is 'another name for the running toad' (1990: 16). But he is not only a theorist: he uses his father's workshop to make a copy of the key to the warehouse. All of this conveys a simple message of the value of intellectual studies in a practical context, a moral point embedded in the narrative and thus a central part of the strip's ideology.

The presentation of Mungatiki, usually called Tiki, is in many ways less clear, certainly when viewed from the perspective of several decades later. There are ways in which his presentation seems patronising at best and racially offensive at worst. He is given odd habits of speech – 'It shall be done, O Toby' and 'Be strong, my arm' – and in the final part contributes to the defeat of the gang by throwing a bargepole, an action which might well be construed as a cultural identification with throwing a spear. We might also regard his advice to Bunny to 'Have faith' when Dickie and Fortynine jump from the warehouse as a patronising view of his religion. These elements need to be seen within the ideology of the time. The late forties saw the encouragement of immigration from the West Indies, with a range of concomitant persecutions and the infamous 'colour-bar' in London and other cities. The East End of London, especially the docks, has always been a multi-cultural area, and the mere presence of Tiki as a member of the group is very significant in spreading the idea of cultural integration at this time. He is an important member of the group, not only in the closing incident already mentioned but in suggesting that they follow Rip to find Dickie (1990: 19). It is probably more legitimate to regard the throwing of the barge-pole as part of the dynamic action of the narrative, and the reference to faith as a dimension of the pervasive Christian ideology of the story – it is not, after all, restricted to Tiki, since we should recall at this point Dickie's kneeling in prayer when he is alone in the burning warehouse. Most striking is the mere presence of Tiki as an member of the Boys' Club: this alone advances an ideology of ethnic integration at a time when this was far from widely accepted.

The particular nature of the Boys' Club as an image of nurture and tolerance can be seen by a brief comparison with perhaps the most famous enclosed society of British comics, the pupils of Greyfriars' School from the *Gem* and *Magnet*. Their privileged world is concerned largely with bullying and snobbery, the former directed against the greedy and selfish figure of Billy Bunter, the latter against the 'yobs' and 'oicks' who do not attend their public school and anyone who has the misfortune not to be born English. By contrast, the world of the Boys' Club is tolerant and nurturing: it accepts Dickie with warmth and immediacy, and there is no suggestion of bullying or exploitation and, though Tiki has a nickname, this is perhaps no different from that of 'Gigs' and certainly has none of the xenophobic force of the 'wops', 'frogs' and 'chinks' that abound in the Greyfriars stories. Presenting such a role model in a comic for boys is a risky business: that it succeeds is shown by the continuing popularity of the Fortynine stories in *Eagle*, the result of the careful embodiment of the ideology within a narrative that is visually dynamic and which employs a range of devices to convey the idea of realism but ultimately works as a subtle moral parable.

It is perhaps impossible for a work of fiction aimed at children successfully to convey a positive moral ideology without also conveying a sense of coercion, as the eventual folding of *Eagle* probably suggests. Yet, given the intentions of Marcus Morris and Frank Hampson, and the extensive circulation of the comic during its peak years, it is hard to conclude that the comic did other than achieve some degree of success in embodying an ideology that was positive and nurturing within a structure that provided excitement and involvement. That the comic lasted for as long as it did suggests that the visual embodiment of a Christian ideology within a comic is not impossible, and that the PC 49 stories provided a strong and compelling contribution to this moral scheme.

8

WORKING-CLASS
F(R)ICTIONS

I go out and along the passage and up the stairs. The carpet's
thick under my feet. The house isn't big but I'm impressed by
the furnishings. It seems Mr Rothwell must have spent a load
of dough making it comfortable for Ingrid and her ma while
he's away on his travels. The bathroom has pink walls with
black tiles to about chest height. Our bath at home stands on
four cast-iron rests like animals' feet but this is one of the
modern boxed-in efforts, in black to match the tiles.

(Barstow 1986: 201–2)

Vic Brown, the narrator and central character of the novel from
which this passage is taken, is waiting nervously for his girlfriend,
Ingrid Rothwell, to undress in her front room so that they can
make love. Unable to do so in front of him, she banishes him to
the bathroom, and as he tries to wait for the ten minutes he has
promised he examines the strange and unfamiliar surroundings in
which he finds himself.

This apparently insignificant paragraph comes from Stan
Barstow's *A Kind of Loving*, first published in 1960 and rapidly
regarded as a prime mover in a new kind of fiction which explores
the experiences of young people in a northern, industrial working-
class environment. The film version directed in 1962 by John
Schlesinger,[1] with a screenplay adapted from the novel by Willis
Hall and Keith Waterhouse, similarly came to be classed as part of
British New Wave realist cinema in its exploration of geographic
and social territory hitherto studiously avoided in mainstream
British fictional film. How the film explores this territory, and
the ways in which it alters and extends the ideas, structure and
ideology of the novel in so doing, offer considerable insight into

154

one further aspect of the process of visualisation: the discourse which results when a realist novel depending on internal monologue is turned into a realist film which, of its nature, externalises the experience that is fundamental to the narrative. And in this, the paragraph which describes Vic's encounter with Ingrid's hallway and bathroom has a far greater significance than the creation of suspense through delay which at first appears to be its chief function.

Vic's account of the hallway, stairs and bathroom might appear to be a straightforward account of the visual surroundings in which he finds himself, as in a way it is, but in the context of the novel as a whole it is much more significant, largely because visual description of this kind is extremely rare. The visual world is taken for granted in Vic's first person, present-tense narrative: it has nothing of the moral and psychological importance that it is given, say, in du Maurier's *Rebecca*. The key locations of the novel – the factory, the drawing office, the town itself – are present merely as a setting through which he passes, something so familiar as to be totally unremarkable and hence totally unremarked. Before the reference to the feet of 'our bath at home', which is there only to stress the contrast with Ingrid's home, there is no description at all of the interior of the house where Vic lives with his parents and younger brother Jim for the first two-thirds of the novel; it is part of the experience of life at such a deep level that it has no separable, visual significance.

By contrast, the account of Ingrid's house is, in the terms of the novel, quite sensuous in its visual duration, to match what is to Vic the strange richness of the interior. The carpet is thick, the furnishings impressive and, most striking of all, the bath is boxed-in and the bathroom is tiled. This is a striking reminder of the setting of the novel: it emphasises by contrast the nature of the writing about the working-class community which is the more forceful because it is constantly understated. The lack of visual stress on the industrial landscape allows us to become part of the environment, seeing it at the level at which Vic sees it, with the visual indifference of someone born and brought up in the same town and for whom it represents the only sort of visual reality. This is a kind of sharing quite different from the sorts of visualisation discussed in other chapters of this book. There is no presentation of key episodes through visual experience, either in the text or in illustrations: instead, we are drawn into Vic's world so completely that we are fully a part of it before we realise how subtly this world has taken control of our responses.

The treatment of the bathroom scene in the film is, inevitably, different. We have already seen Vic's own house, the factory, the drawing office and the visual universe that he inhabits. For this reason, the shock of the middle-class bathroom is immeasurably diminished. In addition, there is no attempt to translate the reference to the boxed-in bath into more strikingly visual terms – perhaps wisely, since it would easily become patronising about Vic's different circumstances, if not openly absurd. We are shown Vic going upstairs, sitting on the bath – the bathroom has marble-effect tiles, not the plain black of the book – and then looking at himself in the mirror. This conveys the primary narrative function of the scene, in adding suspense and tension; but there is nothing of the impact of the scene in the novel.

The reason why this scene is of such significance is that it presents something far more than a statement of visual contrast: it is an embodiment of the totally different territories which are inhabited by Vic and Ingrid at a point just before the pivotal narrative element of the novel. These two territories are constructed from several elements: the material differences so plain in the passage and the physical locations of the two characters' homes at different ends of the town are only the external sites of a complex of oppositions of gender, sexuality and outlook which, taken together, produce a fundamental ideological conflict which is the text's main oppositional force in literary, linguistic and sociological terms.

To Vic, the interior of Ingrid's home is striking not only in itself, but as an image of the family relationship and of its financial status. Not only has Mr Rothwell spent 'a load of dough' on the house; he has done this to make it 'comfortable' for Ingrid and her mother. Money and comfort are both phenomena with which Vic is unfamiliar, as is the idea of the husband and father producing material well-being of this kind: for Vic, it is the mother who is the centripetal and defining force of the family, often in a fairly negative, inquisitorial manner, shown for example in her repeated questionings about Vic's dates with Ingrid. Vic's father – a miner in the novel, an engine-driver in the film – is a fellow-victim with Vic of these inquisitions, content to bring home his wages and enjoy his recreation by playing in a brass band. Ingrid's mother's concerns are different: they are for material well-being in the burgeoning consumer society of the late 1950s, as is stressed by the repeated reference to television quiz-shows. Ingrid's father spends most of his time away from home on business: in the film, he is written out completely so that the widowed Mrs Rothwell takes complete control of the home, a change that, as will become clear, significantly amplifies the clash of ideological territories.

An important further part of the clash is apparent in the couple's attitudes to sex. Vic carries with him a book of pin-ups, 'with a bint on the cover in a suspender belt and black nylons and nothing much else but a you-know-what look' (32); clearly, to him sex is appetitive and exploitative. But for Ingrid, sex is inseparable from marriage, family, security: when she finally convinces Vic that she is pregnant and they agree to marry, she says 'I've always wanted to marry you, Vic.' And now, as Vic sits nervously in the bathroom, while Ingrid undresses nervously in the lounge, in a moment of narrative suspension, the two ideologies are held in metaphoric opposition represented in the visual strangeness of the Rothwells' bathroom. How these conflicting ideologies are presented in the visual structure of the film, and the larger nature of this structure both as narrative discourse and social statement, are the concerns of this chapter.

II

Central to the question of the two territories presented in the film is the position of the viewer. Do we remain outside both, seeing as a dispassionate observer? Do we instead take on the ideology of one of the two territories because of the viewpoint, literal and ideological, from which we see the narrative? What relationship is engendered between the narrative and the visual elements which are both the literal setting and the metaphoric representative of the ideology of which they form a part? All of these are significant questions, which need to be explored if we are to grasp the film's importance as narrative and idiolect.

As I have already made clear, the novel's narrative technique involves us in Vic's working-class experience by assuming its inevitability. Factory, drawing-office and home life are recorded as normal, accepted patterns of existence, aided by the lack of visual detail which becomes apparent only on the rare occasions when visual reality departs from its accepted form, as it does in Ingrid's bathroom. This creates by assumption a bond between writer and reader; we are drawn into Vic's life and experience simply because it is assumed that we know all about it already and do not need to be told. For many readers outside the described milieu, this can be strikingly effective, since we are part of Vic's world before we know it. The technique is considerably enhanced by the directness of the first person narrative. Not only is the narrative presented as told by Vic, in his own idiolect; it is presented in a continuous present. This involves us still further: there is a sense of sharing experience, event and response which we do not have even in the narrative of *Rebecca* and the romantic-historical novels of which it stands representative. In such writing, we know that the story is being told in retrospect: with Vic's story, we are given a continuum of experience and thought apparently as it happens. This use of an inner continuous present is of considerable significance in one further dimension of the novel's ideological geography, as I shall make clear later; but for the moment it is enough to realise that the novel presents Vic's life in a working-class town and his experiences with Ingrid, his opposite in ideology and gender, solely in terms of his own thoughts and immediate existence.

Clearly, any film version of such a narrative technique will differ in one key respect: it cannot take for granted the visual reality of Vic's life, since film is a visual medium – unless it adopt a bare-stage technique favoured in a certain style of Shakespearean theatre, an option that for practical purposes is unlikely to be taken in a mainstream fiction film. Inevitably, then, the assumed will be stated: the working-class setting takes on external form. Not quite so inevitable is the viewpoint. It would be quite possible for the film to be shot subjectively – that is, to present everything from the eyes of Vic himself. This would promote the kind of identity between reader and central character that we have in the novel; and it would also facilitate the presentation of Vic's thoughts in response to the changing circumstances of the narrative. Again, however, this is an unlikely option: mainstream cinema would find it hard to accept a complete film in which the central character did not appear; practical limitations would be placed on the range of physical viewpoints and kinds of shots that could be used; and the visualisation of the external world would still, inevitably, be present, so that the assumptions of ideology and way of life from the novel would be at the least curtailed, if not wholly lost. Not surprisingly, this is not the path pursued by Schlesinger's film, which uses the kind of directorial stance that is the accepted cinematic equivalent of the omniscient narrator in the novel – a presentation of events from an external viewpoint the fiction of which is assumed and accepted by the audience as part of the contract of suspension of disbelief which is fundamental to the viewing process. What now becomes of interest is how, in this approach which stresses external visual forms, the nature of Vic's experiences is presented, and the effect this has on the territorial opposition basic to the novel.

What is striking now about the film is the way in which the surroundings of Vic's life are treated in a manner which makes them almost its dominant feature. Seen thirty years after it was made, the film's use of repeated shots of the industrial landscape in finely contrasted black-and-white gives it a force not held at a time when feature films were always shot in monochrome: seen at the time, its use of the landscape was striking since – with one very important exception – the industrial scene was not something which had appeared in anything but a subordinate, incidental or romanticised way in British films. What in the novel is assumed, in the film is insistent and dominant and this reversal has important effects on every aspect of the narrative.

To the stress on setting which I described earlier as an inevitable result of the change of medium is added another kind of stress which results from a stylistic influence which is apparent repeatedly in the film: the use of a style which derives very clearly and directly from the tradition of British documentary film. This constitutes the important exception to the British cinema's silence about working-class life with anything like sustained or serious attention: beginning in the 1930s, a range of films explored industrial production, housing conditions and a range of other related issues. What it is important to realise, though, is that such films were not the product of an indigenous working-class film culture; they were portraits of working-class life by privileged observers from the outside. Instead of being produced by working-class film-makers for working-class audiences – who, in any case, knew all that they needed to about factory work and slum housing – such films were made by middle-class film-makers for middle-class audiences. Often the film-makers worked with the most honourable of motives. For example, Edgar Anstey and Arthur Elton's *Housing Problems* (1935)[2] sought to reveal the squalor of slum housing in industrial cities. Yet this does not deny the fact that they were fundamentally outside the social territory which they presented. It has been asserted that, as a result, they often presented conditions with a kind of voyeuristic enjoyment in their determination to bring to their audiences new images of what one commentator called 'exotic dirt' (Vesselo 1936: 30), to create the sort of fashionable frisson, perhaps, with which the wealthy viewers of Fildes' *Casual Ward* would have responded in the Royal Academy. *A Kind of Loving* may or may not have that result: but it is clear that the British documentary tradition is a major influence upon its style and structure.

This is apparent in several sequences of the film. One sequence is particularly striking in the way in which it seems to have little explicit connection with the narrative or ideological progress of the film, while making an almost explicit reference to documentary tradition. The scene occurs after Vic and Ingrid have been lying on the grass above the town. Ingrid has told Vic that she thought he wanted to 'go further', and they have spoken about sex briefly, before Ingrid begins to gossip about her workmates and Vic walks off angrily, with Ingrid following and complaining about 'these shoes'. The image fades, and in the next shot the camera pans across the factory yard following the workers walking to the canteen, coming to rest on a menu chalked on a blackboard by the door. Since the camera holds this shot for a full three seconds, it is clearly intended that we read what is written:

Menu

Corned Beef	9d.
Roast Beef	1/3d.
Fish and Mash	1/5d.
Mince Tart	5d.
Cabinet Pudding	5d.

This has no significance in terms of the narrative, and seems to be included largely out of anthropological interest for the film's middle-class audience, as if to provide data on the dietary arrangements of industrial workers. The documentary link is even stronger, since the image is a direct parallel to a sequence in Humphrey Jennings' *Listen to Britain* (1941),[3] one of the most celebrated British documentaries. The sequence in question shows workers in a wartime factory queueing up at a canteen, with a similar lingering on the menu, to the accompaniment of Flanagan and Allen singing at a workers' lunchtime concert. The ideological subtext is concerned with a nation united by war, the menu significant in showing nourishment in adversity – even though these messages are concealed fairly deep within Jennings' subtle, kaleidoscopic montage of sounds and images of the nation which, in itself, is a formal statement of the unity of the country in the war effort.

Schlesinger's use of the menu has no such message; there seems no link between it and the succeeding shot of Vic collecting his food and sitting, not with Ingrid who has saved him a place at the table where she sits with a woman friend, but at the far end of the canteen with his mates. Here it seems that the director's concern for documentary has overcome a concern for the plot and its issues: instead of contributing to the film's portrayal of territorial oppositions, the sequence in a sense puts us outside its ideological territory by presenting us with a sociological detail for our academic consideration.

In many other cases, however, the apparently anthropological aspect of documentary sequences is linked closely with the film's deeper concerns and the pattern of ideological territorialising. One such is the football match which is interpolated into the action shortly before the bathroom sequence already described. This is carefully prepared in a preceding scene: Ingrid waits for Vic one evening, not having seen him for some little while, and asks when they are to meet again. He says that he can't see her on Saturday because of 'the match', stressing its importance as the 'cup tie'. The game is shown from the terraces and in a brief sequence from the touch line; for a period of several seconds the film's single concern is with the football match. But then the camera moves to show Vic and his friend Willy Lomas standing in the crowd at half time. They flirt with a couple of girls standing nearby: Vic asks Willy when he last had sex and, when he looks away and mumbles, Vic comments to the effect that he has only ever done so in his mind.

All of this is important in revealing Vic's ideological territory. Certainly the football match is important; but as part of a much larger pattern of life which includes spending time with male friends, flirting with women, and talking about sex as a form of appetitive conquest rather than human commitment and nurture. That Vic puts off meeting Ingrid to go to the match is as much an assertion of his own working-class, male ideological territory and a rejection of her need for security as a simple desire to watch football: it is part of a tribal loyalty which Ingrid, as a woman, who comes from the ideologically distant land of the middle-class suburbs, cannot be expected to share. Yet the territories are not always mutually exclusive: in the scene that follows, Vic goes into a chemist's to buy contraceptives, only to emerge with a bottle of Lucozade because a woman came out to serve him. Then comes a short scene of the two meeting at the park in the rain; and then they go to the Rothwells' house, in the scene which leads to their love-making in the front room. All of this shows some sort of movement towards an ideological fusion, even if it is incomplete and superficial.

The movement of the whole sequence is clear: the meeting that Ingrid had hoped for as part of her own scheme of middle-class courtship has been changed into the sexual pursuit Vic and Willy have discussed earlier, and central in this movement is the assertion of ideology that is made by the presence of the football match.

Yet if this represents a 'victory' for Vic's ideology in the narrative and visual progress of the film, it is balanced by another sequence in which Ingrid's territory is forcefully dominant. The scene shows the brass band concert in the town hall. There are shots of the conductor in close-up, shown against the background of the capacity audience in the hall, and of various sections of the band, before the camera closes in on the trombones. Vic's father then plays his solo. The music played is an arrangement of nineteenth-century operatic airs of the kind made especially for colliery and works' bands as part of the development of working-class musical culture: this adds an aural dimension to the visual realism of many sequences of the film. Like the scene with the football match, it seems that the sequence is a piece of documentary footage, stressing the traditional working-class cultural pursuit for the anthropological education of the middle-class audience; yet, once again, when it is put into context a larger significance emerges.

In the scene immediately before it, Vic is talking in the kitchen of his mother-in-law's home, where he is now living after marrying Ingrid. He suggests to Ingrid that they go to the concert; her reluctant response is amplified by Mrs Rothwell, close to the camera, saying that Vic must 'make sacrifices' now that he is married. Already angered at the way Mrs Rothwell talks to the window-cleaner, to whom he himself has spoken in a friendly manner through the bedroom window, Vic responds angrily.

162

Then comes the sequence showing the band playing. After showing Vic's father playing his solo, the camera pans across a row of the audience to show his mother and brother, and two empty seats - those for which Vic has shown Ingrid the tickets in the preceding scene. The film then cuts directly to Ingrid and Mrs Rothwell sitting next to each other on a sofa with Vic in an armchair closer to camera; they are watching one of Mrs Rothwell's favourite television game-shows. In itself this shows the displacement of Vic's own cultural values by those of Mrs Rothwell – the domestic, television-dominated concerns of a new consumer society which is seen largely in terms of women and home-building, in opposition to the traditionally male working-class culture based on activities outside the home – the brass band, football and the pub. Seen thus, the band sequence is far more than a mere documentary record: it is another assertion of the narrative's opposition of ideologies.

This is made even clearer by two further aspects of the scene in Ingrid's home. When we are shown the events on the television screen, the question-master is talking to one of the contestants. He announces his home town incorrectly, whereupon the contestant corrects him. The question-master speaks with a plummy middle-class voice; the contestant is a working northerner. It is a small detail, but it significantly poses again the cultural divisions of the film, amplifying them by the implication that the worth of the individual is being eroded by the glossy new middle-class culture. Class values are present again a little later when, as the television glows and fades, Mrs Rothwell complains that the repairman has not been. She talks loudly of 'these people' and how they are 'holding the country to ransom'. 'These people' are those to whom Vic feels the most complete kinship as members of his own class; the opposition felt in the earlier incident with the window-cleaner is rekindled, and Vic storms out of the room. Seen in this setting, the brass band episode is revealed as a key part of the film's narrative and ideological pattern in its contribution to the class opposition on which the whole is founded.

A similar use of what appears to be a documentary style within the film's larger structural pattern appears in a scene which comes between the football and brass band sequences in the film's narrative: the passage showing the firm's annual dance. Ideological opposition is apparent throughout. While the married couples dance, the younger, unmarried men sit together at tables at the side; a banner proclaims 'Soft Drinks Only', while the men walk off to the pub; the boss walks round the groups with his wife intoning ritualistically 'Enjoying yourselves? Jolly good.' The opposition between middle and working class, male and female, married and single is made explicit when one of Vic's friends talks to him about 'security' in marriage, and he makes clear in reply that that is the last thing that he wants.

The most apparent documentary element here is the appearance of the group which the boss introduces over the Tannoy as 'the Dawson Whittakers Formation Team'. These figures, immaculately dressed in dinner suits or sequined gowns, are shown dancing in elaborate formation from a camera high in the roof of the building: for a moment it seems as if, once again, a documentary interlude is revealing the nature of patriarchally dictated recreation at a working-class social function. That this is not so is shown by what comes immediately afterwards.

As Vic and his mates get up to go to the pub, Ingrid follows and calls him back, saying she must talk to him. While the music for the formation dancing continues, the two go into a dark corridor and she tells him that she is pregnant. The formation team is thus revealed as symbolic in its import – suggesting an absurd parody of ritual courtship dances as an ironic contrast to the courtship of Vic and Ingrid which ends in a parody of a proposal instead of the climactic moment for which Ingrid has longed. It is also, of course, symbolic of order and resolution, something which their relationship has lacked and will continue to lack. Once the dancing is seen in terms of symbols, its significance becomes much larger: within the context of the works dance, it is revealed as a middle class ideal, a fantasy of tulle and sequins, in opposition to the disorder of working life shown in the factory. Once again, that which appears as a documentary intrusion is really something of far deeper significance in the visual embodiment of narrative oppositions.

Two further instances where a similar technique is used are worthy of detailed consideration, since they both show adaptations of the conventional techniques of British documentary which are particularly significant in the film's structure. The first is the sequence which follows Ingrid's rejection of Vic's sexual advances. Immediately afterwards, Mrs Rothwell comes in with the new coat she has collected for her daughter. Angered by this, which he sees as evidence that they will never have enough money to live on their own, Vic storms out.

The next shot introduces a lengthy sequence of montage which follows Vic and his friend Conroy as they pub-crawl their way around the town, the editing and presentation becoming progressively less naturalistic as their drunkenness grows. The ideological territory is established straightaway: a barmaid wearing a tight sweater emphasising ice-cream cone breasts is shown over a male voice asking 'Which one have I got to press to get my money back?' Immediately, sex becomes a part of the male world of the pub; it is made predatory, exploitative and quite devoid of any notions either of commitment and nurture or the vague notions of suburban consumerism presented by Ingrid's world. It is an immediate but effective act of transition, as striking as the change of visual setting from the cosily 'feminine' middle-class bedroom to the austerely 'masculine' public bar.

The sequence develops to include Conroy, Vic's former colleague in the drawing office. The dissociation from Ingrid's territory is made complete when he reveals that he was once married but has since cut loose; once this is stated, the pub crawl that he proposes becomes a reassertion of Vic's own ideological territory. It is presented as a series of episodes in different pubs, including the telling of jokes and a political argument; it ends with Vic taking over the microphone on a pub stage and singing 'Down by the Riverside' with Conroy's assistance. The disapproval of the woman pianist when this happens does more than show her anger at the disruption; it is a further statement of ideological conflict to which oppositions of gender are fundamental. As the pub crawl proceeds, the film adopts increasingly a montage technique favoured in earlier British documentaries, and at one stage it uses anticipatory sound editing techniques, where the sound of the next shot is superimposed on the action of the current one, as the voices of Vic and his companions at the bar occur over a sequence showing a pub pianist being given a pint of beer. This technique is used frequently by Humphrey Jennings, most particularly in *Listen to Britain*: once more, Schlesinger uses documentary conventions, but in a manner which can be said to explore the ideological structure of the narrative rather than as a means of anthropological observation, since the overlap adds to the confusion of the pub crawl and so stresses Vic's drunken disorientation.

165

The other sequence which uses documentary techniques occurs shortly after Vic and Ingrid return from their honeymoon. After an establishing long-shot of the suburban estate where they now live, the camera pans round following the progress of a milk float. Over this come the voices of a woman and a shopkeeper from whom she is buying bread and eccles cakes, discussing her needs in detail. The camera comes to rest on a mobile bread-van at which the woman is shown in conversation with the driver. At one level, this is a shot which establishes the new surroundings of the film, just as the sequence before the title, panning round a street of Victorian terraced houses, establishes Vic's environment. Yet at another it presents the goings-on as ridiculously comic, rather like the parodies of garden-wall conversations in the *Monty Python* programmes of the 1970s: the discussion of the day's requirements of bread and eccles cakes at greater length than several of the earlier propositions of Wittgenstein's *Tractatus* makes the scene comically absurd. Is this a statement of the absurdly serious new world in which Vic has found himself? Or is it the presentation of the suburban world with the same kind of documentary detachment seen in the shots of Vic's setting? Is it, even, a satiric comment on the nature of documentary film itself, in presenting a middle-class scene with the kind of anthropological detail used habitually about working-class settings? All of these seem plausible readings: the sequence is a striking moment which seems simultaneously to extend the film's awareness of territories and to undermine the techniques of depiction which it uses itself elsewhere.

This is significant because it raises a larger question about the use of filmic techniques from the tradition of documentary within the film as a whole. Through their purpose in constructing the ideological opposition fundamental to the film, do these techniques allow us to share the dual world so completely as to forget that we are outside spectators, like the middle-class viewers of *Housing Problems*, as we become involved with the film's fictive pattern? Or do they, through viewpoint and content, impose a distance between us and the central figures, in showing us Vic's world as something to be noted and stressed visually, instead of something taken so much for granted that it becomes – as in the novel – unworthy of visual comment? These are important questions, and to answer them – or define the terms in which we may approach them – we need to consider other aspects of the film's construction of the ideologies and territories of Vic and Ingrid.

III

Important though the references to documentary style are in the film, it would be a mistake to regard them as the major way in which its patterns of territorial opposition are established. Fully to answer the question of how effectively we are involved in this conflict and not simply presented with working-class life as privileged outsiders, we need to explore the ways in which the opposition is presented in passages which do not follow overtly the documentary tradition.

Mention has already been made of the opening sequence of the film, in which the camera pans round a Victorian terraced street before reaching the church in which Vic's sister Christine is marrying David. Yet it is a little later on that the opposing territory of Ingrid's physical and ideological home is stated: it is almost as if there is no need to state it, since it is that with which the audience will already be familiar. This initial image must, in 1962, have had considerable shock value as the start of a fictional film because of its working-class setting, and presumably it is images of this sort which engendered the frequent accounts of the film and other similar work such as *Saturday Night and Sunday Morning*[4] as concerned with realistic depictions of working-class life in which words such as 'gritty' and 'grimy' are common. It is not this sequence, however, but one which occurs a little way into the film, which establishes the two main locations of setting and idea.

Vic becomes so engrossed in his conversation with Ingrid on the bus that he misses his stop: as a result, he gets off where Ingrid does. It is a neat suburb on a hill, with trees and hedges in the front gardens of well-ordered 1930s semi-detached houses. This makes clear the larger structural purpose of the establishing shot at the very start of the film: it allows us to draw for ourselves the great contrast between Vic's street and Ingrid's. The full contrast in settings becomes clear a little further on. Vic says goodbye to Ingrid after having arranged to go to the cinema: he turns, and we see him in long shot against the industrial city which is laid out beneath us, seen from Ingrid's hill. What is presented as a simple, 180-degree turn in the viewpoint is immediately effective, emblematising concepts and tensions which are fundamental to the film. To begin with, it makes clear the fact that Ingrid is outside the essential community of the town – the community which is identified as patriarchal, working class, and having at its core all the

167

other features discussed in the preceding paragraphs. In its stead, she has the security of the modern estate, and all its values. Embodying and emblematising the uneasy uniting of these two systems is the central visual element of the film – the industrial town in which they work, whose codes and structures dominate the central characters even if, like Ingrid, they try to reject them. All of this may well not be apparent immediately at first viewing; yet the impact of the turn of viewpoint is very forceful, the sequence one that does not easily remove itself from the visual memory.

What comes after this turnaround is similarly important. Excited and exuberant that Ingrid has agreed to come out with him, Vic runs down the hill into the townscape of factory chimneys and mill buildings, and is next shown walking down a steep flight of stone steps and along a cobbled street, reaching his own terrace just as the lights come on in the early evening, giving a curious halo-effect in the mist which matches Vic's ecstatic mood. The move from one territory to another is thus presented in a visual, temporal and ethical journey: the physical differences of location are all that are visually presented, yet the larger conflicts of ideology are quite implicit to any onlooker with even the slightest awareness of the British system of caste and gender in the late 1950s.

The succeeding sequence emphasises the uneasy shift which Vic seems to have made – and also his position as a draughtsman, not a factory worker, at Dawson Whittaker's. Vic's father is in the kitchen cleaning his trombone, a narrative and ideological clue to the band-concert and its cultural significance to come. This exchange follows:

VIC: Where's tea?
MR BROWN: Tea? Tea? White-collar workers don't get tea. You want to get a day's work before you get tea.

This reveals Vic as, to some extent, caught between separate strata of the system: his parents, home and culture are working class, yet his aspirations are apparently middle class. Coming after the visual statement of the ideological oppositions of territory, the dialogue neatly encapsulates Vic's dilemma.

The visual difference between the territories of Vic and Ingrid is a motif that appears frequently in the film. When Ingrid waits for him in the episode before the football match, she is seen walking up the same steep steps that Vic has run down earlier: now she is out of her own territory, significant because this is the only time that this occurs, and also because she has just complained that it is difficult 'being a girl' and not being able to make the advances in their relationship. Ideologically as well as physically, she is away from home: the shot of her walking awkwardly up the steps shows this well, especially when it is followed by one of Vic walking away from the spot, confident in his ownership not only of the territory but of his freedom in attending the cup tie.

The separation is also generated by the houses of the two characters. If Vic's sense of being out of place is not made clear in the film's portrayal of the strangeness of Ingrid's bathroom, it is shown clearly in other forms of conflict. Shortly after the passage of dialogue quoted above, the film cuts sharply from a shot of Vic in Jimmy's bedroom, where he tries to borrow his younger brother's tie, to one of Ingrid's bedroom, where she is making-up for the date. Mrs Rothwell's questions about Vic and where he comes from add another dimension to the ideological difference already apparent in the two rooms: Vic's is austere, male and working class, Ingrid's cosily female in the fashion of the day, with a valanced dressing-table and elaborate make-up preparations on which even Mrs Rothwell comments, albeit in the middle of describing a television quiz-show. These two scenes, of course, are significant in advancing the narrative in showing the two characters preparing for the outing to the cinema as a significant stage in their relationship: yet they also reveal the difference in ideology, and prepare us for the presentation of Vic in a quite alien environment when he lives with Ingrid in Mrs Rothwell's house. Ideology and narrative are seamlessly united in the film's visual progress.

One key part of the film's exploration of the two territories is the attitudes it presents towards sex. Much of the scene showing Vic with Jimmy before the cinema outing is concerned with a discussion of sex and marriage. This is occasioned by Jimmy's discovery of a book of pin-ups which Vic has in his inside jacket pocket. Jimmy looks through the book, and three or four of the images are shown on camera: they show women posing with naked breasts. In looking at them on film, we are drawn directly into the scopophilic view of women that is part of the gender-ideology of Vic and his mates, seen also in his exchanges with Willy Lomas, his mates in the drawing-office and at the staff social. Yet Vic's attitude to the book reveals an ambivalence in his approach to sexuality:

169

JIMMY: I bet you wish you were married to her!
VIC: These are the kind you joke about with your mates. When
it comes to marrying a bird you want something different.

He goes on to say that, when it comes to marriage, he wants a girl
'like Christine', his sister.

Yet later it becomes clear that this is far from what he seems to
want from Ingrid. The pin-up book plays a significant part in the
scene where Vic and Ingrid make love: she finds the book, and
they discuss the women's features, Vic saying that Ingrid's breasts
are as lovely as those of the women in the photographs. Just before
she begins to undress, and the film cuts to Vic in the bathroom,
Ingrid picks up the book and looks at it for a moment; this seems a
clear signal that she is about to take on the identity of a fantasy pin-
up woman in the sex which follows. In so doing, she is entering
Vic's sexual ideology: from the sequence following the sex, which
shows Vic fully dressed and Ingrid in her mac, sitting on separate
chairs, it is clear that her excursion into his territory is just as
desolate as his appears to have been into hers. The sex is an act of
ideological penetration as much as physical entry: the fact that it is
not shown except in terms of its results – a symbolic dying fire in
the grate and the two figures sitting apart – makes clear that it is
something furtive and unsatisfying, an embodiment of scopophilia
rather than an act of mutual tenderness. The absence of visual
representation is, of course, the result of contemporary notions of
censorship; but here they work to the film's advantage by locating
the act within the lexicon of adolescent male smut: Ingrid's
emotional territory has been invaded and spoiled, just as her front
room has been invaded by the sexual ideology of Vic and his
mates. Once again the narrative makes clear the ideological
conflicts of the characters in its visual structure, here by what it
does not show as much as by what it does.

IV

Ideology, and especially sexual ideology, is thus revealed as
fundamental in the film's visual structure, and this should reassure
us that the documentary element is not the only way in which the
visual sense operates to present the moral structure of the work.
We may well feel that this compensates for the apparent
intrusiveness of the viewpoint, which acts to keep us outside the

action rather than feel part of it – as we invitably do, of course, in the novel, because of the continuous present-tense, first-person narrative from Vic himself. What we now have to consider is the ways in which the film compensates for this change of viewpoint, to explore how far we enter into the character of Vic himself. Much of the novel is concerned with the thoughts and responses of Vic to his changing situation with Ingrid: his delight at her agreeing to come out with him, for example, rapidly shifts to a feeling of uncertainty about what he feels for her, which grows to fear and anger at being ensnared in her world of suburban values, new coats and television quizzes. In the film, this is shown clearly enough in his conversations with Ingrid and her mother. Vic's ambivalent attitude towards Ingrid is shown frequently enough in his conversations and actions – when he doesn't sit next to her in the canteen, for example, when he accepts with ill grace that now she has 'got me', and when he storms out of the house after arguing with Ingrid and her mother. More extreme moments are also clear: before they make love in the front room, Vic asks Ingrid if she wants to 'pack it in', and she replies that she never knows how he feels; while they are arguing in the bedroom, a little before Ingrid's miscarriage, Vic replies to his wife's question 'Perhaps you're sorry you married me' with 'There's no perhaps about it.'

Yet these are all external statements: we are told things, but do not experience them. How far does the film succeed in letting us share the confused feelings of Vic towards Ingrid in its use of visual techniques and viewpoints, and so extend the sense of involvement we have in the novel because of its narrative voice? Several scenes suggest a move towards a visual equivalent of this verbal technique. The sequence showing Vic and Ingrid lying on the grass above the town begins with Vic's face in close-up, and only a little later is Ingrid revealed next to him: his face and eyes when she talks to him about 'going further' are not directed to hers, and it is clear that his mind is elsewhere. This prepares us well for the next shot in which Ingrid begins gossiping about her workmate: when Vic gets up and walks away, the action is only a confirmation of the lack of interest we have seen implied before.

A similar technique of focusing on Vic's face in close-up is used again to show his uncertainties about Ingrid and the security that she represents. After the scene in which Ingrid brings her friend Dorothy with her when she is going out with Vic, we are shown the Brown family having tea at David and Christine's new flat. The opening shows Vic's parents discussing marriage with the young couple, while the camera holds Vic's face, which moves uneasily to reveal his disquiet. Yet when Jimmy gives him the note from Ingrid, he runs off to meet her: his uncertainty and rapid mood changes are shown clearly enough for those who choose to note them. More directly apparent, perhaps, is the scene in the coffee bar where Vic meets Ingrid after his blood donating session. As she begins to talk about the television serial *Call Dr Martin*, Vic loses interest, and his gaze wanders around the café. The viewpoint then becomes subjective as we see, through Vic's eyes, young couples talking and then an older couple silent and morose: it is a clear indication of Vic's thoughts about the future course of his relationship with Ingrid, which is given immediacy by the use of a purely visual technique to convey his mood and fears.

The scene which explores Vic's feelings in greatest depth avoids this subjective technique, however, and instead employs a mixture of symbolic location which seems to return to the idea of ideological territories for its main thrust. When Vic leaves the house after being sick in Mrs Rothwell's front room – a powerful enough symbolic rejection of an alien territory in both the novel and the film – he walks through the town and, after passing through the arcade where he met Ingrid and her friend, comes to the railway station. As he looks at the timetable, a railway engine passes and the platform is covered with steam. The camera then moves to a close-up of Vic holding his head in his hands, in a sequence of several seconds' duration which is accompanied by a plangent solo clarinet. The locomotive which has passed before moves back; the platform again fills with smoke; and Vic then lies on the bench to sleep. The concentration on Vic's face suggests his mental turmoil; the placing of the scene in the railway station suggests a return to his own territory and is perhaps a hint of his turning to his father for advice – his father is an engine-driver in the film. More important perhaps is the symbolic presence of the railway engine, which moves forward and backward without reaching a destination just as, we assume, do Vic's thoughts. Reversal of direction is made more explicit in the scene which follows, which shows the railway marshalling yards coming alive in the dawn as Vic walks up the slope and across a narrow footbridge away from us: the bridge is the same one which he has crossed towards us in a long tracking shot where he is shown with his father, who talks to him about a man's need to move on, in an earlier sequence. The balance in both visual and narrative terms between these scenes suggests that the move away from his own territory is now reversed as Vic tries to retreat from the world of Ingrid to which he has unwillingly and incompletely committed himself.

Whether this actually allows us to enter Vic's mind and experience is, of course, a question of personal judgement. Inevitably, the visual nature of the film medium will result in greater stress being laid on the external reality of the working-class setting: ultimately, each viewer must decide whether the constant presence of the industrial town allows us to share its visual identity or whether the film is a repeated act of cultural voyeurism. As Vic and Ingrid lie above the town, the sound of shunting comes up the valley to them; as they make clumsy moves towards sexual contact in the park shelter, a man in a cloth cap walks his whippet past them against the background of the factory chimneys. The images do more than interrupt their sexual explorings: they keep us outside the sense of involvement with Vic that we have in the novel. In terms of the moral and social values of the film, this is turned to good use: both Mrs Brown and Christine make clear to Vic that he has no understanding of Ingrid's suffering, and that he must face his responsibilities towards her. Yet this does not solve one key problem of the cinematic adaptation of the novel: the continuous present of the narrative of Vic's thoughts which reveal him as what social psychologists would call a 'present-dweller' in his fundamentally irresponsible attitude is not recreated in the visual continuum of film, because the viewpoint cannot constantly remain that of the central character, and because the visual surroundings which are taken for granted in the novel inevitably become a central force in the film.

Schlesinger's *A Kind of Loving* makes sensitive use of the industrial setting, and uses the contrast between it and Ingrid's suburban home as an embodiment of the ideological opposition which is fundamental to the discourse. There are many fine moments where the visual nature of the film explores areas untouched by the novel, the best of which is probably the sequence in the shelter where, to the sound of Vic and Ingrid's sexual explorations, the camera pans around the back of the shelter to place them in the larger context of the couples who have chalked their initials there – even if the point is perhaps overdone by the inclusion of 'I love Adam.' Yet for all this, the visual narrative never quite succeeds in letting us share the experiences of Vic, however superficial and irresponsible they may be, as we do in the novel. Visualisation, in this sense, is too explicit: the discourse ultimately presents a form of narrative separation from which, ironically, we are excluded as onlookers rather than involved as participants.

NOTES

1 THE NATURE AND FUNCTION OF VISUALISATION

1 This is strange, since the study of popular art forms was not in itself foreign to either F.R. Leavis or Q.D. Leavis. The former's *Mass Civilization and Minority Culture* (with Denys Thompson, 1930) and the latter's *Fiction and the Reading Public* (1932) both discuss the arts of the people, not always with the sense of dismay that the incautious reader might expect; yet neither looks at the effects of illustrations in these works, or in the more celebrated studies which celebrate the canon.

2 The course is *A102: An Arts Foundation Course*, which discusses Dickens' *Hard Times*.

3 These are listed in the bibliography or cited in succeeding chapters as relevant.

4 Hogarth, subscription ticket for *The Four Stages of Cruelty*.

5 That the article has illustrations by Fred Walker, himself an illustrator of Thackeray and a painter who influenced figures such as Luke Fildes and the illustrators of the *Graphic*, is a further example of the complex links between visual and verbal texts of all kinds in the middle years of the nineteenth century.

6 *Shakespeare Sacrificed – or – the Offering to Avarice*, 20 June 1789. The Boydell Gallery was a collection of paintings commissioned by Alderman James Boydell from most of the leading artists of the day depicting subjects from Shakespeare's plays, subsequently issued in engraved form.

7 Gilpin wrote a series of books beginning with *The Wye and South Wales*, 1782 which became the basis of Picturesque and, later, Romantic tourism. In satirising them, Rowlandson was showing a literary sensibility at least equal to that of Gillray in his attacks on Boydell and Lewis.

8 Its full title was *Life in London: or, the Day and Night Scenes of Jerry Hawthorn Esq., and his Elegant Friend Corinthian Tom. Accompanied by Bob Logic, the Oxonian, in their Rambles and Sprees through the Metropolis*. This in itself is a striking statement of the publisher's desire to appeal to as

175

wide a range of readers as possible – the fashionable, the elegant, those with academic pretensions, and those with an interest in metropolitan low-life are neatly gathered in here.

9 For an account of some of these and an illustration of a pirated twopenny version, see Neuberg (1977), pp. 144–8.

10 For a discussion of the founding of this magazine, see Bratton (1981) pp. 39–40 and Scott Bennett, 'Revolutions in Thought: Serial Publication and the Mass Market for Reading', in Shattock and Wolff (1982), pp. 234–53. For an example of its illustrations, see Ivins (1953) plate 55.

11 The most famous of these personal styles was the 'Roxburgh' binding, named after the club of that name.

12 The full circumstances are discussed in Patten (1978), pp. 62–8.

13 Full details of printings and sales of *Pickwick* and Dickens' other serial novels are given in Patten (1978), Appendix B.

14 See Gettman (1960) for a full examination of the paper's circulation.

15 See the Memorandum of Agreement between Ainsworth and Cruikshank dated 19 November 1839 reproduced in Harvey (1970), p. 38.

16 In the Widener Collection, Harvard College Library, Boston, MA.

17 Ainsworth shared Dickens' respect for Hogarth. In *Jack Sheppard* there is a scene where Jack is visited in prison by Hogarth, who draws him as the basis of *Industry and Idleness*; the novel is referred to elsewhere by the writer as 'a sort of Hogarthian novel' (letter quoted in Ellis (1911: I, 328)).

18 Further evidence of the relationship between Dickens and his illustrators can be found in his letters (Storey *et al.*: 1965–93).

19 The shift is helpfully summarised in Rees and Borzello (ed.) (1986).

20 See Barthes (1977) pp. 91–7 for Barthes' own elucidation of the system.

21 For an exploration of this in greater depth, see Chapter 4.

22 For a discussion of Dickens' response to this illustration and the group of which it forms a part, see Harvey (1970), pp. 118–21.

23 See above, p. 11.

24 This is explored in more detail, though without reference to the illustrations and their placing, in Williams (1973), pp. 198–201.

4 ILLUSTRATED MAGAZINES

1 Most recently by John Carey (1992).

2 A writer in *What's What* (Quilter 1902) complained of the illustrations that 'the manner in which they are inserted, their numbers and their relation to the literary matter is either bad, excessive or perfunctory', going on to talk of how the pages are 'disfigured' by the addition of illustrations in a way which 'habitually makes the page ugly' (pp. 872–3). These words are anonymous, but may well be by the editor of the volume, Harry Quilter – a London barrister and journalist who had

written enthusiastically of the illustrated journalism of *The Graphic* (1888: 94–104).

3 See above, pp. 18–19, and Barthes (1977), pp. 38–40.

4 See 'Myth today', in Barthes, trans. Lavers (1973), pp. 150–1.

5 *GONE TO EARTH* AND TWENTIES LANDSCAPE IDEOLOGY

1 For ease of reference, page numbers are given for both Hepple's illustrated edition and the most easily available paperback edition, which shares the pagination of the Florin edition of 1932. To make this less cumbersome, page numbers are not given for quotations taken from the same page as the last words quoted.

2 In 1920 there were less than 200,000 private cars registered in England; in 1930, there were 1 million. Between 1930, when the 20 mph speed limit was abolished, and 1934, when a 30 mph one was imposed, speed was unrestricted.

3 See, for example, the discussion in Wiener (1980).

4 In the series of poems collected as *Idylls of the King*; see Tennyson, Ricks, ed. (1987).

5 The first anthology, *Georgian Poetry 1911–1912*, appeared in 1912; further collections were published in 1915, 1917, 1919 and 1922. All were edited by Edward Marsh.

6 For example, Edric Holmes' *London's Countryside*, which appeared in 1927, with 102 line-drawings by the author. Other similar volumes included *Seaward Sussex: the South Downs from End to End* (1920) and *Wanderings in Wessex* (1922).

7 For example, Humphrey Pakington's *English Villages and Hamlets*, 1934, illustrated with drawings by Sydney R. Jones and photographs by Will F. Taylor. An account of the series is given by Brian Cook Batsford (1987).

8 Built in 1859; the chimney-piece is illustrated in Pevsner (1960: 58).

6 THE ROMANTIC CONTINUUM: *REBECCA* AND INTERNAL VISUALISATION

1 This is the title and subject of a complete chapter (1932: 235–73), as well as being a concern which underpins a great deal of her discussion of the modern bestseller in distinction from that of the eighteenth and nineteenth centuries.

2 Q.D. Leavis gives four reasons why novels are read: '1 To pass time not unpleasantly. 2 To obtain vicarious satisfaction or compensation for life. 3 To obtain assistance in the business of living. 4 To enrich the quality of living by extending, deepening, refining, co-ordinating experience' (1932: 48). It is significant that her subsequent comments

centre on the second of these, to the extent of having a whole chapter titled 'Living at the novelist's expense', where the element of reading for a fantasy life is stressed and that of reading for some form of moral guide ignored.

8 WORKING-CLASS F(R)ICTIONS

1 Warner Home Video, *The 60s Revisited* series, WTB 38096.
2 John Grierson, for the British Commercial Gas Association, 15 minutes, 1935.
3 Ian Dalrymple for the Crown Film Unit, Ministry of Information, 20 minutes, 1941. Available, with Jennings' *The Heart of Britain* and *A Diary for Timothy* in *Listening to Britain: A Jennings Trilogy*, Imperial War Museum 1991. (ISBN 0–901627–80–1).
4 Karel Reisz, 1960.

REFERENCES AND FURTHER READING

Acton, Harold, 1977, *Introduzione all mostra del libro Inglese illustrato dell'Ottocento, Gabinetto Scientifico Litterario G.P. Vieusseux*, Florence: G.P. Vieusseux.

Allingham, William, 1855, *The Music Master, A Love Story, and Two Series of Day and Night Songs*, London: Routledge.

Altick, Richard D., 1957, *The English Common Reader: A Social History of the Mass Reading Public 1800–1900*, Chicago and London: University of Chicago Press.

Applebee, Arthur N., 1978, *The Child's Concept of Story*, Chicago and London: University of Chicago Press.

Avery, Gillian, 1965, *Nineteenth-Century Children, Heroes and Heroines in English Children's Stories*, London: Hodder and Stoughton.

Bailey, Peter, 1978, *Leisure and Class in Victorian England: Rational Recreation and the Contest for Control 1830-1885*, London: Routledge and Kegan Paul.

Barstow, Stan, 1986, *A Kind of Loving*, London: Transworld Publishers.

Barthes, Roland, 1973, *Mythologies*, trans. Annette Lavers, London: Paladin.

———— 1977, *Image, Music, Text: Essays Selected and Translated by Stephen Heath*, trans. Stephen Heath, London: Fontana.

———— 1982, *Camera Lucida – Reflections on Photography*, trans. Richard Howard, London: Cape.

Batsford, Brian Cook, 1987, *The Britain of Brian Cook Batsford*, London: Batsford.

Beetham, Margaret, 1989, 'Open and Closed: the Periodical as Publishing Genre', *Victorian Periodicals Review* 22(3): 96–100.

Bettelheim, Bruno, 1976, *The Uses of Enchantment: The Meaning and Importance of Fairy Tales*, London: Thames and Hudson.

Bratton, J.S., 1981, *The Impact of Victorian Children's Fiction*, London: Croom Helm and Totowa, NJ: Barnes & Noble.

Buchan, John, 1916, *The Battle of the Somme: First Phase*, London: Nelson.

———— 1915, *The Thirty-Nine Steps*, Edinburgh and London: W. Blackwood and Sons.

Carey, John, 1992, *The Intellectuals and the Masses*, London: Faber and Faber.

REFERENCES

Carroll, Lewis, 1982, *The Complete Works of Lewis Carroll*, Harmondsworth: Penguin.
Cecil, David, 1932, *Early Victorian Novelists*, London: Constable.
Cohen, Jane R., 1969, '"All-of-a-Twist" – The Relationship of George Cruikshank and Charles Dickens', *Harvard Library Bulletin* 17(2): 169–94; (3): 320–42.
Coleridge, S.T., 1907, *Biographia Literaria*, ed. James Shawcross, 2 vols, Oxford: Clarendon.
Copede, Maurizio, Silvia Bettocchi and Graziano Braschi (comp.), 1977, *Mostra del libro Inglese illustrato dell'Ottocento*, Florence: G.P. Vieusseux.
Copley, Esther, 1841, *The Poplar Grove*, London: Thomas Tegg.
Cowley, Robert, 1983, *Marriage-à-la-mode: A Re-view of Hogarth's Narrative Art*, Manchester: Manchester University Press.
Crane, Walter, 1874, *Walter Crane's Toy Books, Shilling Series*, London: Routledge.
——— 1881, *The First of May: A Fairy Masque*, London: Henry Sotheran.
Crocetti, Luigi, ed., 1986, *Caricaturisti Inglesi dai libri illustrati dell 'Ottocento*, Florence: G.P. Vieusseux (exhibition catalogue).
Dickens, Charles, 1948 repr. 1978, *The Personal History of David Copperfield* (Oxford Illustrated Dickens), intro. R.H. Malden, Oxford: Oxford University Press.
——— 1949 repr. 1987, *Oliver Twist* (Oxford Illustrated Dickens), intro. Humphrey House, Oxford: Oxford University Press.
——— 1950 repr. 1987, *Dealings With the Firm of Dombey and Son, Wholesale Retail and for Exportation* (Oxford Illustrated Dickens), intro. H.W. Garrod, Oxford: Oxford University Press.
——— 1951 repr. 1987, *The Old Curiosity Shop* (Oxford Illustrated Dickens), intro. The Earl of Wicklow, Oxford: Oxford University Press.
——— 1977, *Bleak House* (Oxford Illustrated Dickens), eds George Ford and Sylvere Monod, Oxford: Oxford University Press.
——— 1986, *The Pickwick Papers* (the Clarendon Dickens), Oxford: Clarendon.
Dolman, Frederick, 1900, 'Illustrated Interviews LXX – Hubert Herkomer, R.A.', *Strand Magazine* 19: 434–44.
du Maurier, Daphne, 1938 repr. 1975, *Rebecca*, London: Pan Books.
du Maurier, George, 1895, *Trilby*, London: Osgood, McIlvaine and Co.
Egan, Pierce, 1820–1, *Life in London; or, the Day and Night Scenes of Jerry Hawthorn Esq., and his Elegant Friend Corinthian Tom. Accompanied by Bob Logic, the Oxonian, in their Rambles and Sprees through the Metropolis*, London: Sherwood, Neely and Jones.
Ellegård, Alvar, 1957, *The Readership of the Periodical Press in Mid-Victorian Britain*, Acta Universitatis Gotheburgensis, Göteborgs Universitets Årsskrift, 63: 3.
Ellis, S.M., 1911, *William Harrison Ainsworth and his Friends*, 2 vols, London and New York: John Lane.
Feather, John, 1988, *A History of British Publishing*, London: Croom Helm.
Fildes, L.V., 1968, *Luke Fildes, R.A.: A Victorian Painter*, London: Joseph.
Fish, Stanley, 1980, *Is There A Text in This Class? The Authority of Interpretive Communities*, Cambridge, MA: Harvard University Press.

Forster, E.M., 1910, *Howards End*, London: Edward Arnold.

Forster, John, 1872–4, *Life of Charles Dickens*, 3 vols, London: Chapman & Hall.

Fox, Celina, 1977, 'The Development of Social Reportage in English Periodical Illustration during the 1840s and Early 1850s', *Past and Present* 74: 90–111.

Garrigan, Kristine Ottesen, 1989, 'Bearding the Competition: John Ruskin's *Academy Notes*', *Victorian Periodicals Review* 22(4): 148–56.

George, M. Dorothy, 1967, *Hogarth to Cruikshank: Social Change in Graphic Satire*, London: Allen Lane.

Gettmann, Royal Alfred, 1960, *A Victorian Publisher: A Study of the Bentley Papers*, Cambridge: Cambridge University Press.

Gibbons, Stella, 1932, *Cold Comfort Farm*, London, Longman.

Gifford, Dennis, 1984, rev. edn 1990, *The International Book of Comics*, London: Hamlyn.

Gombrich, Ernst, 1960, *Art and Illusion*, Oxford: Phaidon.

Greenaway, Kate, 1879, *Under the Window*, London: Routledge.

Griest, Guinevere L., 1970, *Mudie's Circulating Library and the Victorian Novel*, Bloomington and London: Indiana University Press.

Haggard, H. Rider, 1887, *She*, London: Longman.

—— 1905, *Ayesha*, London: Ward Lock.

Harris, R.W., 1969, *Romanticism and the Social Order 1780–1830*, Blandford: London.

Harvey, J.R., 1970, *Victorian Novelists and their Illustrators*, London: Sidgwick and Jackson.

Hodnett, Edward, 1982, *Image and Text: Studies in the Illustration of English Literature*, Scolar Press: London.

Holme, Brian, 1976, *The Kate Greenaway Book*, London: Warne.

Holmes, Edric, 1920, *Seaward Sussex: the South Downs from End to End*, London: Robert Scott.

—— 1922, *Wanderings in Wessex*, London: Robert Scott.

—— 1927, *London's Countryside*, London: Robert Scott.

How, Harry, 1893, 'Illustrated Interviews XXV – Mr. Luke Fildes, R.A.', *The Strand Magazine* 25: 110–27.

Iser, Wolfgang, 1978, *The Art of Reading: A Theory of Aesthetic Response*, London: Routledge.

Ivins, William M., Jr, 1953, *Prints and Visual Communication*, Cambridge, MA: Massachusetts Institute of Technology Press.

James, P., 1947, *English Book Illustration 1800–1900*, Harmondsworth and New York: Penguin.

Jefferies, Richard, 1885, *After London*, London: Cassell.

Jerome, Jerome K., 1989, *Three Men in a Boat*, Bristol: Arrowsmith.

Johannsen, A., 1956, *Phiz: Illustrations from the Novels of Charles Dickens*, Chicago: University of Chicago Press.

Kipling, Rudyard, 1906, 'Puck of Pook's Hill', *The Strand Magazine* 31–32, June–October.

—— 1906, *Puck of Pook's Hill*, London: Macmillan.

Kitton, F.G., 1899, *Dickens and his Illustrators*, London: G. Redway.

Knight, Charles, 1854, *The Old Printer and the Modern Press*, London: John Murray.

Lang, Andrew, 1890, *The Red Fairy Book*, London: Longman.

———— 1897, *The Pink Fairy Book*, London: Longman.

Leavis, F.R. and Denys Thompson, 1930, *Mass Civilization and Minority Culture*, Cambridge: Gordon Fraser.

Leavis, Q.D., 1932, *Fiction and the Reading Public*, London: Chatto and Windus.

MacDonald, George, 1871, *The Princess and the Goblin*, London: Blackie.

Maclean, Ruari, ed., 1967, *The Reminiscences of Edmund Evans*, Oxford: Clarendon.

Mayhew, Augustus, 1858, *Paved with Gold, or the Romance and Reality of the London Streets*, London: Ward Lock.

Mayhew, Henry, 1851, *London Labour and the London Poor*, III, *The London Street Folk*, London: Griffin, Bohn and Company.

Mayo, Robert, 1962, *The English Novel in the Magazines 1740–1815: With a Catalogue of 1375 Magazine Novels and Novelettes*, Evanston: Northwestern University Press and London: Oxford University Press.

Mills, J. Saxon, 1923, *Life and Letters of Sir Hubert Herkomer C.V.O., R.A.: A Study in Struggle and Success*, London: Hutchinson.

Morris, the Rev. Marcus, 1949, '"Comics" That Take Horror Into The Nursery', *Sunday Dispatch* 13 February, 4.

Morris, William, 1890, *News From Nowhere*, Boston, MA: Roberts Bros.

Myers, Bernard, 1982, 'Studies for Houseless and Hungry and the Casual Ward by Luke Fildes, R.A.', *Apollo*, July, 36–43.

Nesbit, E., 1901, *The Would-be-goods*, London: T. Fisher Unwin.

———— 1902, *Five Children and It*, London: T. Fisher Unwin.

———— 1902, 'The Psammead', *The Strand Magazine* April–December.

———— 1904, *The New Treasure-Seekers*, London: T. Fisher Unwin.

———— 1905, 'Molly, the Measles and the Missing Will', *Windsor* November.

———— 1906, *The Story of the Amulet*, London: T. Fisher Unwin.

Neuberg, Victor E., 1977, *Popular Literature: A History and Guide*, Harmondsworth: Penguin.

North, Michael, 1991, *The Political Aesthetic of Yeats, Eliot and Pound*, Cambridge: Cambridge University Press.

Orwell, George, 1940, 'Boys' Weeklies', *Horizon* March, in *The Penguin Essays of George Orwell*, 1984, Harmondsworth: Penguin.

Pakington, Humphrey, 1934, *English Villages and Hamlets*, London: Batsford.

Patten, Robert L., 1978, *Charles Dickens and his Publishers*, Oxford: Clarendon.

Paulson, Ronald, 1975, *Emblem and Expression: Meaning in English Art of the Eighteenth Century*, London: Thames and Hudson.

Peppin, Bridgid, 1975, *Fantasy Book Illustration 1860–1920*, London: Studio Vista.

Pevsner, Nikolaus, 1960, *Pioneers of Modern Design*, Harmondsworth: Penguin.

Pointon, Marcia R., 1970, *Milton and English Art: A Study in the Pictorial Artist's Use of a Literary Source*, Manchester: Manchester University Press.

Poole, Stephen, ed., 1982, *A Passion for Work – Sir Hubert von Herkomer 1849–1914*, Watford: Watford Borough Council.

Quilter, Harry, 1888, 'Some "Graphic" Artists', *Universal Review* 2: 94–104.

Quilter, Harry, 1902, *What's What: A Guide for To-day to Life as It Is and Things as They Are*, London: Sonnenschein.

Rees, A.L., and F. Borzello, eds, 1986, *The New Art History*, London: Camden Press.

Reid, Forrest, 1928, *Illustrators of the Eighteen Sixties: An Illustrated Survey of the Work of 58 British Artists*, London: Faber and Gwyer.

Reynolds, A.M. (1912) *The Life and Work of Frank Holl*, London: Methuen.

Ruskin, John, 1903–12, *Complete Works*, ed. E.T. Cook and A.D.O. Wedderburn, 39 vols, London: George Allen.

Salway, Lance, ed., 1976, *A Peculiar Gift: Nineteenth-Century Writings on Books for Children*, Harmondsworth: Penguin.

Schapiro, Meyer, 1973, *Words and Pictures: On the Literal and Symbolic in the Illustration of a Text*, The Hague and Paris: Mouton.

Scott, Walter, 1824, *Novels and Romances of the Author of Waverley*, 7 vols, Edinburgh: Archibald Constable.

―――― 1859, *The Waverley Novels*, 20 vols, Edinburgh: A. and C. Black.

Shattock, Joanne and Michael Wolff, eds, 1982, *The Victorian Press: Samplings and Soundings*, Leicester: University of Leicester Press.

Shepard, Leslie, 1973, *The History of Street Literature*, Newton Abbot: David and Charles.

Spectator, The, 1712, 315, March.

Stevens, J., 1967, '"Woodcuts Dropped into the Text": The Illustrations in *The Old Curiosity Shop* and *Barnaby Rudge*', *Studies in Bibliography* 20: 113–34.

Storey, Graham, Kathleen Tillotson and Angus Easson, eds, 1965–93, *The Letters of Charles Dickens*, 7 vols, Oxford: Clarendon Press.

Stranks, Alan, 1951, *PC 49*, London: Juvenile Publications.

―――― 1952, *On Duty with PC 49*, London: Juvenile Publications.

―――― 1953, *On the Beat PC 49*, London: Juvenile Publications.

Stranks, Alan, and John Worsley, 1953, *PC49 Eagle Strip Cartoon Book*, London: Juvenile Publications.

―――― 1990, *The Adventures of P.C. 49*, intro. Norman Wright, London: Hawk Books Ltd.

Sutherland, J.A., 1976, *Victorian Novelists and Publishers*, London: Athlone Press.

Tennyson, Alfred, 1857, *Poems*, London: Moxon.

―――― 1987, *The Poems of Tennyson*, ed Christopher Ricks, 3 vols, Harlow: Longman.

Thackeray, William Makepeace, 1853, *The English Humourists of the Eighteenth Century. A Series of Lectures delivered in England, Scotland and the United States of America*, London: Smith, Elder and Co.

―――― 1878, *Vanity Fair: A Novel Without a Hero (The Works of W.M. Thackeray)*, London: Smith, Elder and Co.

Thomas, W.L., 1888, 'The Making of "The Graphic"', *Universal Review* 2: 80–93.

Thompson, David Croal, 1895, 'Luke Fildes, R.A., His Life and Work', *The Art Annual (Art Journal)*, 4–6.

Tillotson, Kathleen, 1954, *Novels of the Eighteen-Forties*, Oxford: Oxford University Press.

Tillotson, G. and K. Tillotson, 1965, *Mid-Victorian Studies*, London: Athlone Press.

Tompkins, J.M.S., 1932, *The Popular Novel in England, 1770–1800*, London: Constable.

Town and Country Homes, 1930, Ideal Home Exhibition Number, April.

Townsend, John Rowe, 1974, rev. edn, *Written for Children*, Harmondsworth: Penguin.

Treuhertz, Julian, 1987, *Hard Times: Social Realism in Victorian Art*, London: Lund Humphries.

Twyman, Michael, 1970, *Printing 1770–1970: An Illustrated History of its Use and Development in England*, London: Eyre and Spottiswoode.

Vesselo, Arthur, 1936, *Sight and Sound*, 5, 18, Summer.

Warden, Florence, 1905, 'Lady Anne's Trustee', *Windsor*, November.

Watt, Ian, 1963, *The Rise of the Novel*, Harmondsworth: Penguin.

Webb, Mary, 1978, *Precious Bane*, London: Virago.

Webb, Mary, 1928, *Precious Bane* (The Collected Works of Mary Webb), ill. Rowland Hilder, London: Cape.

———— 1930, *Gone to Earth*, (The Collected Works of Mary Webb), ill. Norman Hepple, London: Cape.

———— 1978, *Gone to Earth*, London: Virago.

Wiener, Martin, 1980, *English Culture and the Decline of the Industrial Spirit*, Cambridge: Cambridge University Press.

Williams, Raymond, 1973, *The Country and the City*, London: Chatto and Windus.

Woolf, Virginia, 1925, *Mrs. Dalloway*, London: Hogarth Press.

Wolff, Michael and Celina Fox, 1973, 'Pictures from the Magazines', in H.J. Dyos and Michael Wolff (eds) *The Victorian City: Images and Realities*, II, London: Routledge.

Wrenn, D.P.H., 1964, *Goodbye to Morning: A Biographical Study of Mary Webb*, Shrewsbury: Wilding and Co.

INDEX